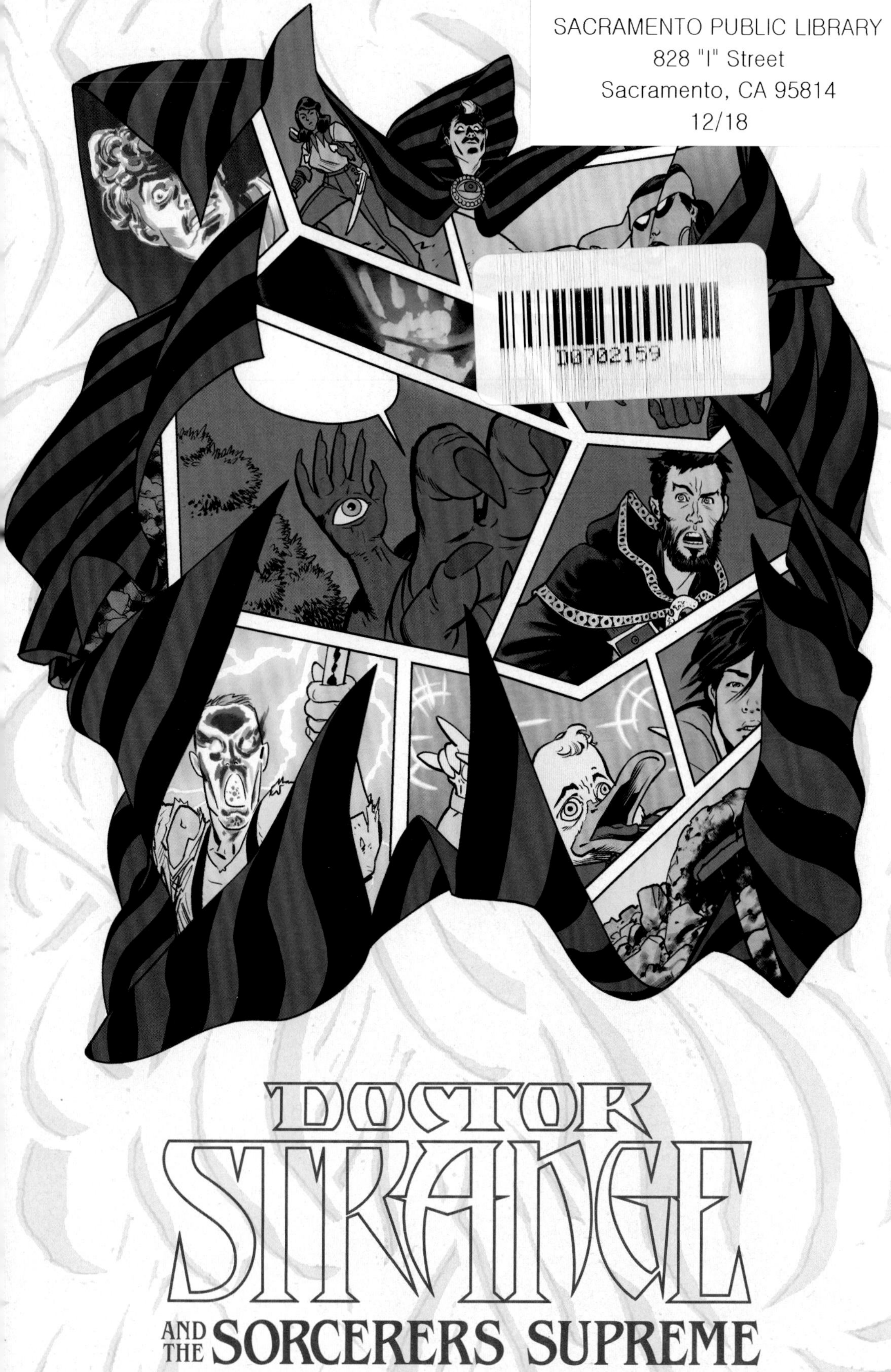

DOCTOR STRANGE AND THE SORCERERS SUPREME

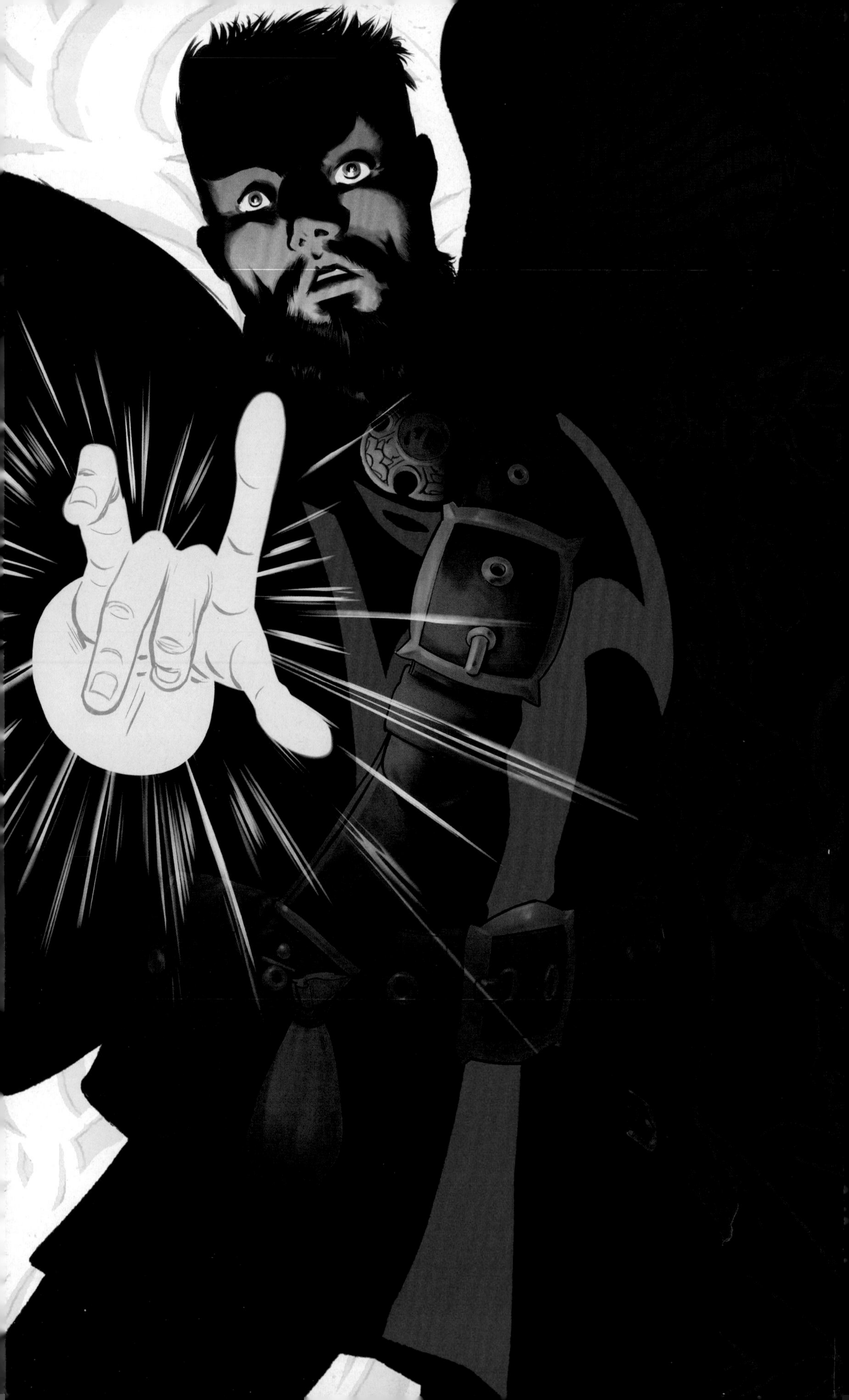

IN EVERY AGE. THERE IS ONE PERSON WHO POSSESSES GREATER MAGICAL SKILL AND POWER THAN ANY OTHER BEING.
THIS PERSON IS THE **SORCERER SUPREME**, AND THEY ARE THIS DIMENSION'S PROTECTOR AGAINST ANY MYSTICAL MAYHEM THAT THREATENS IT.

MERLIN, THE SORCERER SUPREME OF THE MIDDLE AGES, TRAVELED THROUGH TIME TO RECRUIT SORCERERS SUPREME FROM VARIOUS ERAS,
INCLUDING DOCTOR STRANGE, TO COMBAT A POWERFUL FOE CALLED THE FORGOTTEN. ONE OF THOSE SORCERERS, SIR ISAAC NEWTON,
USED THE WORD OF GOD – FORBIDDEN MAGIC – TO DEFEAT THE FORGOTTEN AND FREE THE MAGICIANS TRAPPED WITHIN IT. HOWEVER, HE
THEN TURNED ON THE SORCERERS, STEALING THE SPIRIT OF VENGEANCE FROM THE DEMON RIDER AND CUTTING OFF THE YOUNG ANCIENT
... BEFORE LOCKING THEM ALL IN THE FORGOTTEN'S PRISON CELL. JOÃO, THE
... OM THE DESTRUCTION OF THE FORGOTTEN. HE LIBERATED THE SORCERERS
... P SET BY NEWTON. FORTUNATELY, THEY MANAGED TO ESCAPE, AND FOUND
... VENGERS LAY DEFEATED BY NONE OTHER THAN NEWTON!

DOCTOR STRANGE AND THE SORCERERS SUPREME

~ *After Time* ~

Thompson
WRITER

~ ISSUES #10-12 ~

Nathan Stockman
ARTIST

Tamra Bonvillain (#10) &
Jim Campbell (#11-12)
COLORISTS

VC's Joe Caramagna
LETTERER

Javier Rodriguez & *Álvaro López*
COVER ART

Allison Stock
ASSISTANT EDITOR

Darren Shan
ASSOCIATE EDITOR

Nick Lowe
EDITOR

~ DOCTOR STRANGE CREATED BY **STAN LEE** & **STEVE DITKO** ~

COLLECTION EDITOR: **JENNIFER GRÜNWALD**
ASSISTANT EDITOR: **CAITLIN O'CONNELL**
ASSOCIATE MANAGING EDITOR: **KATERI WOODY**
EDITOR, SPECIAL PROJECTS: **MARK D. BEAZLEY**
VP PRODUCTION & SPECIAL PROJECTS: **JEFF YOUNGQUIST**
SVP PRINT, SALES & MARKETING: **DAVID GABRIEL**
BOOK DESIGNER: **ADAM DEL RE**

EDITOR IN CHIEF: **AXEL ALONSO**
CHIEF CREATIVE OFFICER: **JOE QUESADA**
PRESIDENT: **DAN BUCKLEY**
EXECUTIVE PRODUCER: **ALAN FINE**

DCTOR STRANGE AND THE SORCERERS SUPREME VOL. 2: TIME AFTER TIME. Contains material originally published in magazine form as DOCTOR STRANGE AND THE SORCERERS SUPREME #7-12. First printing 2017. ISBN# 978-1-302-
)591-0. Published by MARVEL WORLDWIDE, INC., a subsidiary of MARVEL ENTERTAINMENT, LLC. OFFICE OF PUBLICATION: 135 West 50th Street, New York, NY 10020. Copyright © 2017 MARVEL No similarity between any of the names,
aracters, persons, and/or institutions in this magazine with those of any living or dead person or institution is intended, and any such similarity which may exist is purely coincidental. **Printed in Canada.** DAN BUCKLEY, President, Marvel
tertainment; JOE QUESADA, Chief Creative Officer; TOM BREVOORT, SVP of Publishing; DAVID BOGART, SVP of Business Affairs & Operations, Publishing & Partnership; C.B. CEBULSKI, VP of Brand Management & Development, Asia; DAVID
ABRIEL, SVP of Sales & Marketing, Publishing; JEFF YOUNGQUIST, VP of Production & Special Projects; DAN CARR, Executive Director of Publishing Technology; ALEX MORALES, Director of Publishing Operations; SUSAN CRESPI, Production
anager; STAN LEE, Chairman Emeritus. For information regarding advertising in Marvel Comics or on Marvel.com, please contact Vit DeBellis, Integrated Sales Manager, at vdebellis@marvel.com. For Marvel subscription inquiries, please

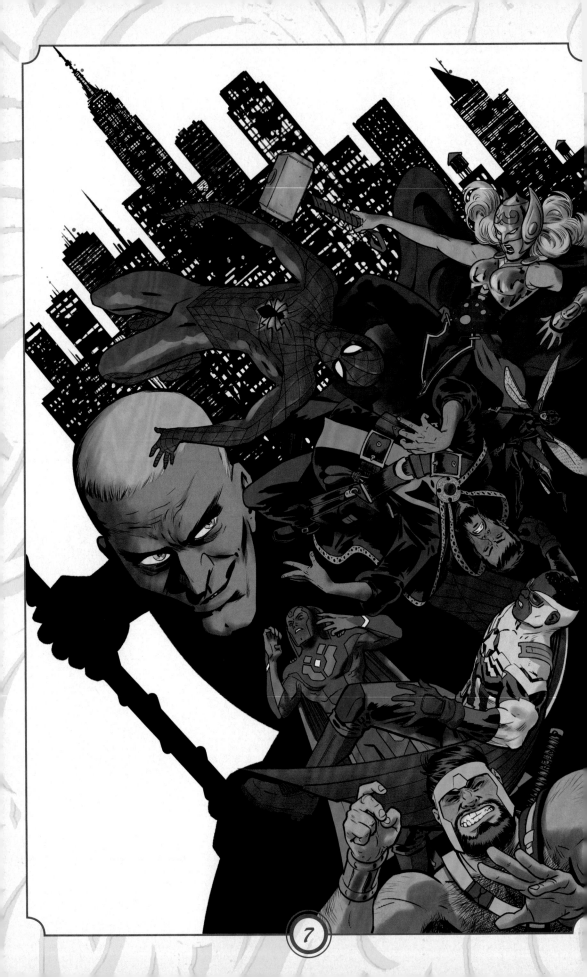

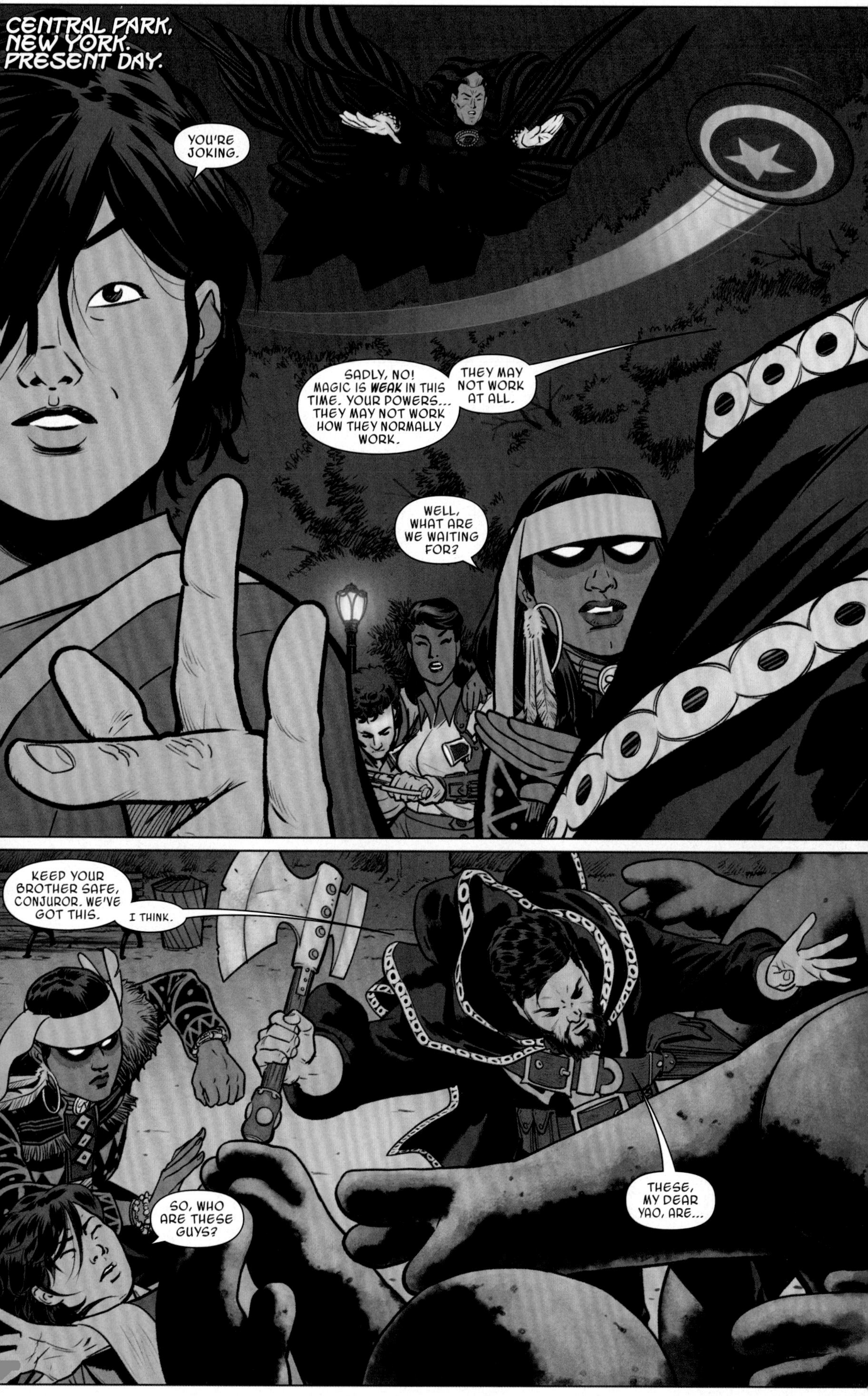
CENTRAL PARK, NEW YORK. PRESENT DAY.
YOU'RE JOKING.
SADLY, NO! MAGIC IS WEAK IN THIS TIME. YOUR POWERS... THEY MAY NOT WORK HOW THEY NORMALLY WORK.
THEY MAY NOT WORK AT ALL.
WELL, WHAT ARE WE WAITING FOR?
KEEP YOUR BROTHER SAFE, CONJUROR. WE'VE GOT THIS.
I THINK.
SO, WHO ARE THESE GUYS?
THESE, MY DEAR YAO, ARE...

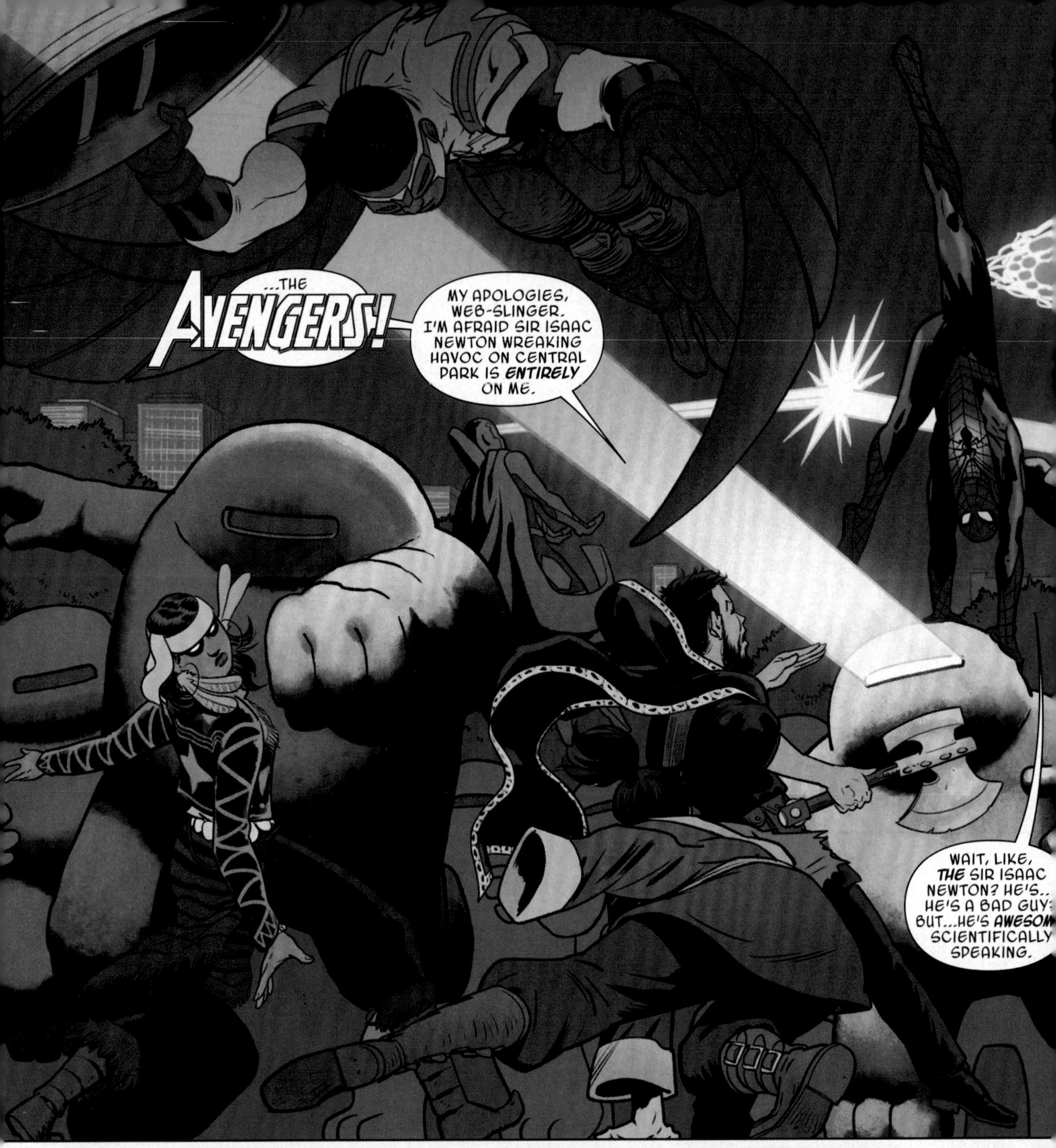
...THE AVENGERS!
MY APOLOGIES, WEB-SLINGER. I'M AFRAID SIR ISAAC NEWTON WREAKING HAVOC ON CENTRAL PARK IS ENTIRELY ON ME.
WAIT, LIKE, THE SIR ISAAC NEWTON? HE'S.. HE'S A BAD GUY? BUT...HE'S AWESOM SCIENTIFICALLY SPEAKING.

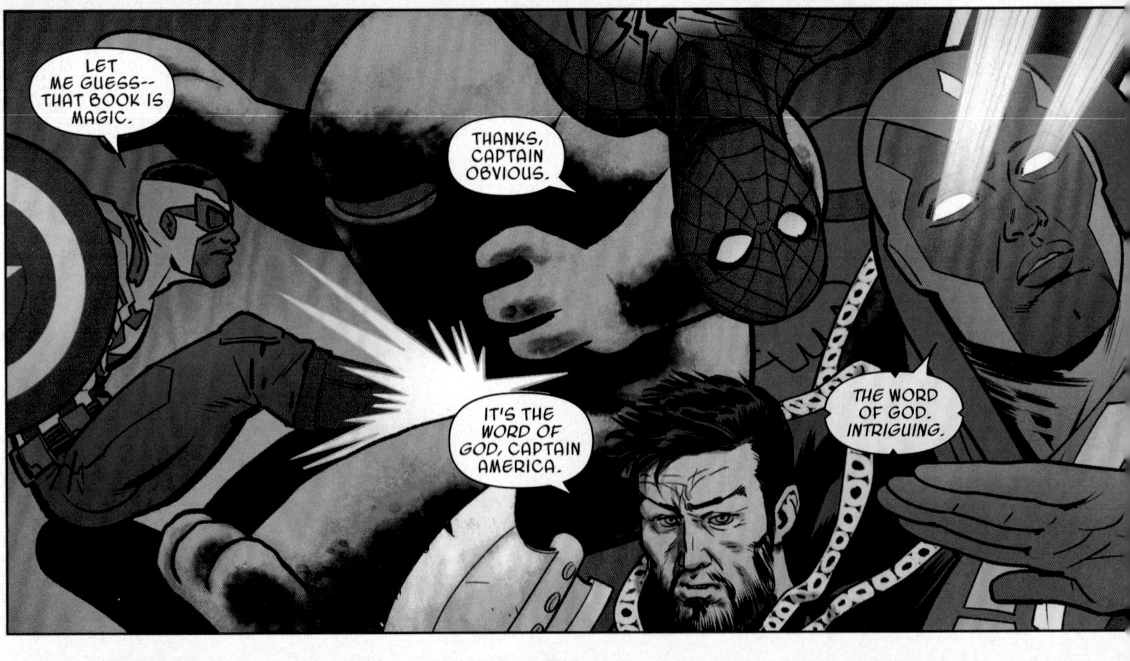
LET ME GUESS-- THAT BOOK IS MAGIC.
THANKS, CAPTAIN OBVIOUS.
IT'S THE WORD OF GOD, CAPTAIN AMERICA.
THE WORD OF GOD. INTRIGUING.

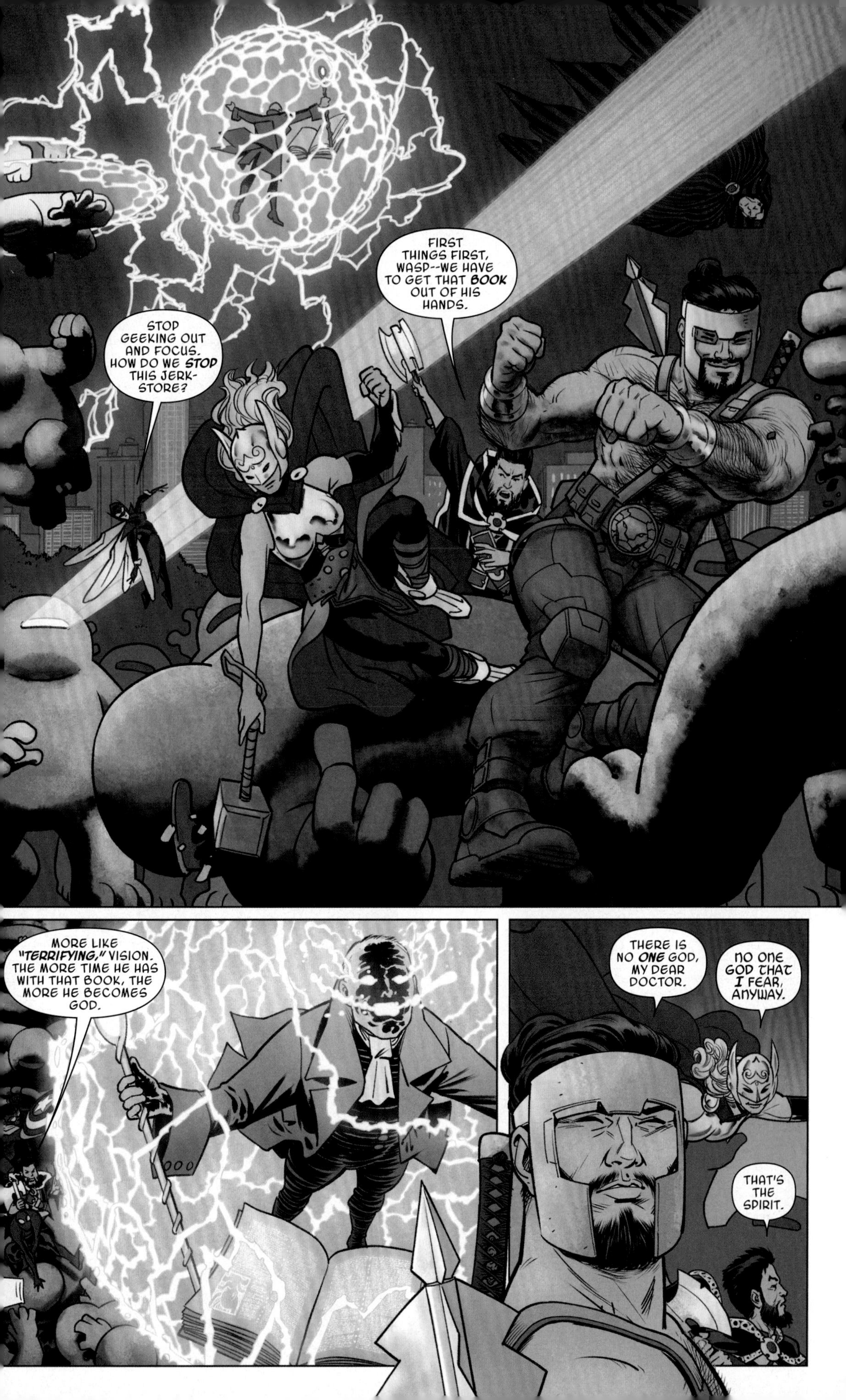
STOP GEEKING OUT AND FOCUS. HOW DO WE STOP THIS JERK-STORE?
FIRST THINGS FIRST, WASP--WE HAVE TO GET THAT BOOK OUT OF HIS HANDS.
MORE LIKE "TERRIFYING," VISION. THE MORE TIME HE HAS WITH THAT BOOK, THE MORE HE BECOMES GOD.
THERE IS NO ONE GOD, MY DEAR DOCTOR.
NO ONE GOD THAT I FEAR, ANYWAY.
THAT'S THE SPIRIT.

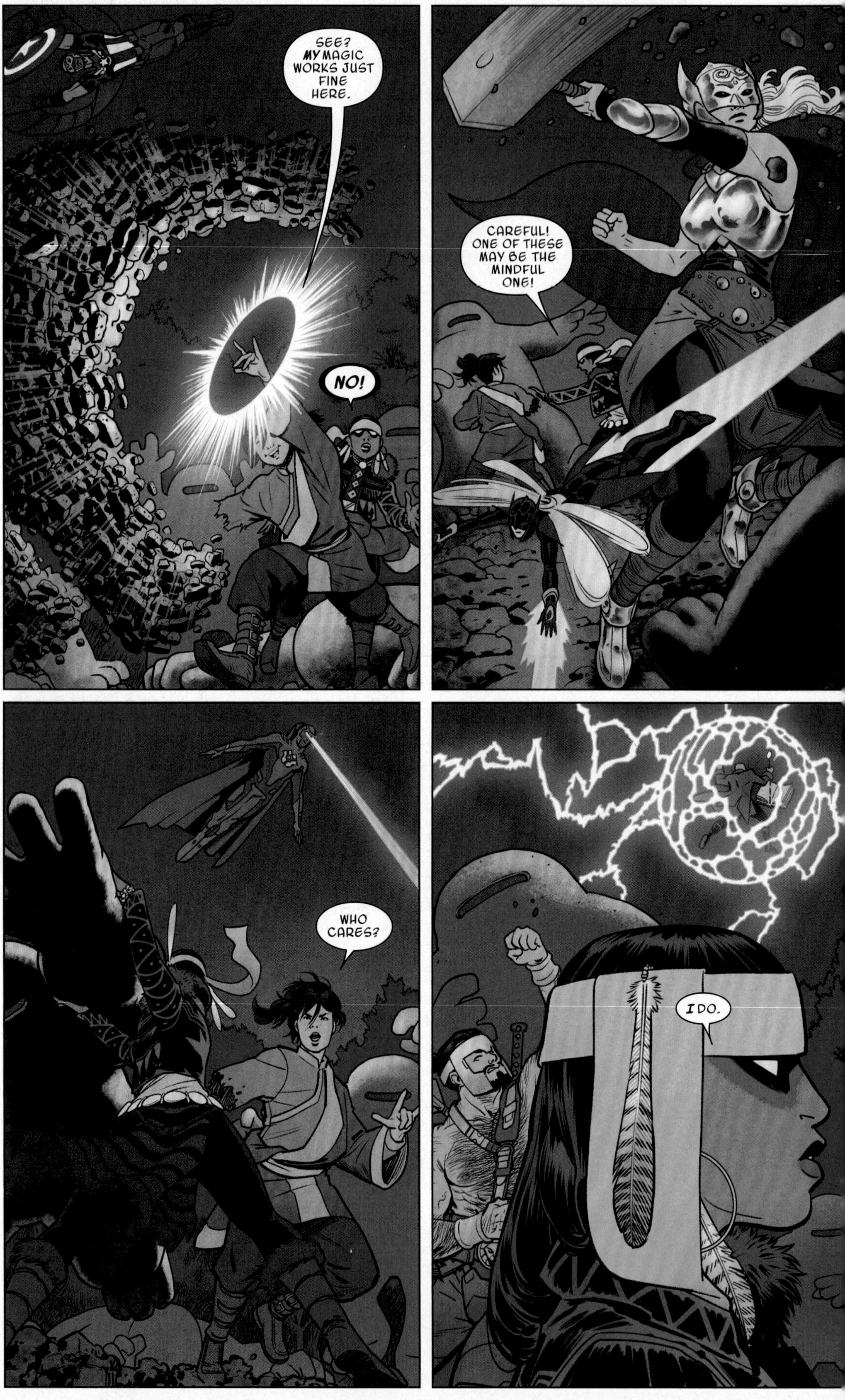
SEE? MY MAGIC WORKS JUST FINE HERE.
NO!
CAREFUL! ONE OF THESE MAY BE THE MINDFUL ONE!
WHO CARES?
I DO.

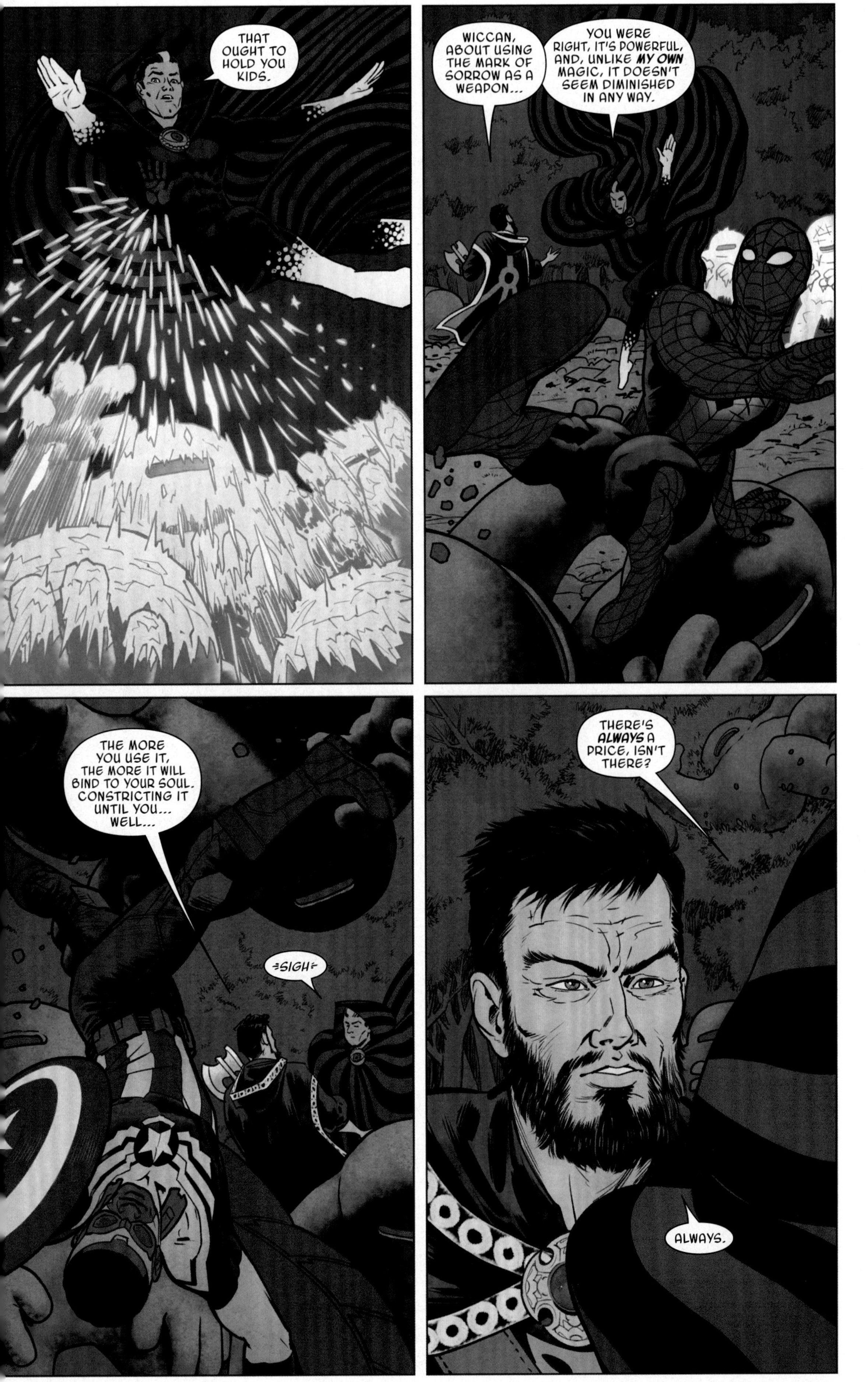
THAT OUGHT TO HOLD YOU KIDS.
WICCAN, ABOUT USING THE MARK OF SORROW AS A WEAPON...
YOU WERE RIGHT, IT'S POWERFUL, AND, UNLIKE MY OWN MAGIC, IT DOESN'T SEEM DIMINISHED IN ANY WAY.
THE MORE YOU USE IT, THE MORE IT WILL BIND TO YOUR SOUL. CONSTRICTING IT UNTIL YOU... WELL...
SIGH
THERE'S ALWAYS A PRICE, ISN'T THERE?
ALWAYS.

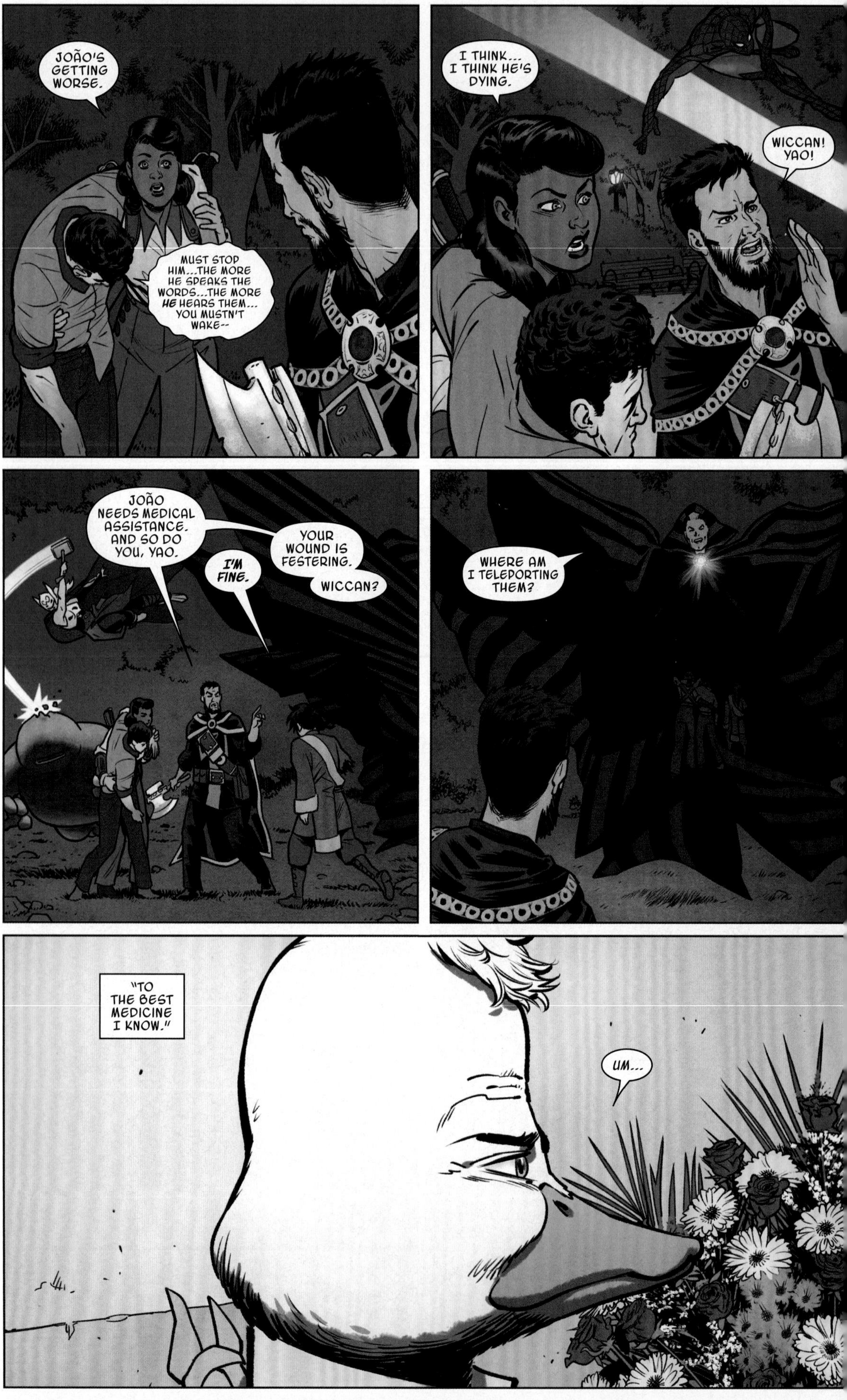
JOÃO'S GETTING WORSE.
MUST STOP HIM...THE MORE HE SPEAKS THE WORDS...THE MORE HE HEARS THEM... YOU MUSTN'T WAKE--
I THINK... I THINK HE'S DYING.
WICCAN! YAO!
JOÃO NEEDS MEDICAL ASSISTANCE. AND SO DO YOU, YAO.
YOUR WOUND IS FESTERING.
I'M FINE.
WICCAN?
WHERE AM I TELEPORTING THEM?
"TO THE BEST MEDICINE I KNOW."
UM...

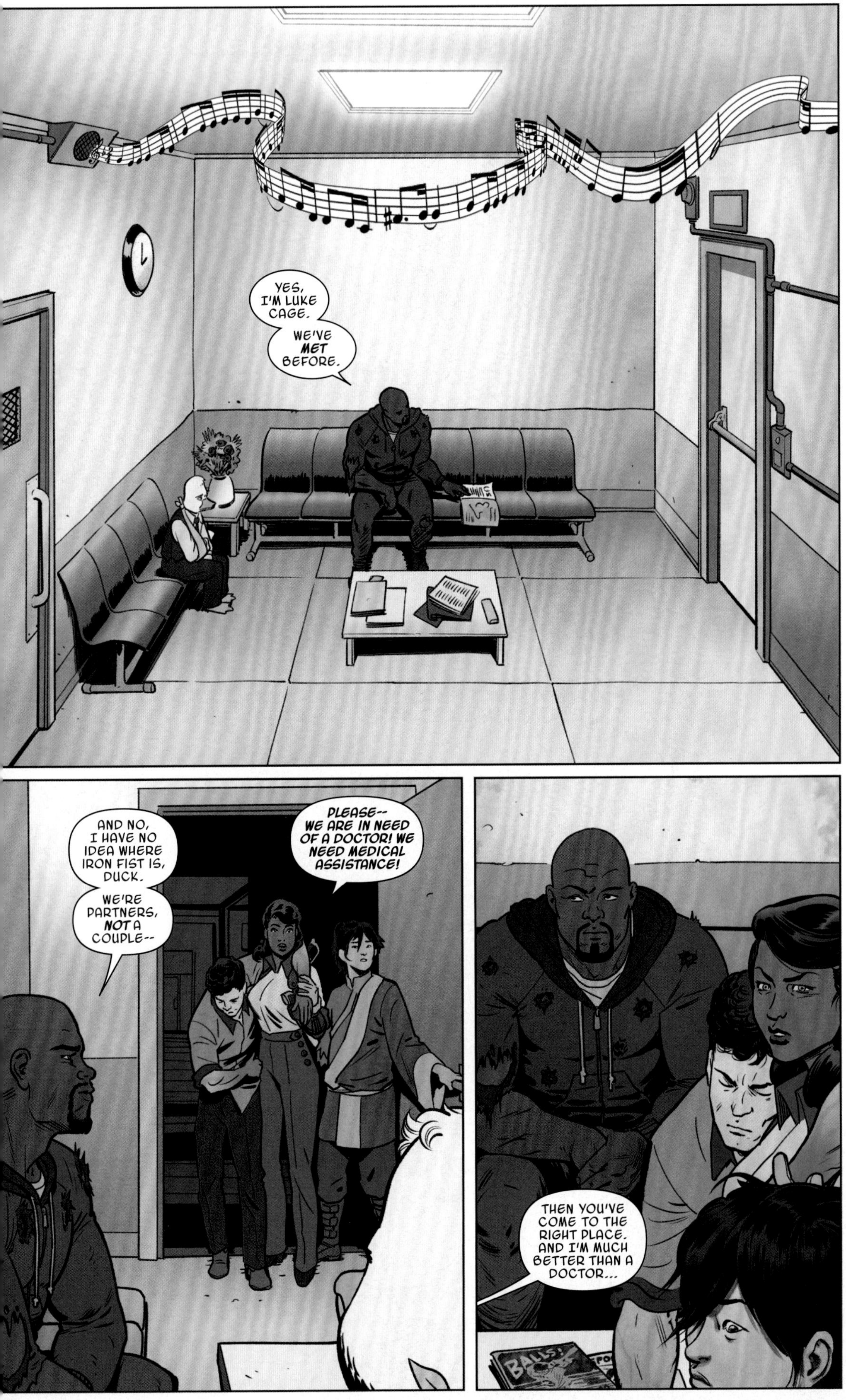
YES, I'M LUKE CAGE.
WE'VE MET BEFORE.
AND NO, I HAVE NO IDEA WHERE IRON FIST IS, DUCK.
WE'RE PARTNERS, NOT A COUPLE--
PLEASE-- WE ARE IN NEED OF A DOCTOR! WE NEED MEDICAL ASSISTANCE!
THEN YOU'VE COME TO THE RIGHT PLACE. AND I'M MUCH BETTER THAN A DOCTOR...

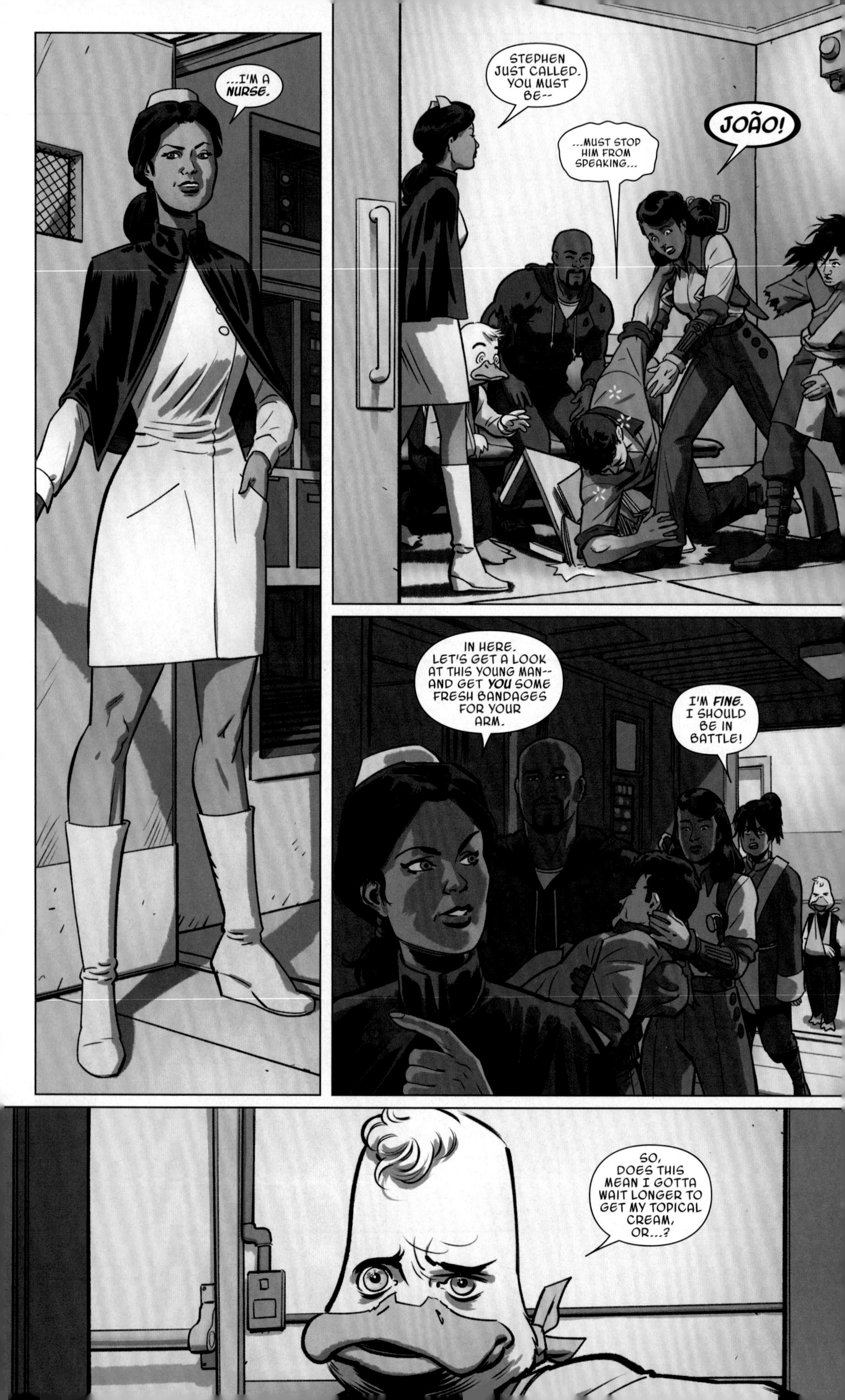
...I'M A NURSE.
STEPHEN JUST CALLED. YOU MUST BE--
...MUST STOP HIM FROM SPEAKING...
JOÃO!
IN HERE. LET'S GET A LOOK AT THIS YOUNG MAN-- AND GET YOU SOME FRESH BANDAGES FOR YOUR ARM.
I'M FINE. I SHOULD BE IN BATTLE!
SO, DOES THIS MEAN I GOTTA WAIT LONGER TO GET MY TOPICAL CREAM, OR...?

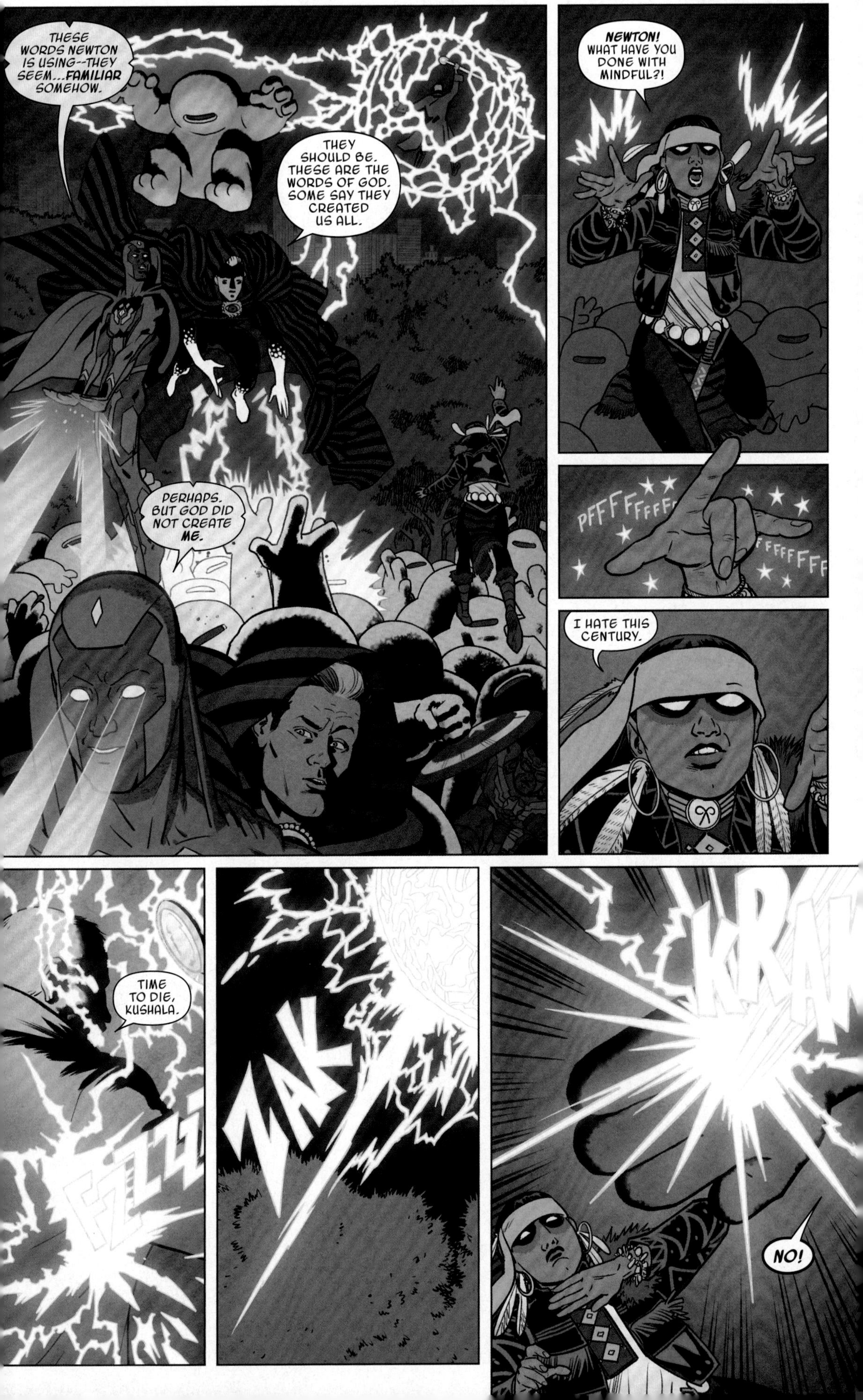
THESE WORDS NEWTON IS USING--THEY SEEM...FAMILIAR SOMEHOW.
THEY SHOULD BE. THESE ARE THE WORDS OF GOD. SOME SAY THEY CREATED US ALL.
PERHAPS. BUT GOD DID NOT CREATE ME.
NEWTON! WHAT HAVE YOU DONE WITH MINDFUL?!
PFFFFFFFF
FFFFFFFF
I HATE THIS CENTURY.
TIME TO DIE, KUSHALA.
FZZZ
ZAK
KRA
NO!

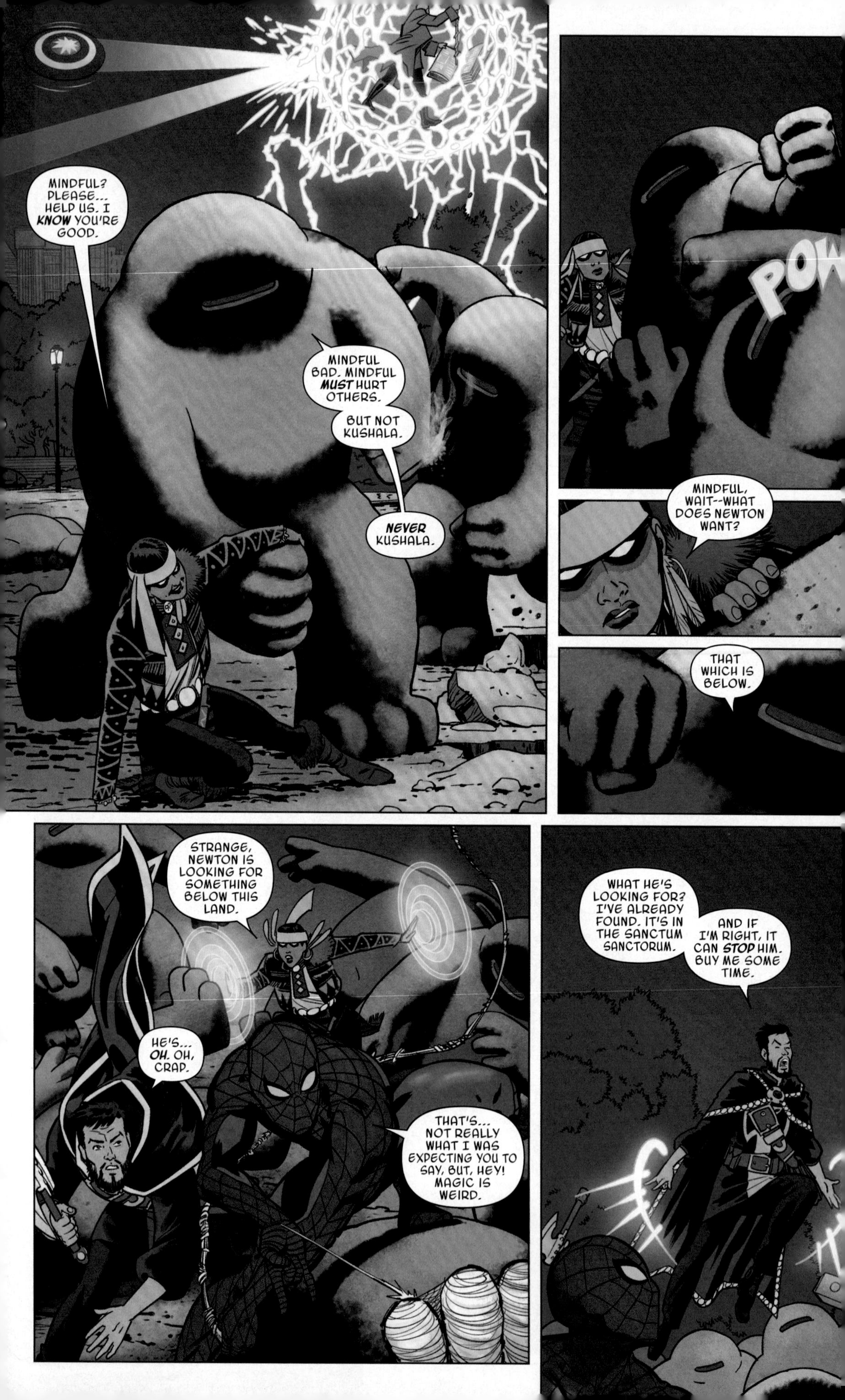
MINDFUL? PLEASE... HELP US. I KNOW YOU'RE GOOD.
MINDFUL BAD. MINDFUL MUST HURT OTHERS.
BUT NOT KUSHALA.
NEVER KUSHALA.
POW
MINDFUL, WAIT--WHAT DOES NEWTON WANT?
THAT WHICH IS BELOW.
STRANGE, NEWTON IS LOOKING FOR SOMETHING BELOW THIS LAND.
HE'S... OH. OH, CRAP.
THAT'S... NOT REALLY WHAT I WAS EXPECTING YOU TO SAY, BUT, HEY! MAGIC IS WEIRD.
WHAT HE'S LOOKING FOR? I'VE ALREADY FOUND. IT'S IN THE SANCTUM SANCTORUM.
AND IF I'M RIGHT, IT CAN STOP HIM. BUY ME SOME TIME.

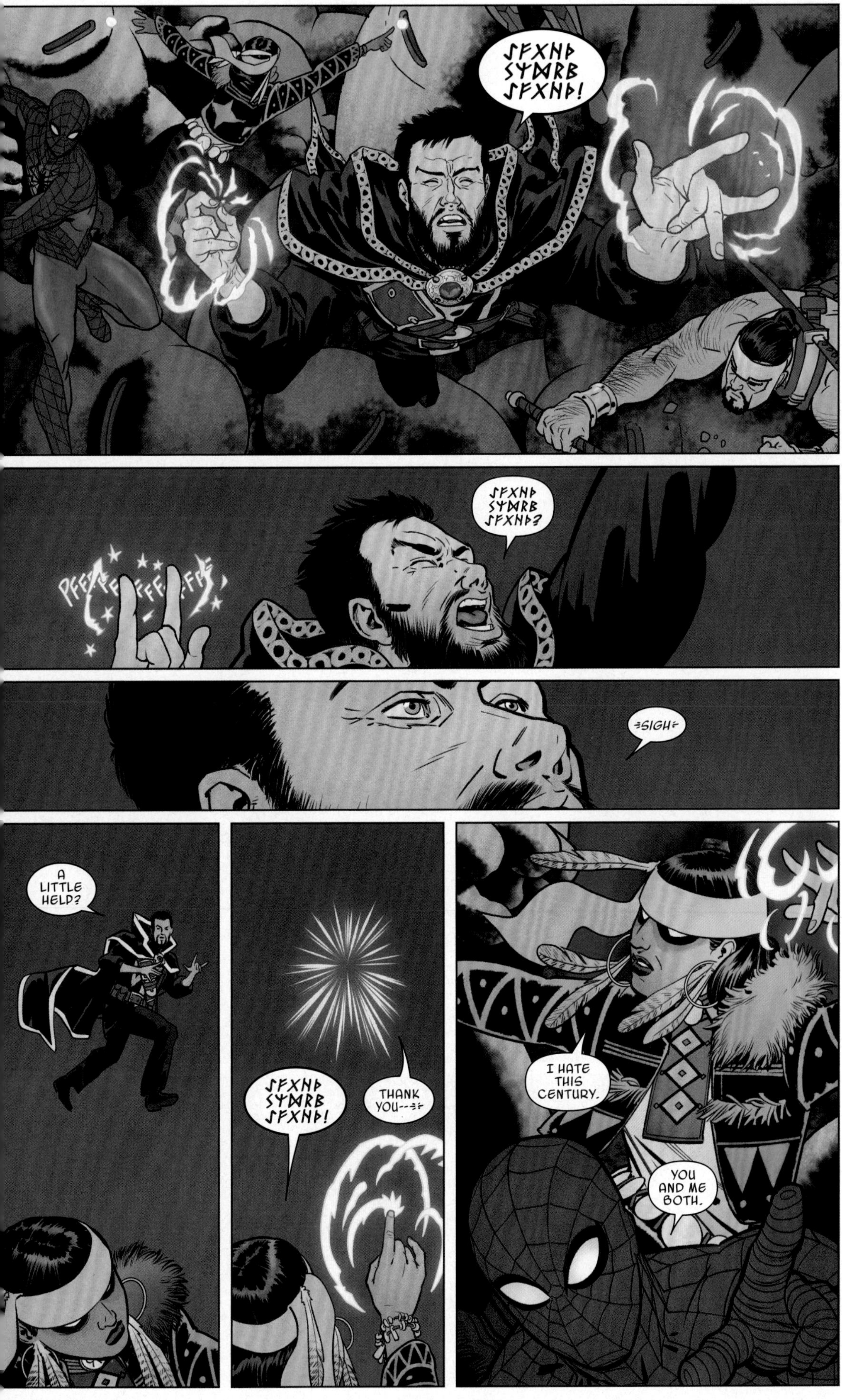
=SIGH=
A LITTLE HELP?
THANK YOU--=
I HATE THIS CENTURY.
YOU AND ME BOTH.

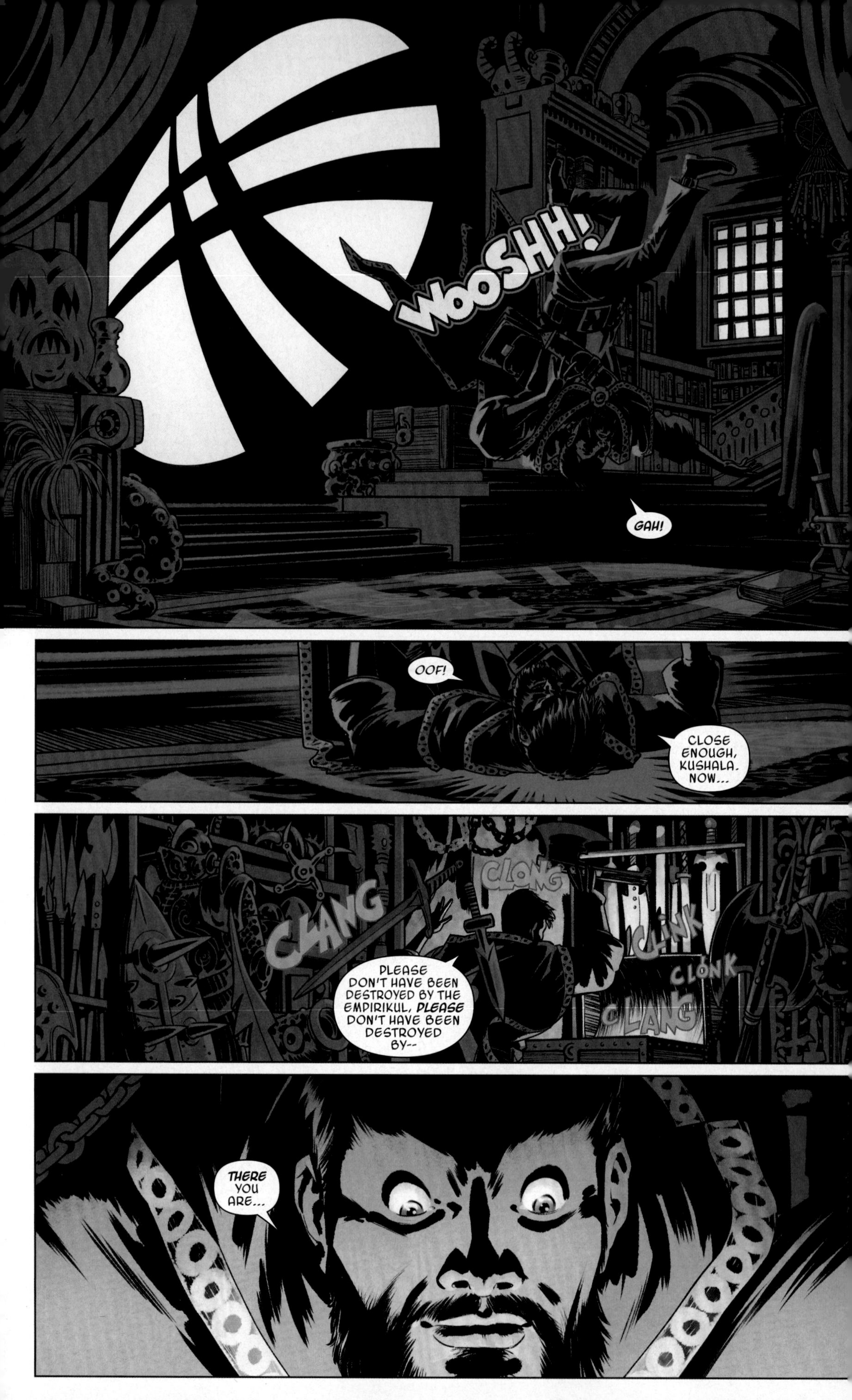
WOOSHH!
GAH!
OOF!
CLOSE ENOUGH, KUSHALA. NOW...
CLANG
CLONG
CLINK
CLONK
CLANG
PLEASE DON'T HAVE BEEN DESTROYED BY THE EMPIRIKUL, PLEASE DON'T HAVE BEEN DESTROYED BY--
THERE YOU ARE...

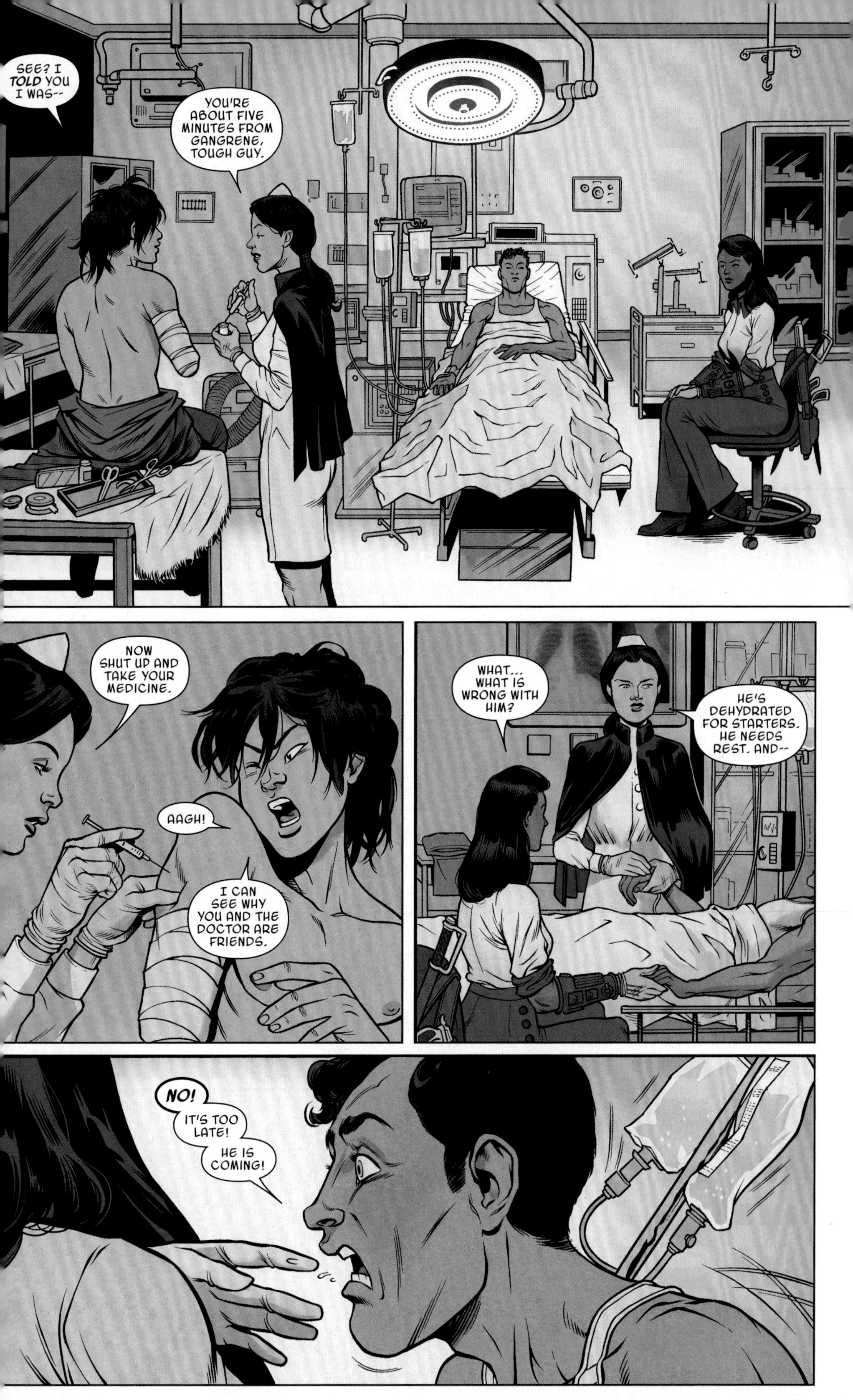
SEE? I TOLD YOU I WAS--
YOU'RE ABOUT FIVE MINUTES FROM GANGRENE, TOUGH GUY.
NOW SHUT UP AND TAKE YOUR MEDICINE.
AAGH!
I CAN SEE WHY YOU AND THE DOCTOR ARE FRIENDS.
WHAT... WHAT IS WRONG WITH HIM?
HE'S DEHYDRATED FOR STARTERS. HE NEEDS REST. AND--
NO!
IT'S TOO LATE!
HE IS COMING!

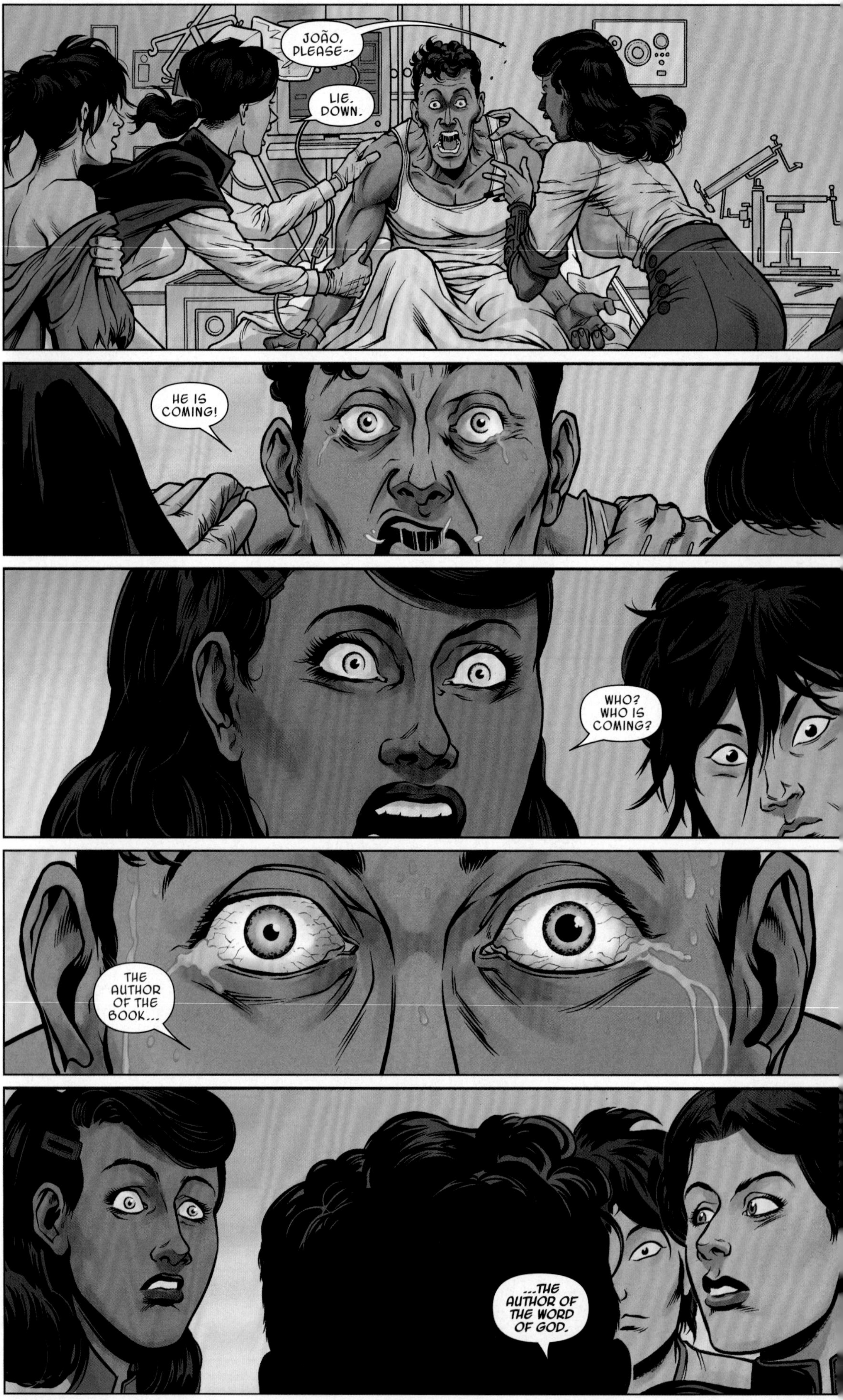
JOÃO, PLEASE--
LIE. DOWN.
HE IS COMING!
WHO? WHO IS COMING?
THE AUTHOR OF THE BOOK...
...THE AUTHOR OF THE WORD OF GOD.

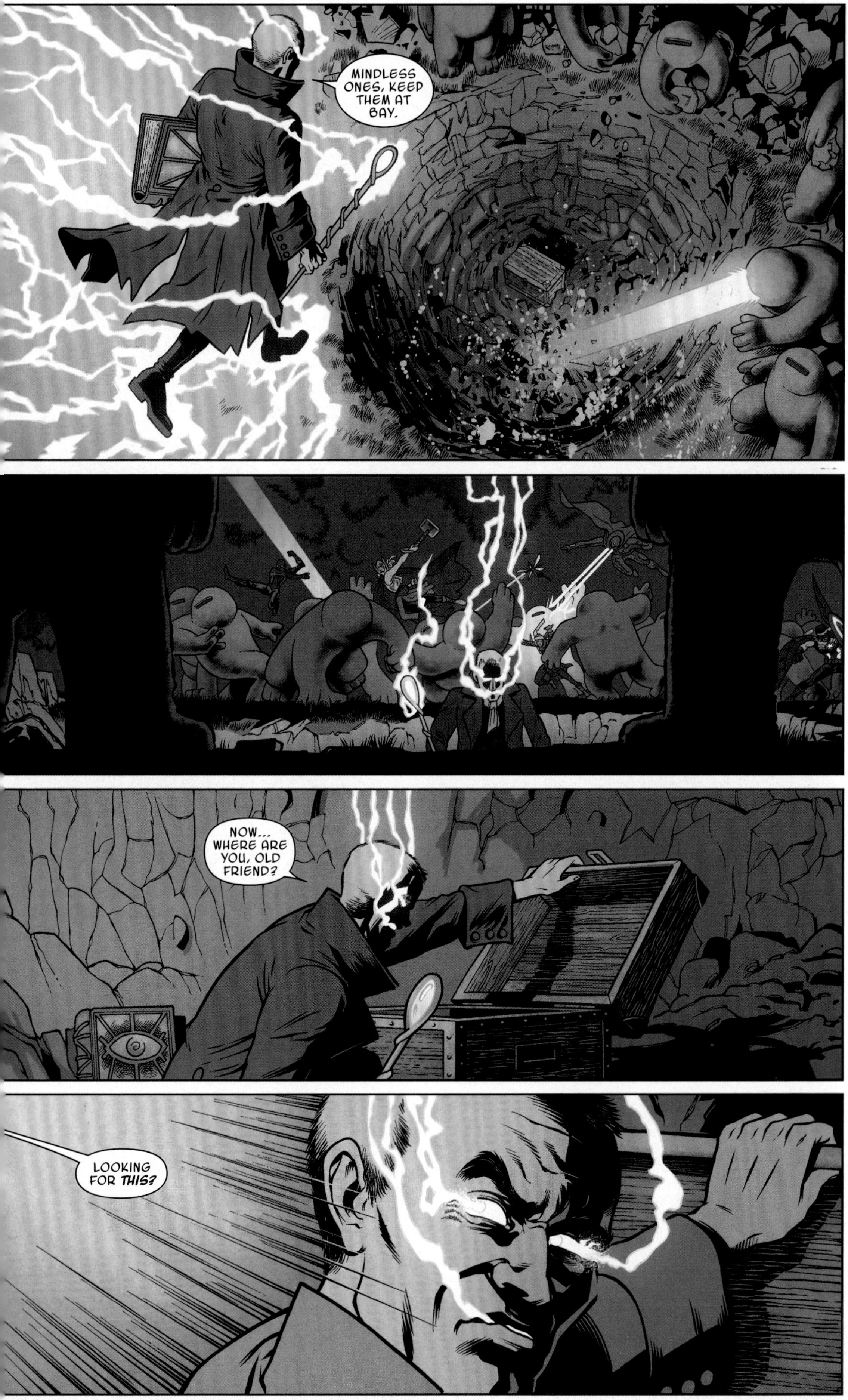
MINDLESS ONES, KEEP THEM AT BAY.
NOW... WHERE ARE YOU, OLD FRIEND?
LOOKING FOR THIS?

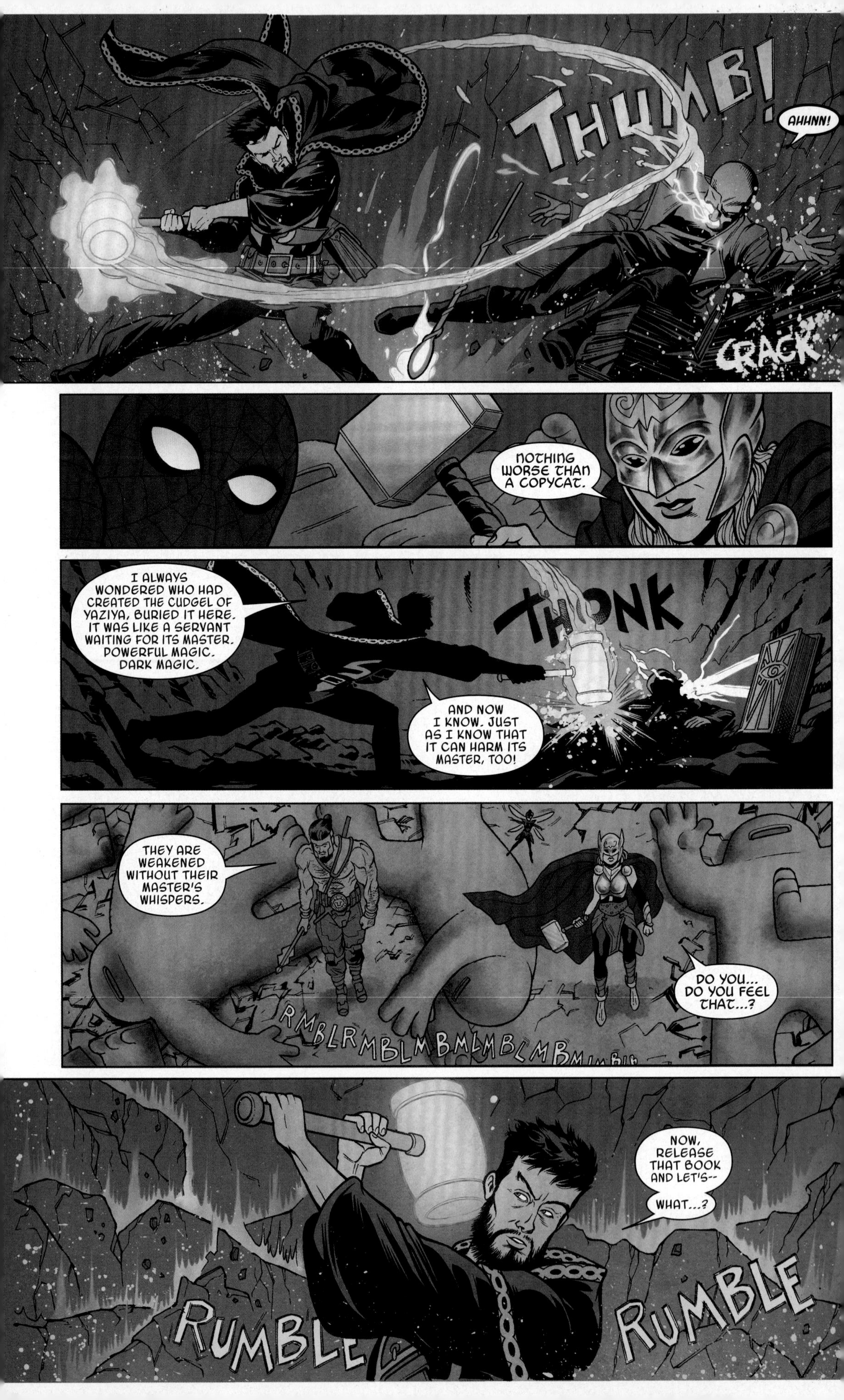
THUMB!
AHHNN!
CRACK
NOTHING WORSE THAN A COPYCAT.
I ALWAYS WONDERED WHO HAD CREATED THE CUDGEL OF YAZIYA, BURIED IT HERE. IT WAS LIKE A SERVANT WAITING FOR ITS MASTER. POWERFUL MAGIC. DARK MAGIC.
THONK
AND NOW I KNOW. JUST AS I KNOW THAT IT CAN HARM ITS MASTER, TOO!
THEY ARE WEAKENED WITHOUT THEIR MASTER'S WHISPERS.
DO YOU... DO YOU FEEL THAT...?
NOW, RELEASE THAT BOOK AND LET'S--
WHAT...?
RUMBLE
RUMBLE

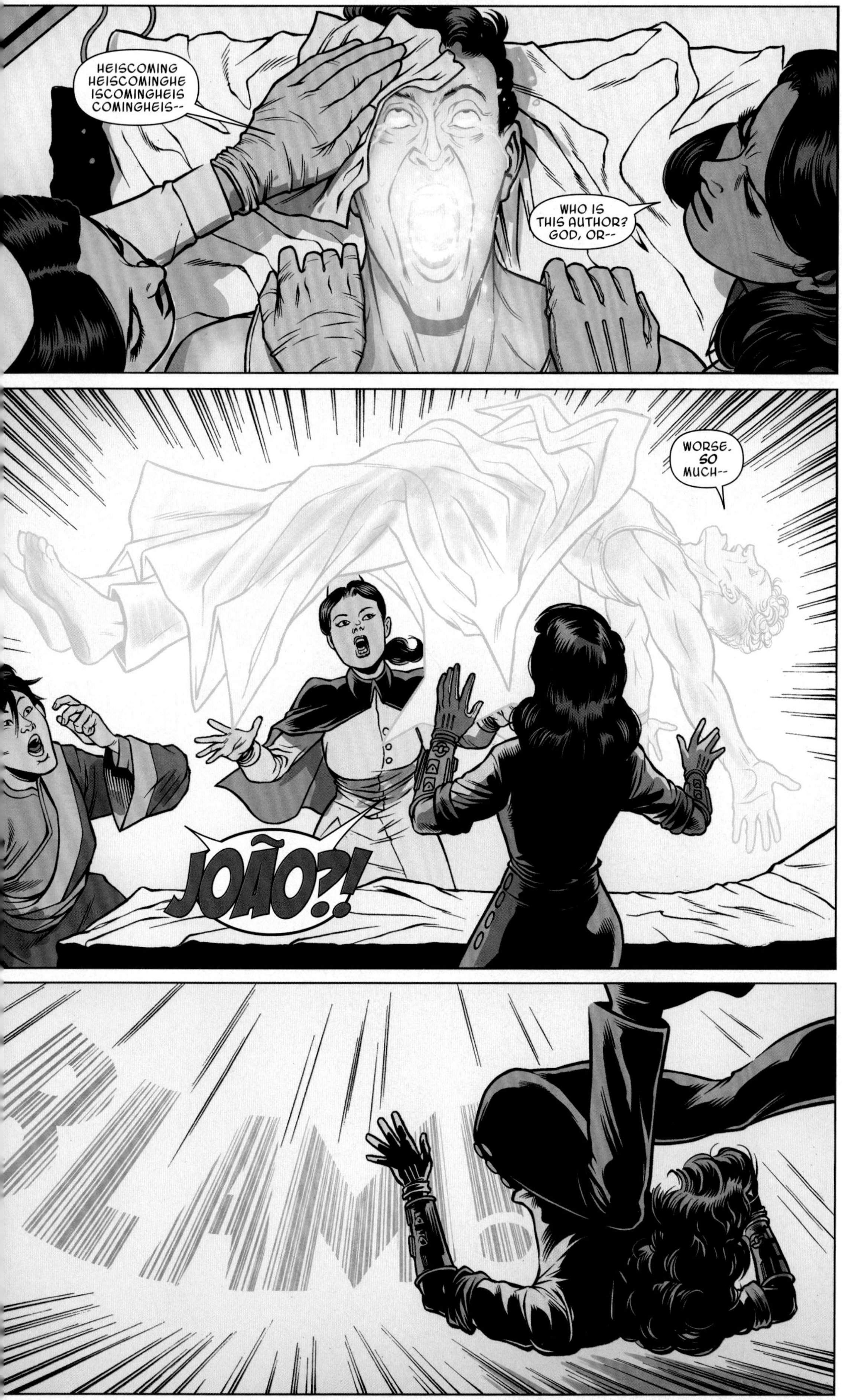

HEISCOMING HEISCOMINGHE ISCOMINGHEIS COMINGHEIS--
WHO IS THIS AUTHOR? GOD, OR--
WORSE. SO MUCH--
JOÃO?!

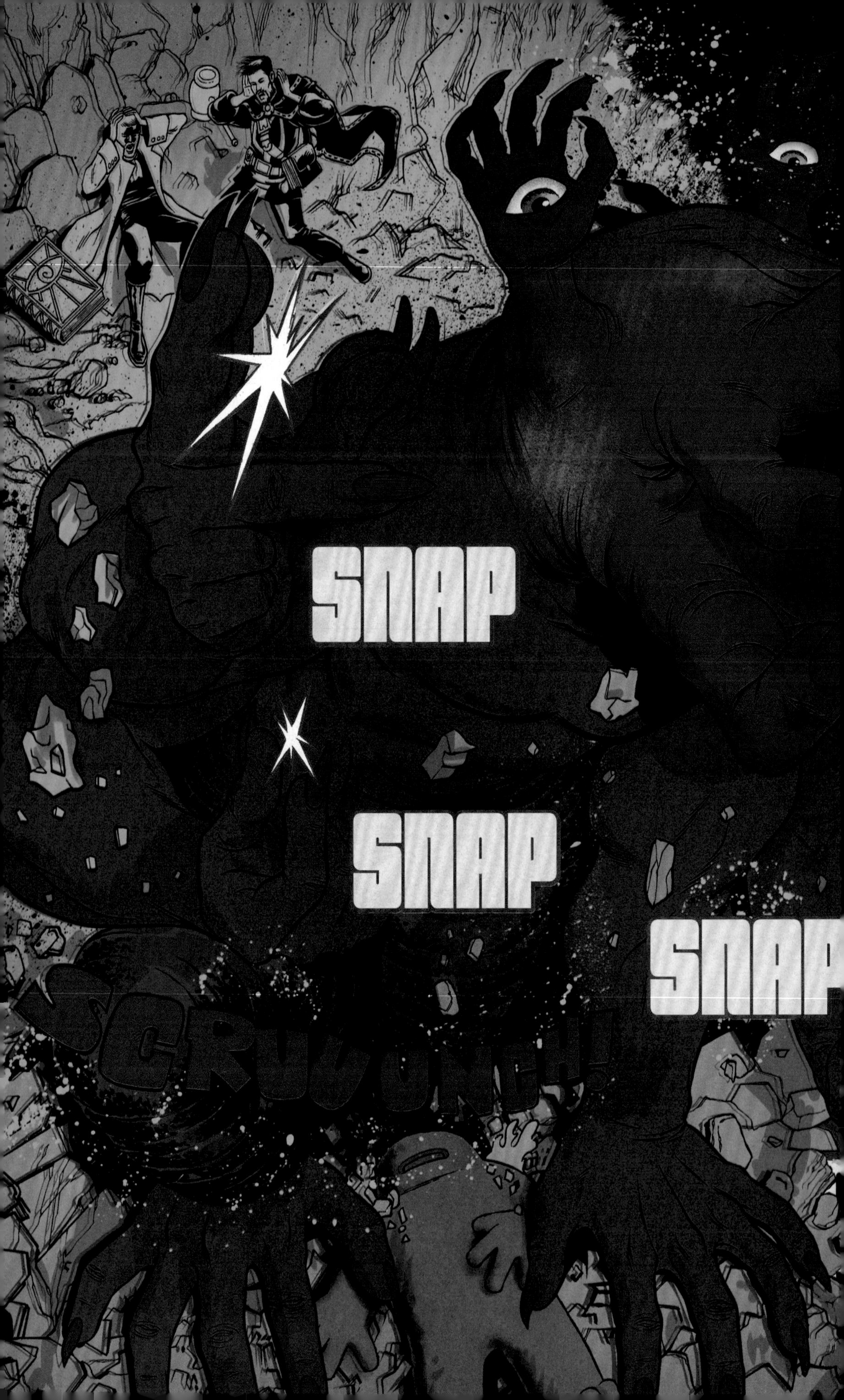

SNAP
SNAP
SNAP
CRUUUNCH!

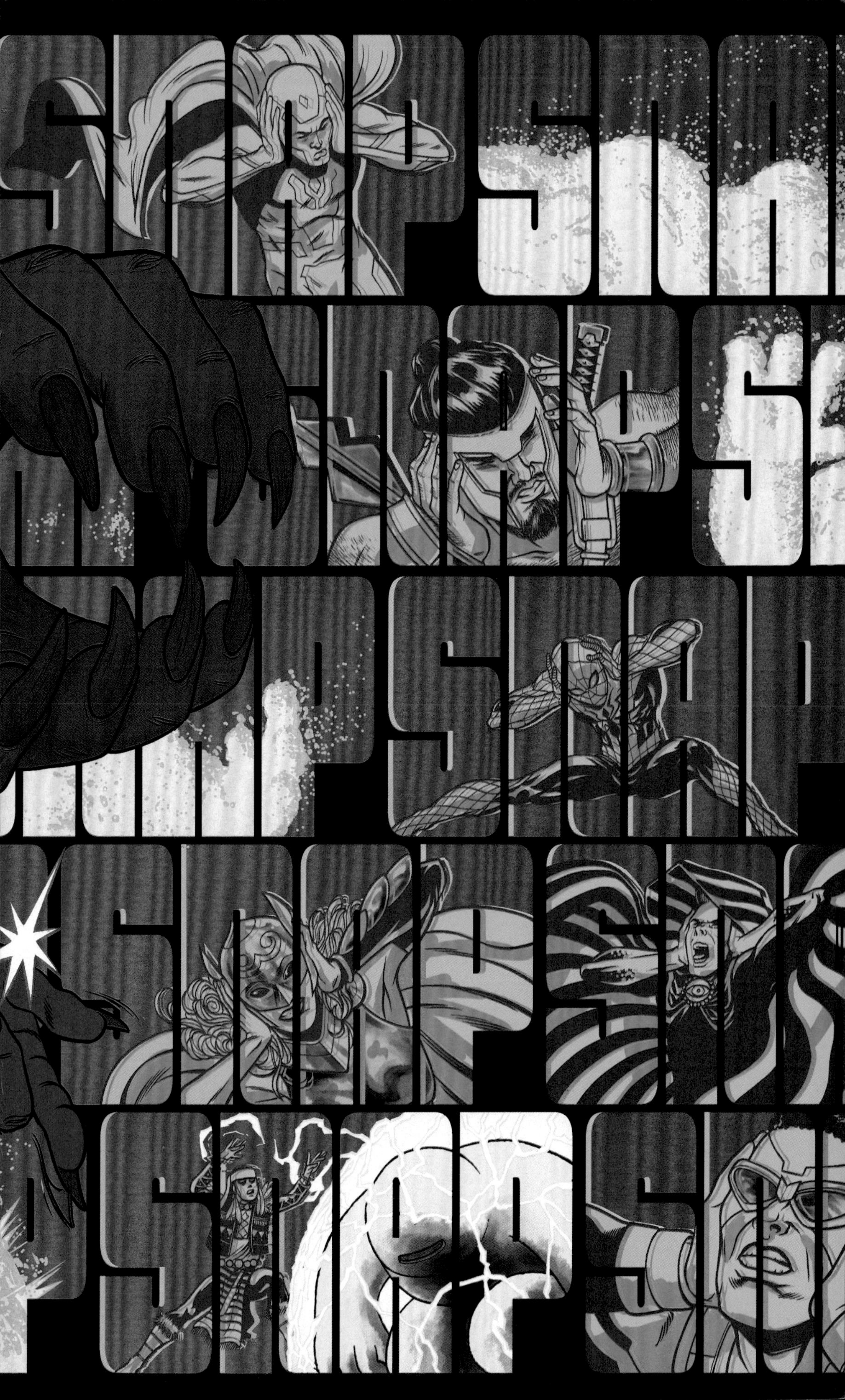

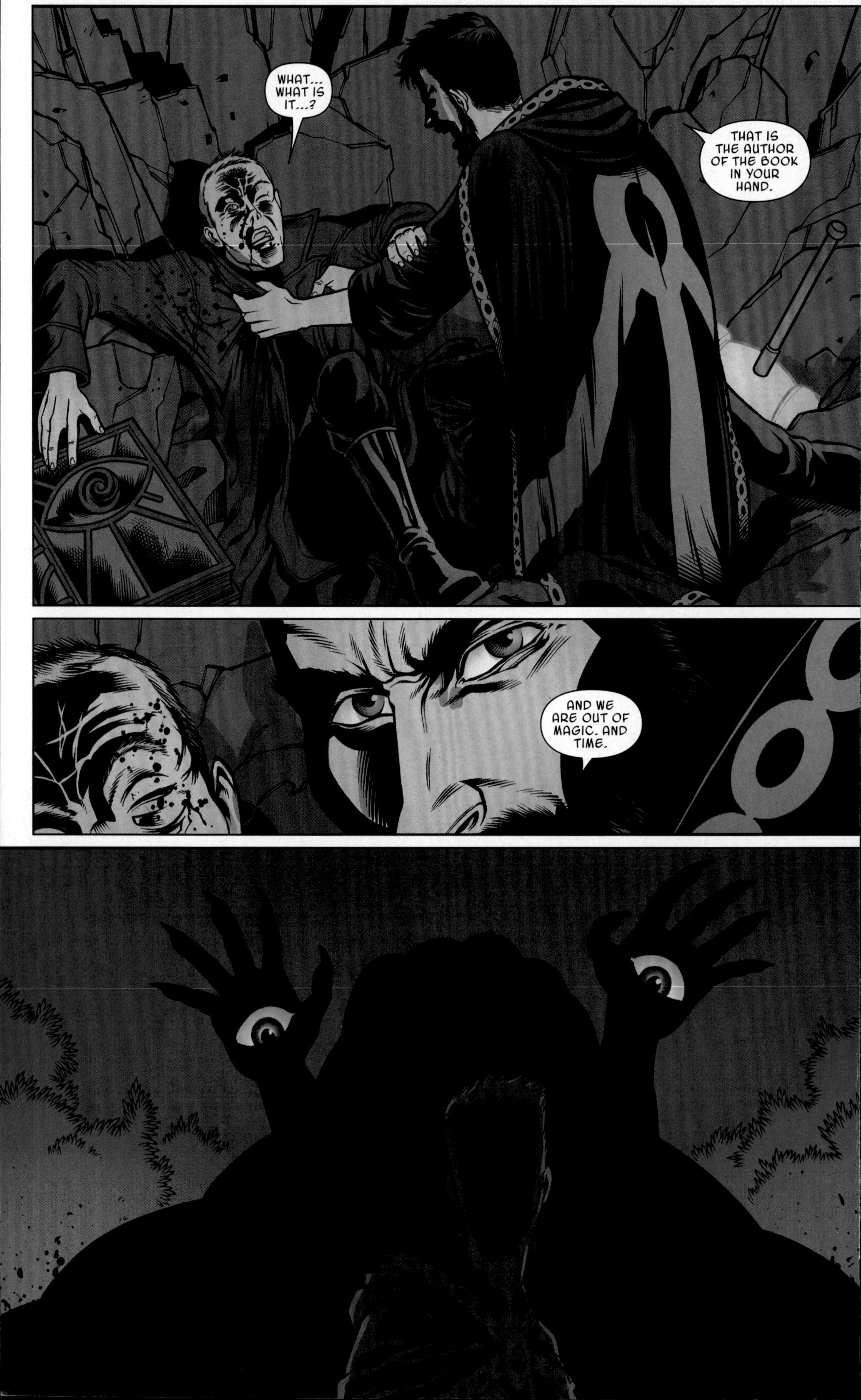
WHAT... WHAT IS IT...?
THAT IS THE AUTHOR OF THE BOOK IN YOUR HAND.
AND WE ARE OUT OF MAGIC. AND TIME.

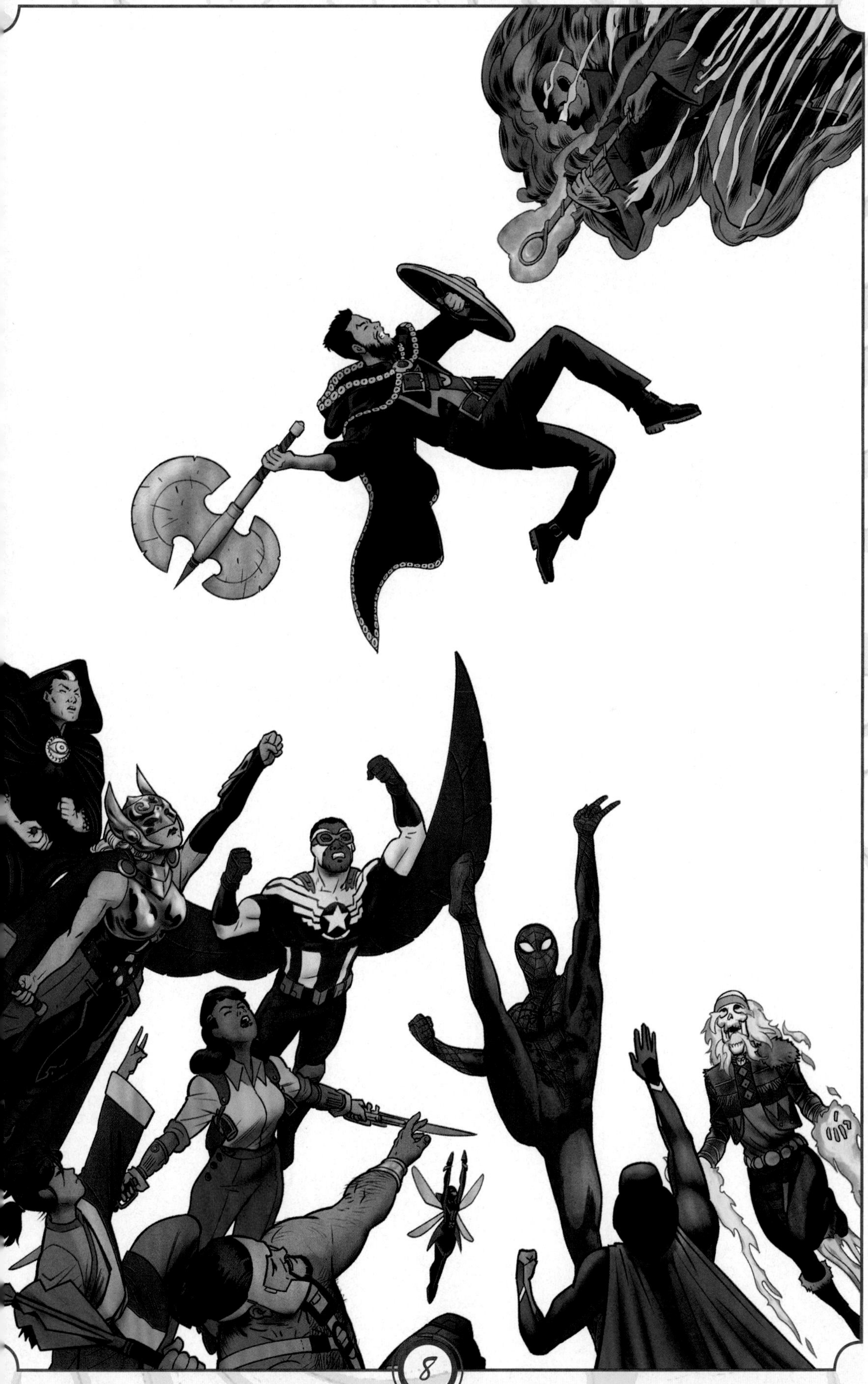

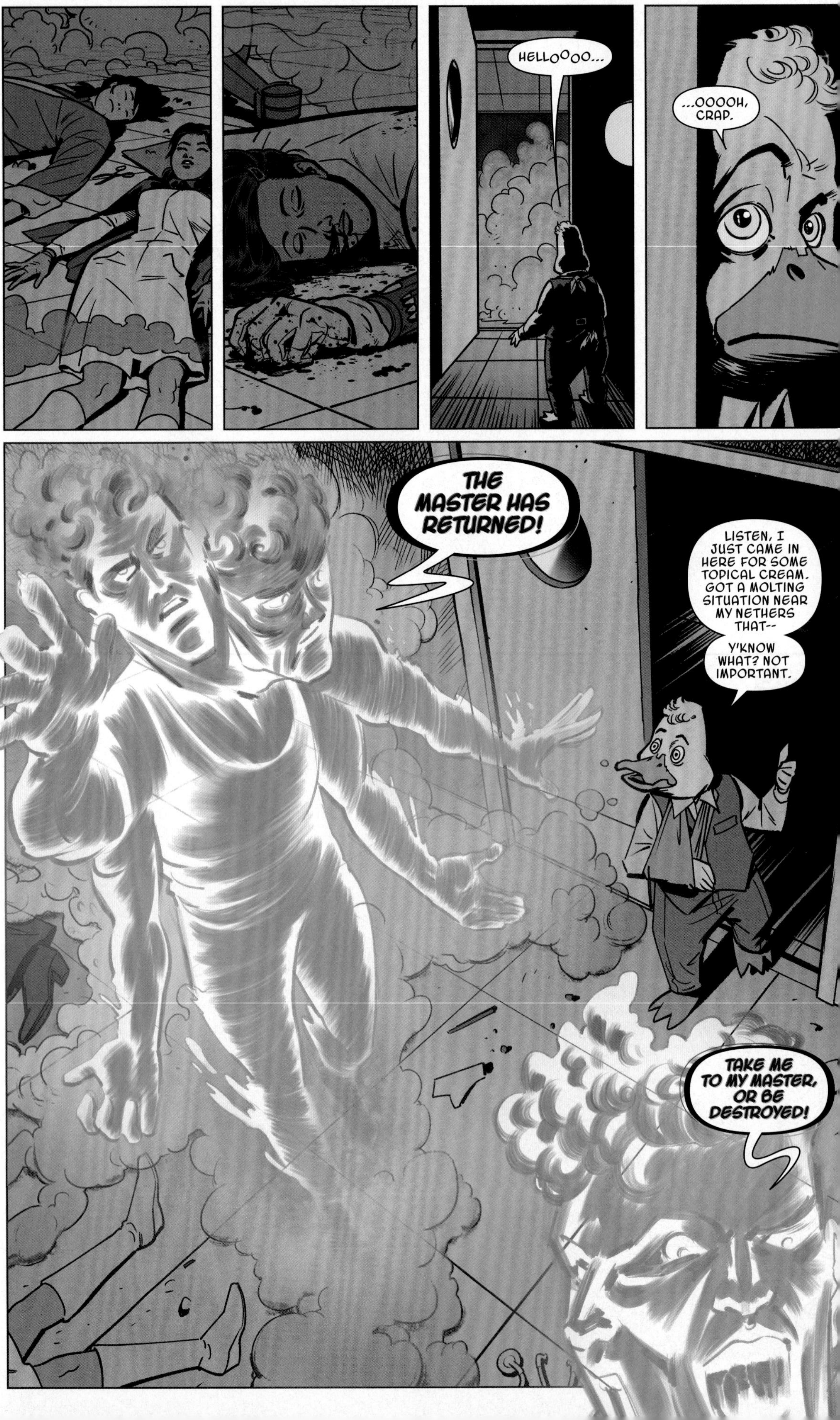
HELLOOOO...
...OOOOH, CRAP.
THE MASTER HAS RETURNED!
LISTEN, I JUST CAME IN HERE FOR SOME TOPICAL CREAM. GOT A MOLTING SITUATION NEAR MY NETHERS THAT--
Y'KNOW WHAT? NOT IMPORTANT.
TAKE ME TO MY MASTER, OR BE DESTROYED!

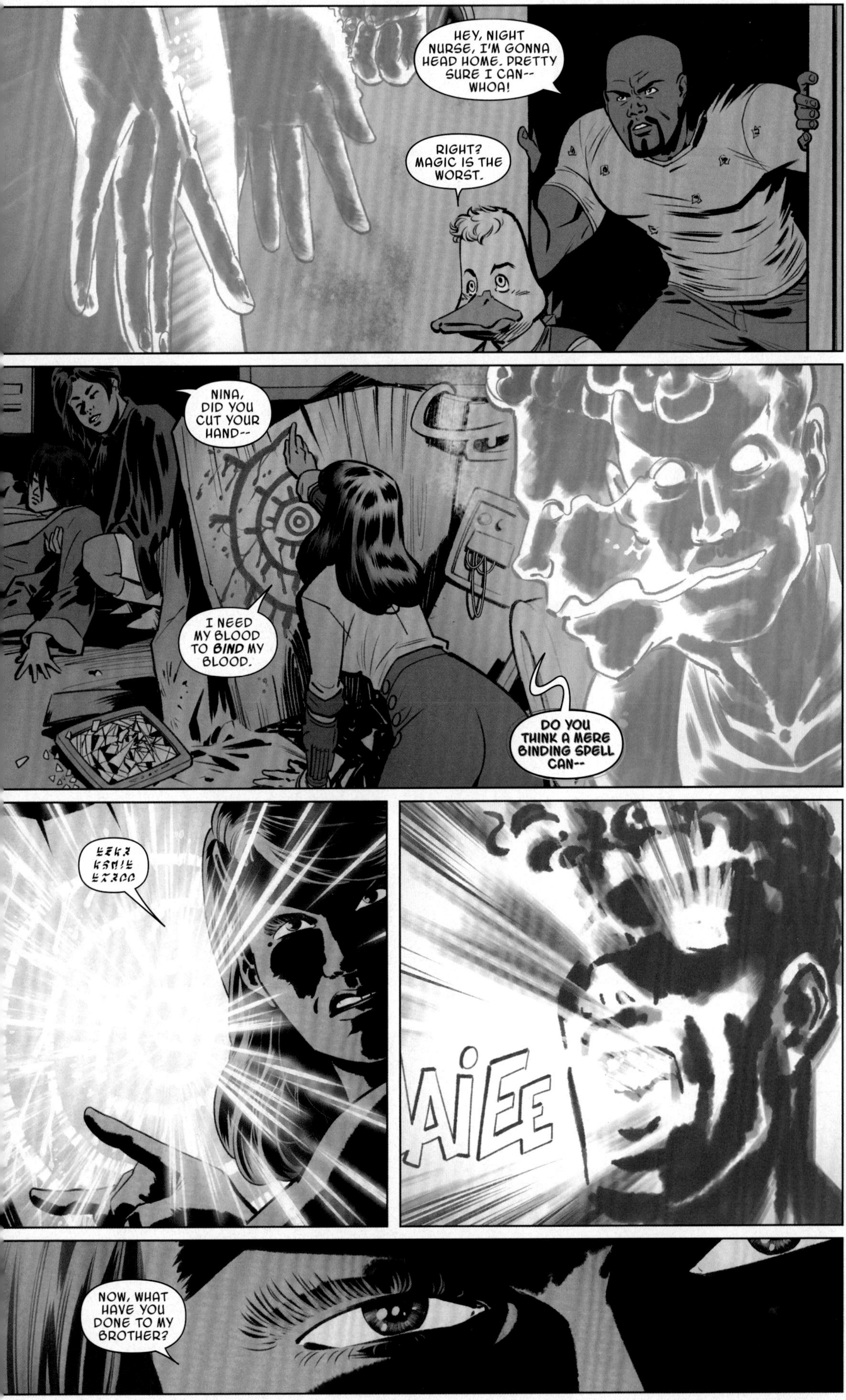
HEY, NIGHT NURSE, I'M GONNA HEAD HOME. PRETTY SURE I CAN-- WHOA!
RIGHT? MAGIC IS THE WORST.
NINA, DID YOU CUT YOUR HAND--
I NEED MY BLOOD TO BIND MY BLOOD.
DO YOU THINK A MERE BINDING SPELL CAN--
AIEE
NOW, WHAT HAVE YOU DONE TO MY BROTHER?

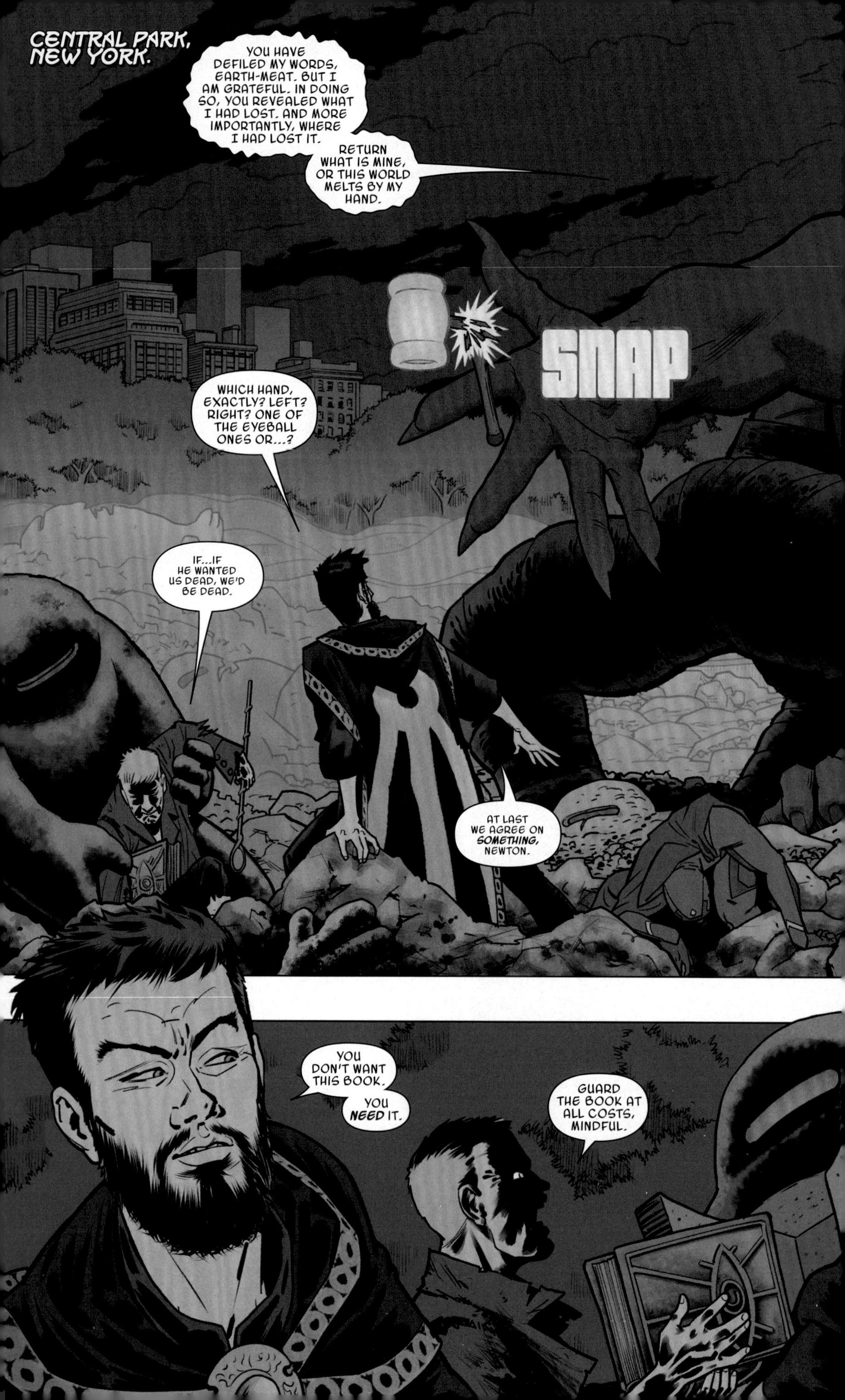
CENTRAL PARK, NEW YORK.
YOU HAVE DEFILED MY WORDS, EARTH-MEAT. BUT I AM GRATEFUL. IN DOING SO, YOU REVEALED WHAT I HAD LOST. AND MORE IMPORTANTLY, WHERE I HAD LOST IT.
RETURN WHAT IS MINE, OR THIS WORLD MELTS BY MY HAND.
SNAP
WHICH HAND, EXACTLY? LEFT? RIGHT? ONE OF THE EYEBALL ONES OR...?
IF...IF HE WANTED US DEAD, WE'D BE DEAD.
AT LAST WE AGREE ON SOMETHING, NEWTON.
YOU DON'T WANT THIS BOOK.
YOU NEED IT.
GUARD THE BOOK AT ALL COSTS, MINDFUL.

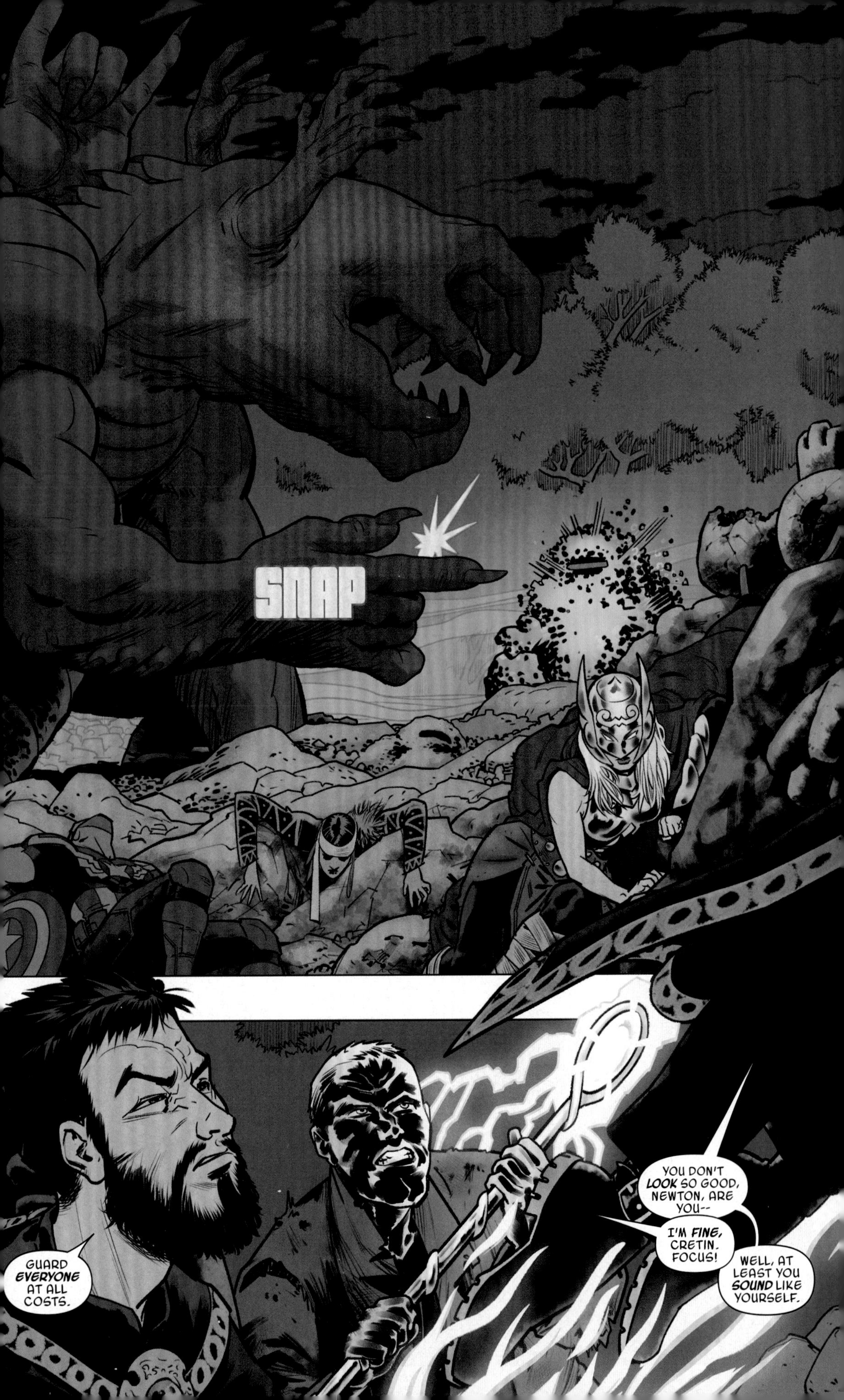
SNAP
GUARD EVERYONE AT ALL COSTS.
YOU DON'T LOOK SO GOOD, NEWTON, ARE YOU--
I'M FINE, CRETIN. FOCUS!
WELL, AT LEAST YOU SOUND LIKE YOURSELF.

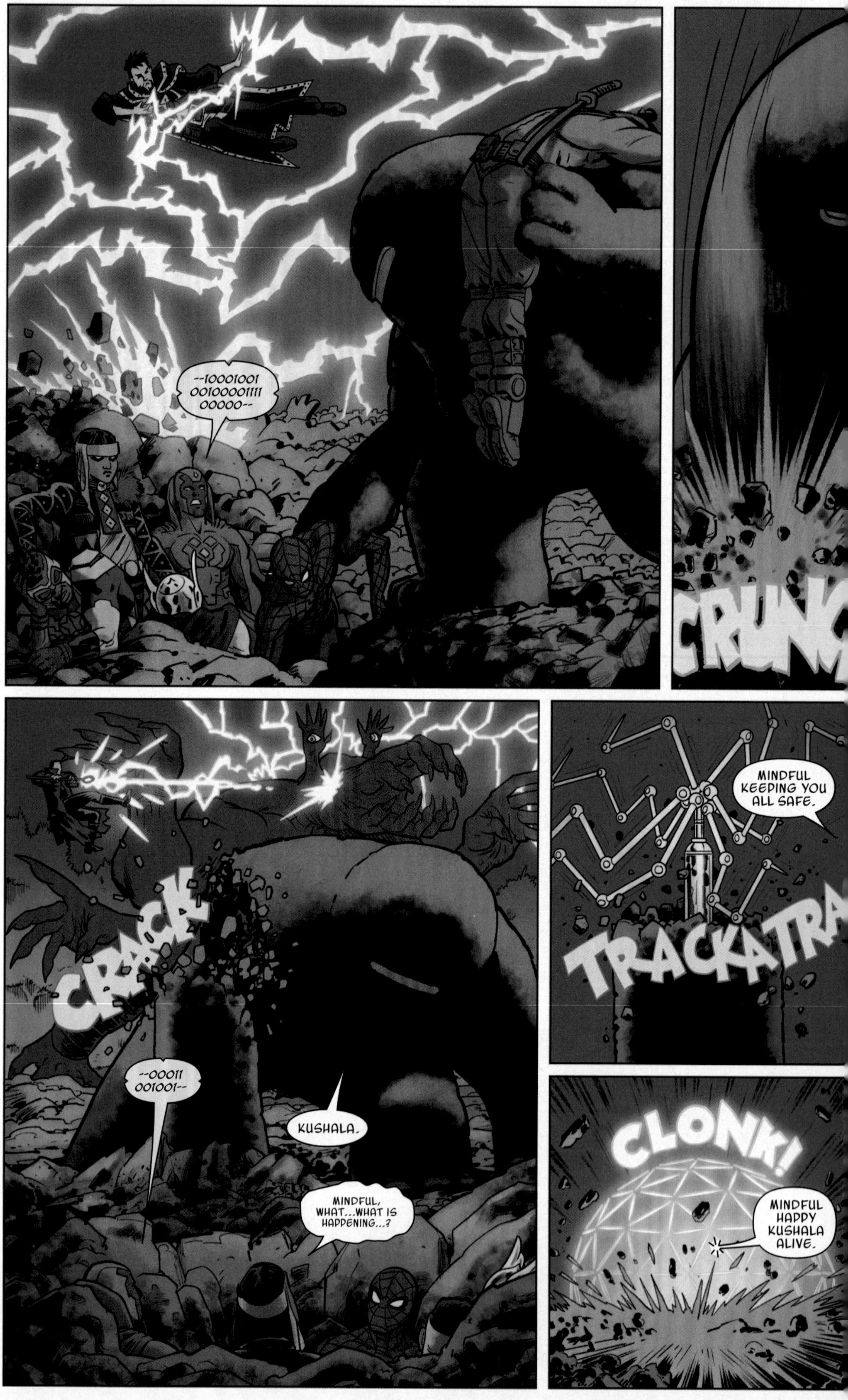
--10001001 00100001111 00000--
CRUNC
CRACK
--00011 001001--
KUSHALA.
MINDFUL, WHAT...WHAT IS HAPPENING...?
MINDFUL KEEPING YOU ALL SAFE.
TRACKATRA
CLONK!
MINDFUL HAPPY KUSHALA ALIVE.

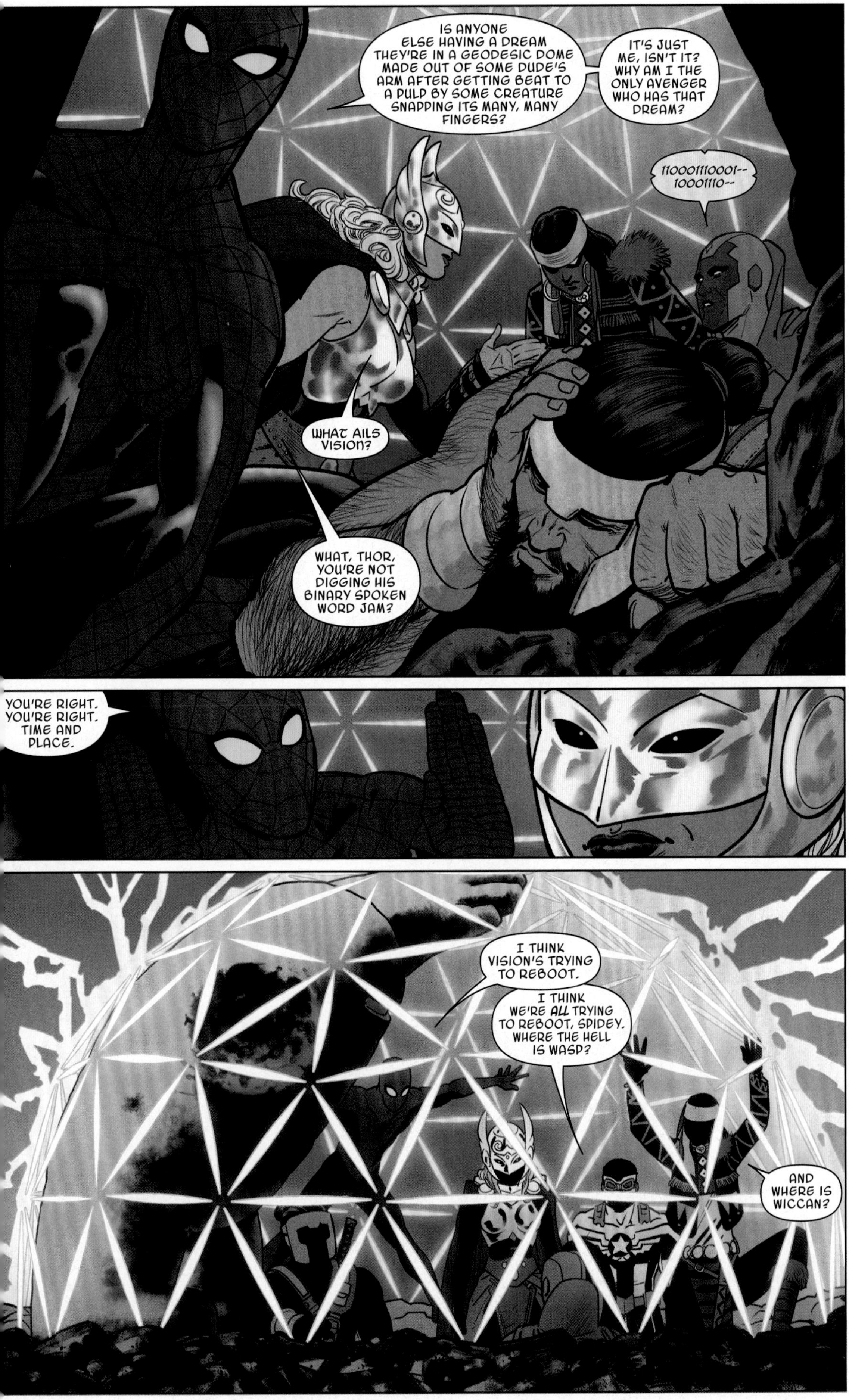
IS ANYONE ELSE HAVING A DREAM THEY'RE IN A GEODESIC DOME MADE OUT OF SOME DUDE'S ARM AFTER GETTING BEAT TO A PULP BY SOME CREATURE SNAPPING ITS MANY, MANY FINGERS?
IT'S JUST ME, ISN'T IT? WHY AM I THE ONLY AVENGER WHO HAS THAT DREAM?
110001110001-- 1000111O--
WHAT AILS VISION?
WHAT, THOR, YOU'RE NOT DIGGING HIS BINARY SPOKEN WORD JAM?
YOU'RE RIGHT. YOU'RE RIGHT. TIME AND PLACE.
I THINK VISION'S TRYING TO REBOOT.
I THINK WE'RE *ALL* TRYING TO REBOOT, SPIDEY. WHERE THE HELL IS WASP?
AND WHERE IS WICCAN?

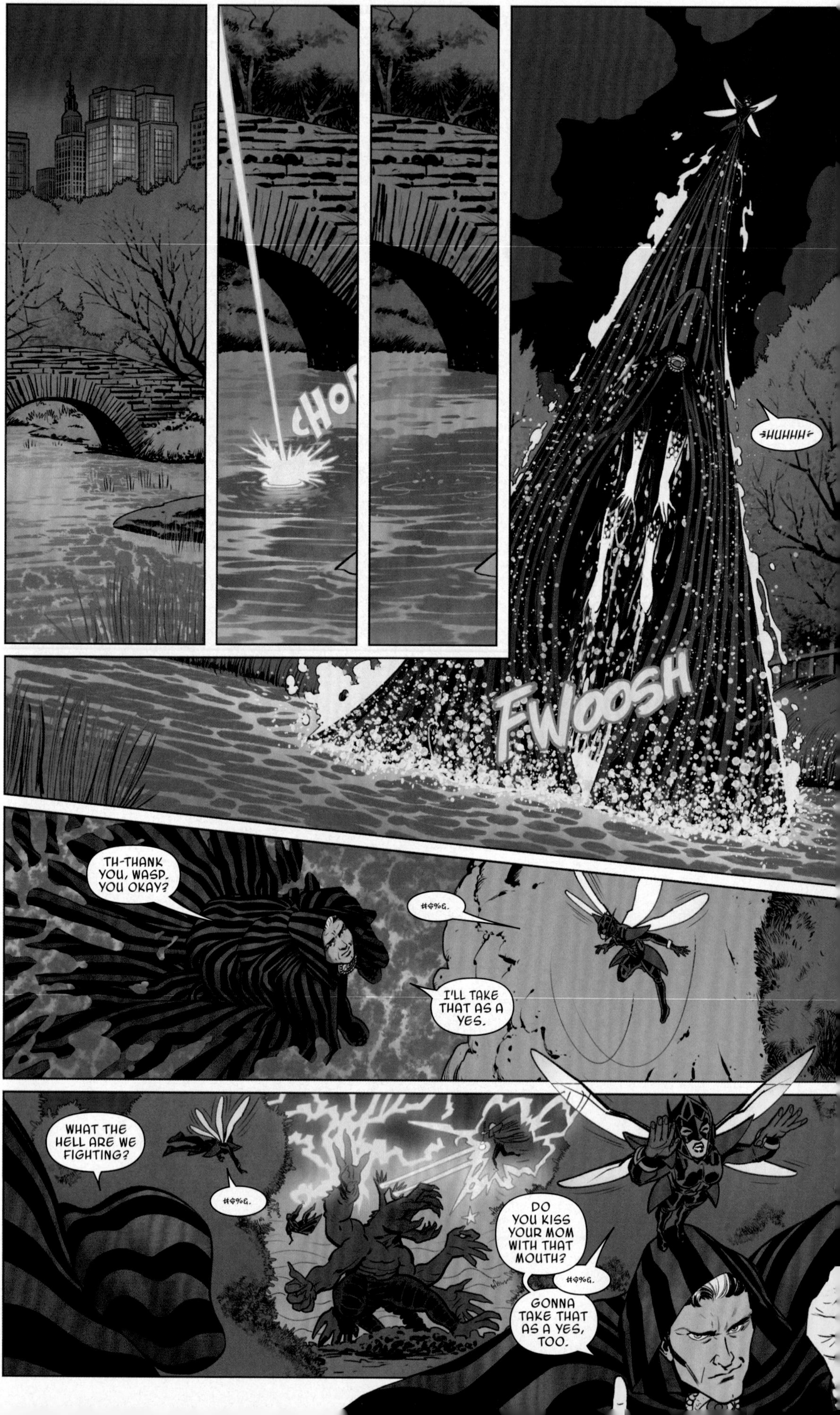
CHOP
-HUHHH-
FWOOSH
TH-THANK YOU, WASP. YOU OKAY?
#$%&.
I'LL TAKE THAT AS A YES.
WHAT THE HELL ARE WE FIGHTING?
#$%&.
DO YOU KISS YOUR MOM WITH THAT MOUTH?
#$%&.
GONNA TAKE THAT AS A YES, TOO.

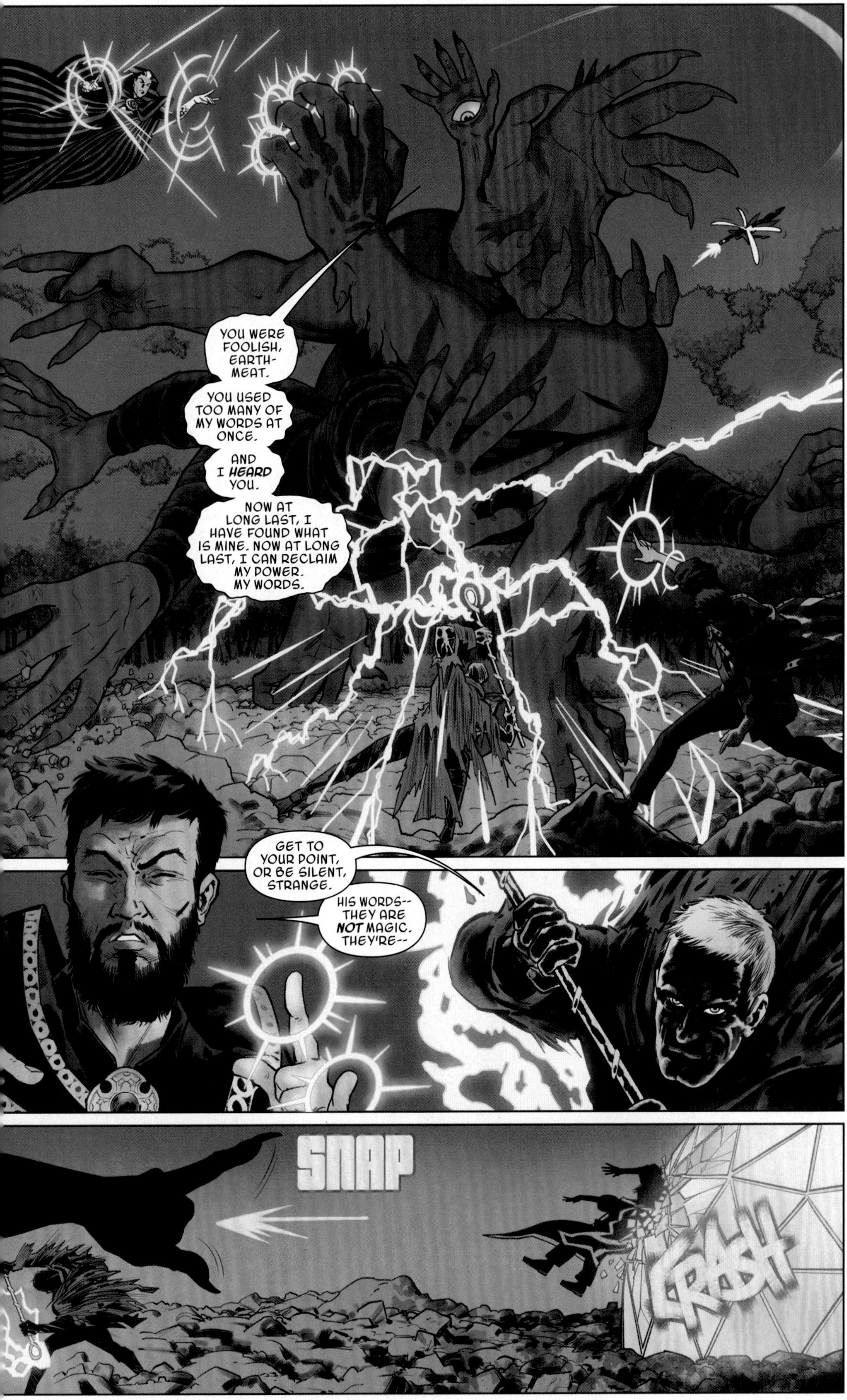
YOU WERE FOOLISH, EARTH-MEAT.
YOU USED TOO MANY OF MY WORDS AT ONCE.
AND I HEARD YOU.
NOW AT LONG LAST, I HAVE FOUND WHAT IS MINE. NOW AT LONG LAST, I CAN RECLAIM MY POWER. MY WORDS.
GET TO YOUR POINT, OR BE SILENT, STRANGE.
HIS WORDS-- THEY ARE NOT MAGIC. THEY'RE--
SNAP
CRASH

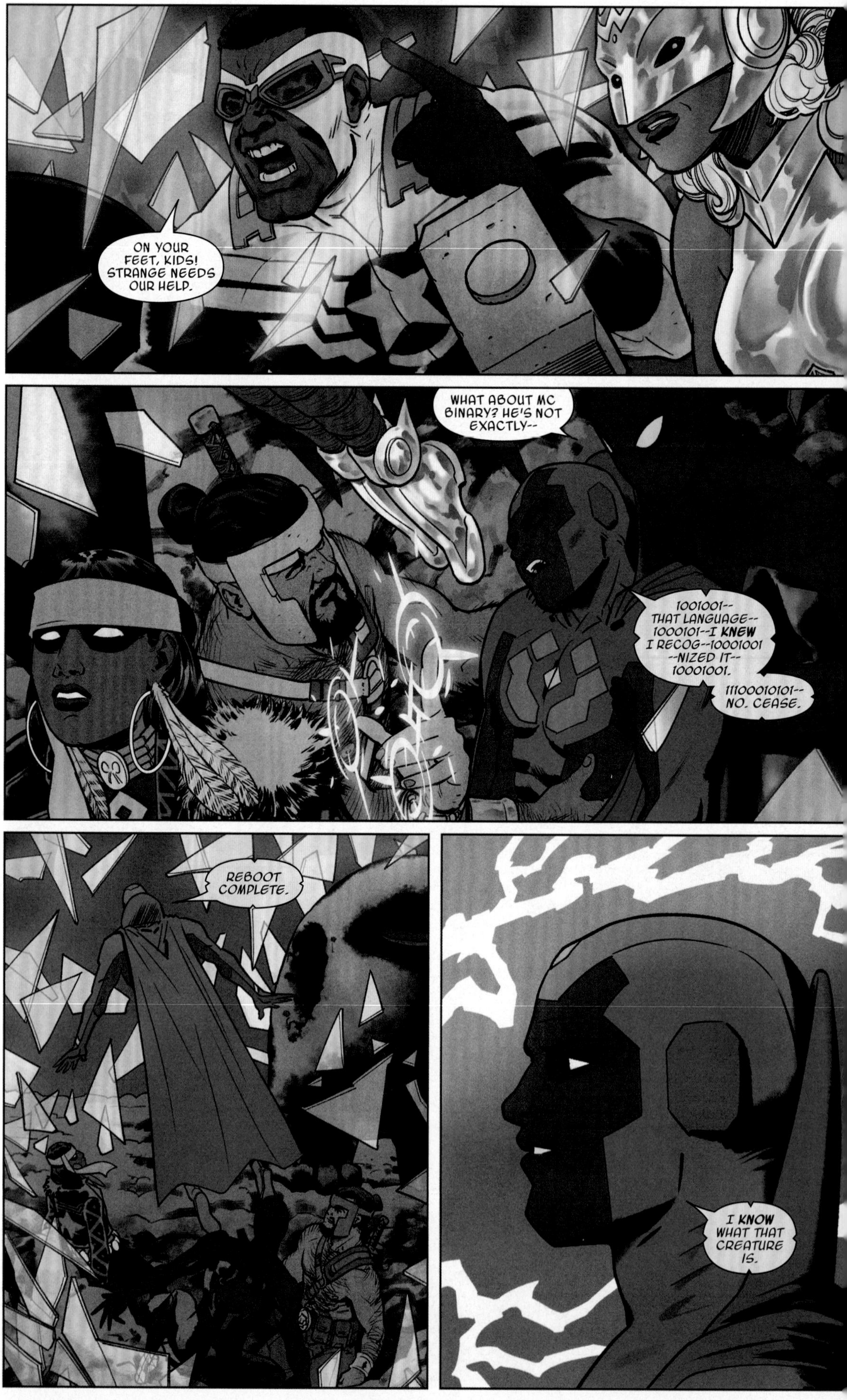
ON YOUR FEET, KIDS! STRANGE NEEDS OUR HELP.
WHAT ABOUT MC BINARY? HE'S NOT EXACTLY--
1001001-- THAT LANGUAGE-- 1000101--I **KNEW** I RECOG--10001001 --NIZED IT-- 10001001.
11100010101-- NO. CEASE.
REBOOT COMPLETE.
I **KNOW** WHAT THAT CREATURE IS.

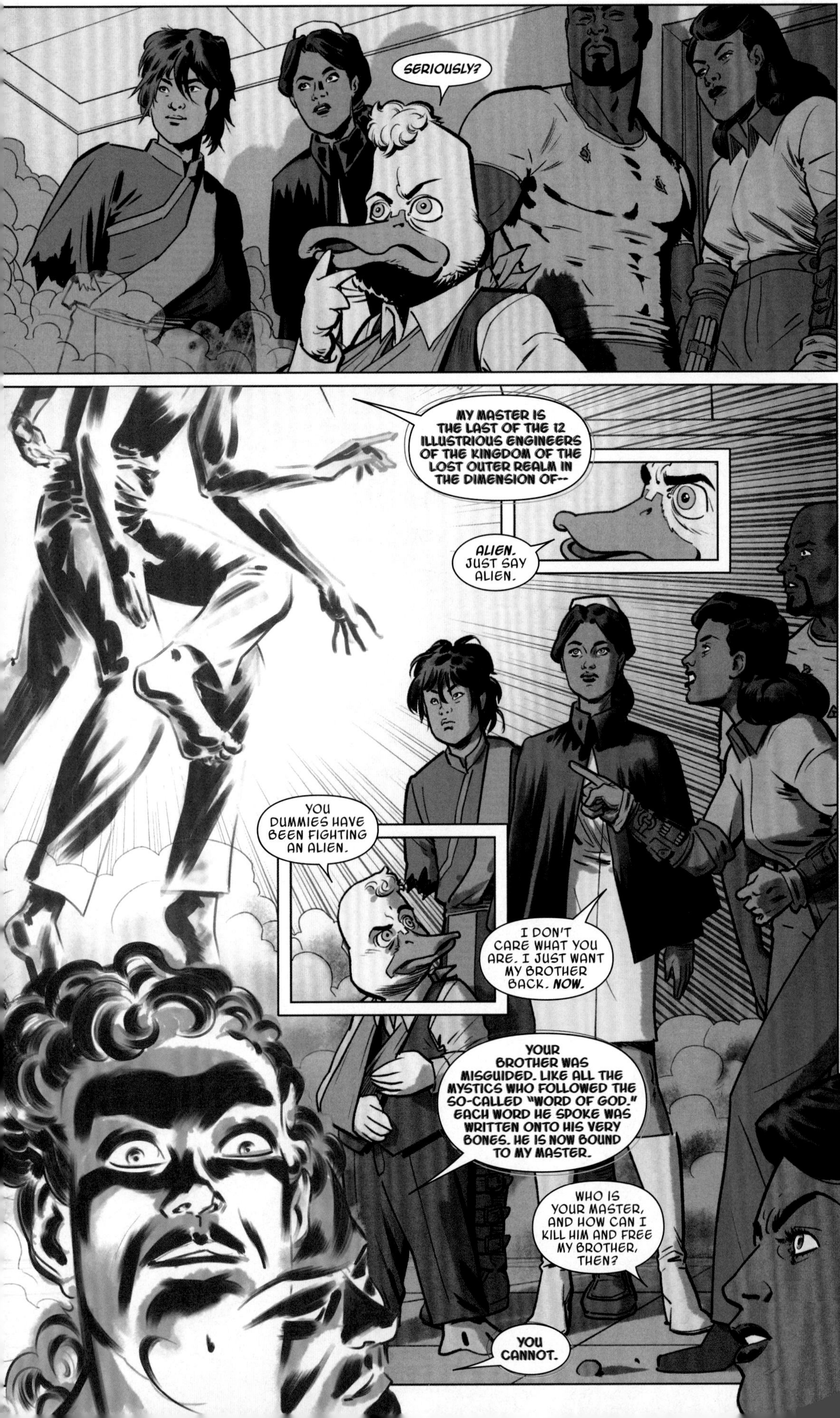
SERIOUSLY?
MY MASTER IS THE LAST OF THE 12 ILLUSTRIOUS ENGINEERS OF THE KINGDOM OF THE LOST OUTER REALM IN THE DIMENSION OF--
ALIEN. JUST SAY ALIEN.
YOU DUMMIES HAVE BEEN FIGHTING AN ALIEN.
I DON'T CARE WHAT YOU ARE. I JUST WANT MY BROTHER BACK. NOW.
YOUR BROTHER WAS MISGUIDED. LIKE ALL THE MYSTICS WHO FOLLOWED THE SO-CALLED "WORD OF GOD." EACH WORD HE SPOKE WAS WRITTEN ONTO HIS VERY BONES. HE IS NOW BOUND TO MY MASTER.
WHO IS YOUR MASTER, AND HOW CAN I KILL HIM AND FREE MY BROTHER, THEN?
YOU CANNOT.

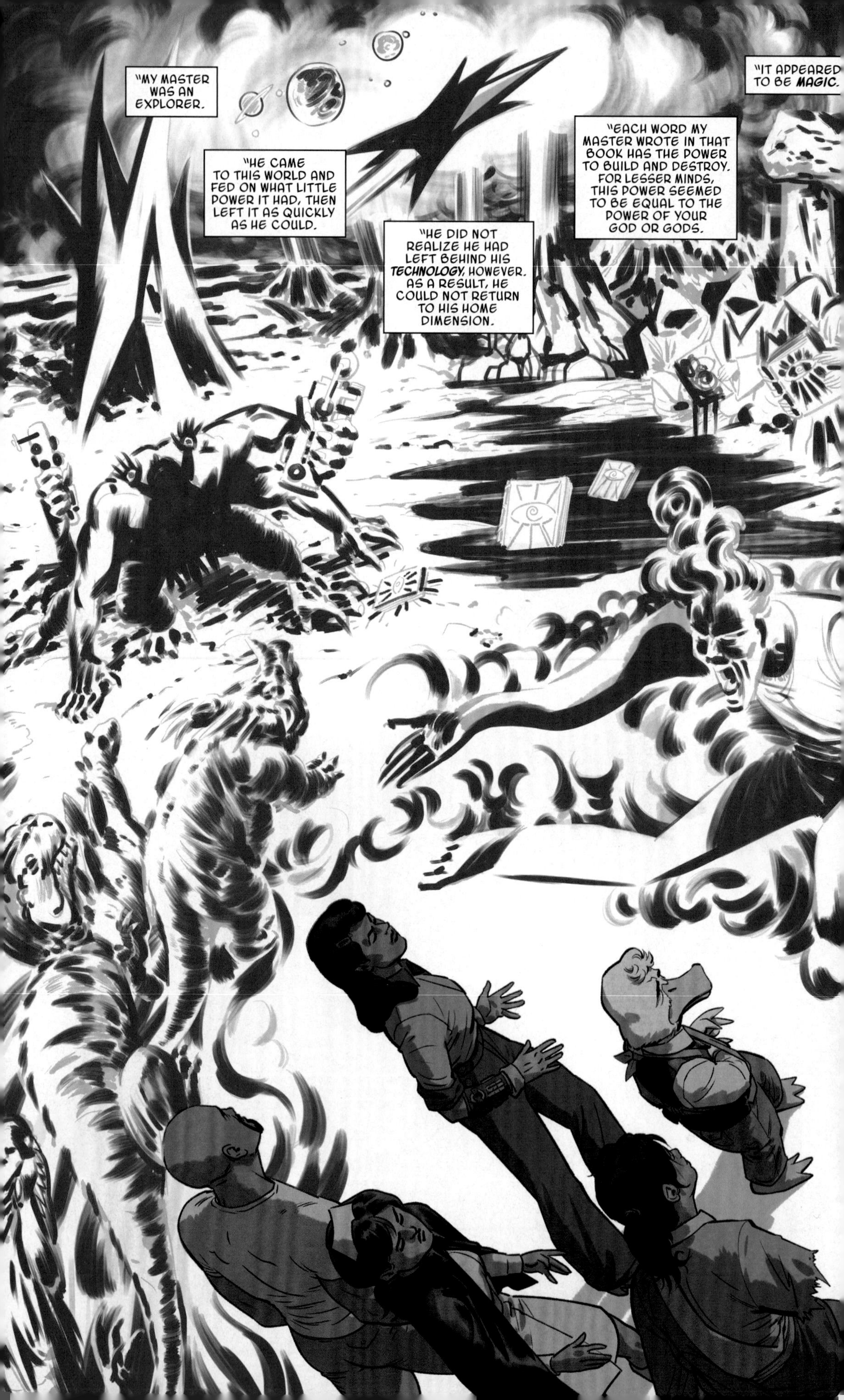

"MY MASTER WAS AN EXPLORER.
"HE CAME TO THIS WORLD AND FED ON WHAT LITTLE POWER IT HAD, THEN LEFT IT AS QUICKLY AS HE COULD.
"HE DID NOT REALIZE HE HAD LEFT BEHIND HIS TECHNOLOGY, HOWEVER. AS A RESULT, HE COULD NOT RETURN TO HIS HOME DIMENSION.
"EACH WORD MY MASTER WROTE IN THAT BOOK HAS THE POWER TO BUILD AND DESTROY. FOR LESSER MINDS, THIS POWER SEEMED TO BE EQUAL TO THE POWER OF YOUR GOD OR GODS.
"IT APPEARED TO BE MAGIC.

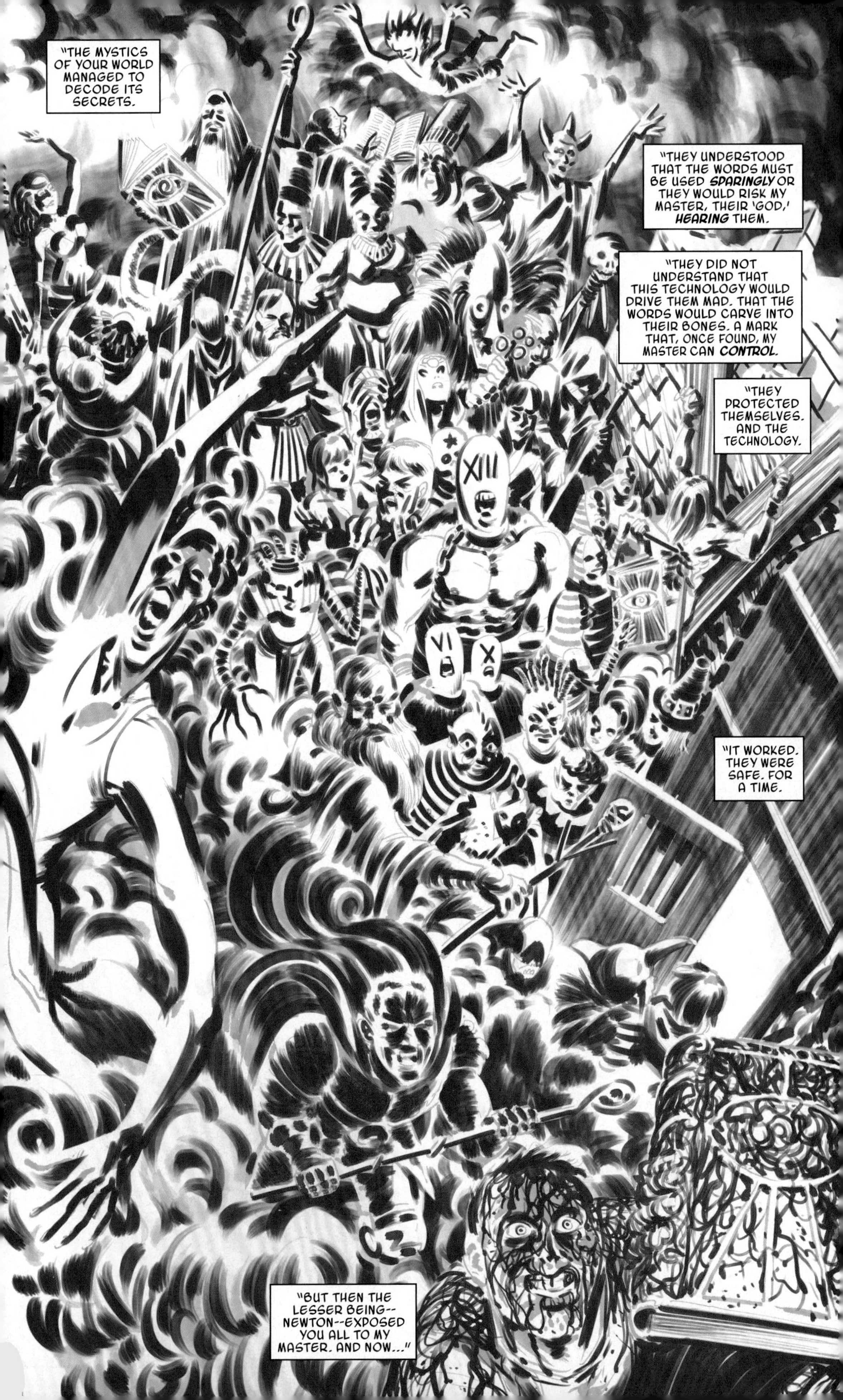
"THE MYSTICS OF YOUR WORLD MANAGED TO DECODE ITS SECRETS.
"THEY UNDERSTOOD THAT THE WORDS MUST BE USED **SPARINGLY** OR THEY WOULD RISK MY MASTER, THEIR 'GOD,' **HEARING** THEM.
"THEY DID NOT UNDERSTAND THAT THIS TECHNOLOGY WOULD DRIVE THEM MAD. THAT THE WORDS WOULD CARVE INTO THEIR BONES. A MARK THAT, ONCE FOUND, MY MASTER CAN **CONTROL**.
"THEY PROTECTED THEMSELVES. AND THE TECHNOLOGY.
XIII
VI
X
"IT WORKED. THEY WERE SAFE. FOR A TIME.
"BUT THEN THE LESSER BEING--NEWTON--EXPOSED YOU ALL TO MY MASTER. AND NOW..."

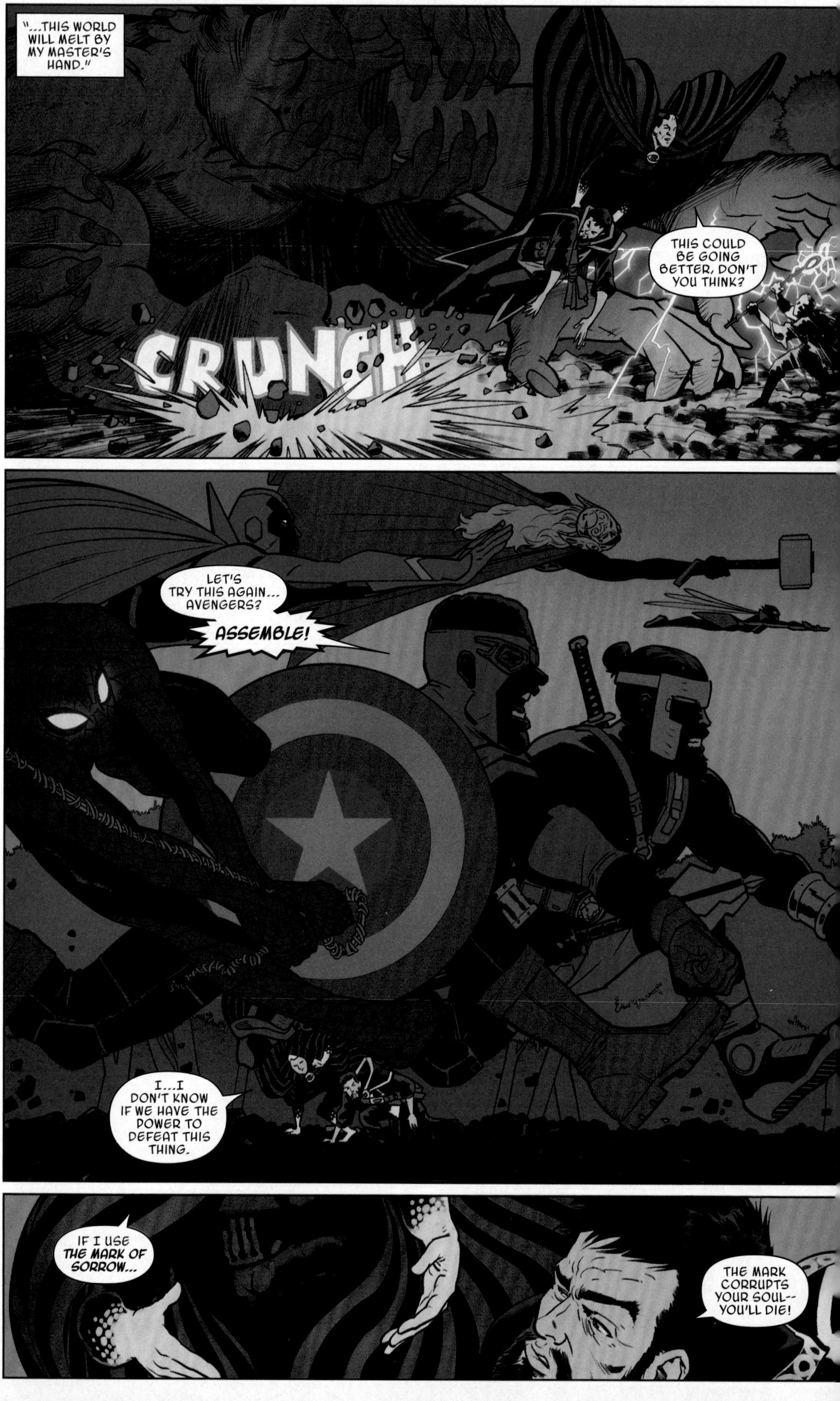
"...THIS WORLD WILL MELT BY MY MASTER'S HAND."
CRUNCH
THIS COULD BE GOING BETTER, DON'T YOU THINK?
LET'S TRY THIS AGAIN... AVENGERS?
ASSEMBLE!
I...I DON'T KNOW IF WE HAVE THE POWER TO DEFEAT THIS THING.
IF I USE THE MARK OF SORROW...
THE MARK CORRUPTS YOUR SOUL-- YOU'LL DIE!

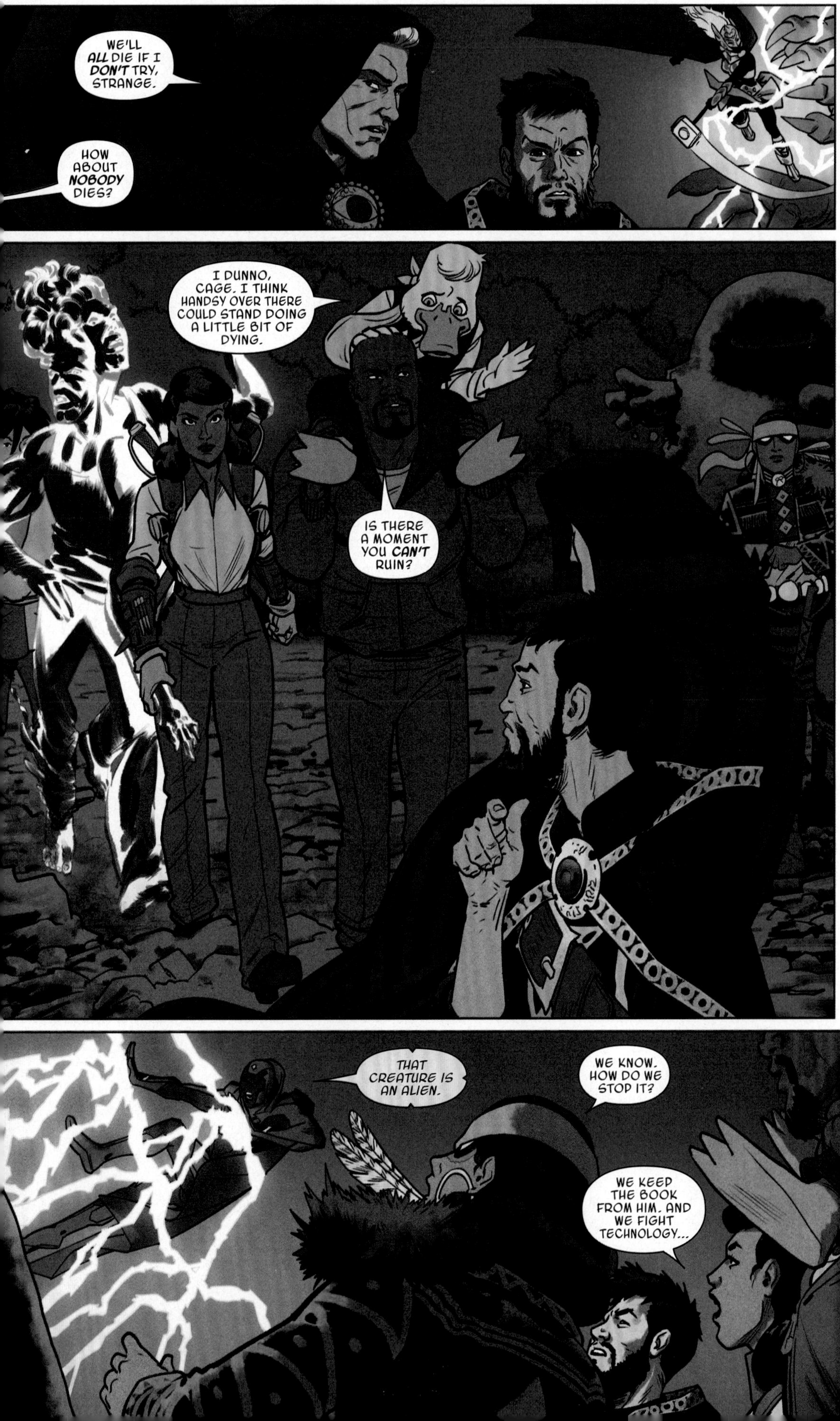
WE'LL ALL DIE IF I DON'T TRY, STRANGE.
HOW ABOUT NOBODY DIES?
I DUNNO, CAGE. I THINK HANDSY OVER THERE COULD STAND DOING A LITTLE BIT OF DYING.
IS THERE A MOMENT YOU CAN'T RUIN?
THAT CREATURE IS AN ALIEN.
WE KNOW. HOW DO WE STOP IT?
WE KEEP THE BOOK FROM HIM. AND WE FIGHT TECHNOLOGY...

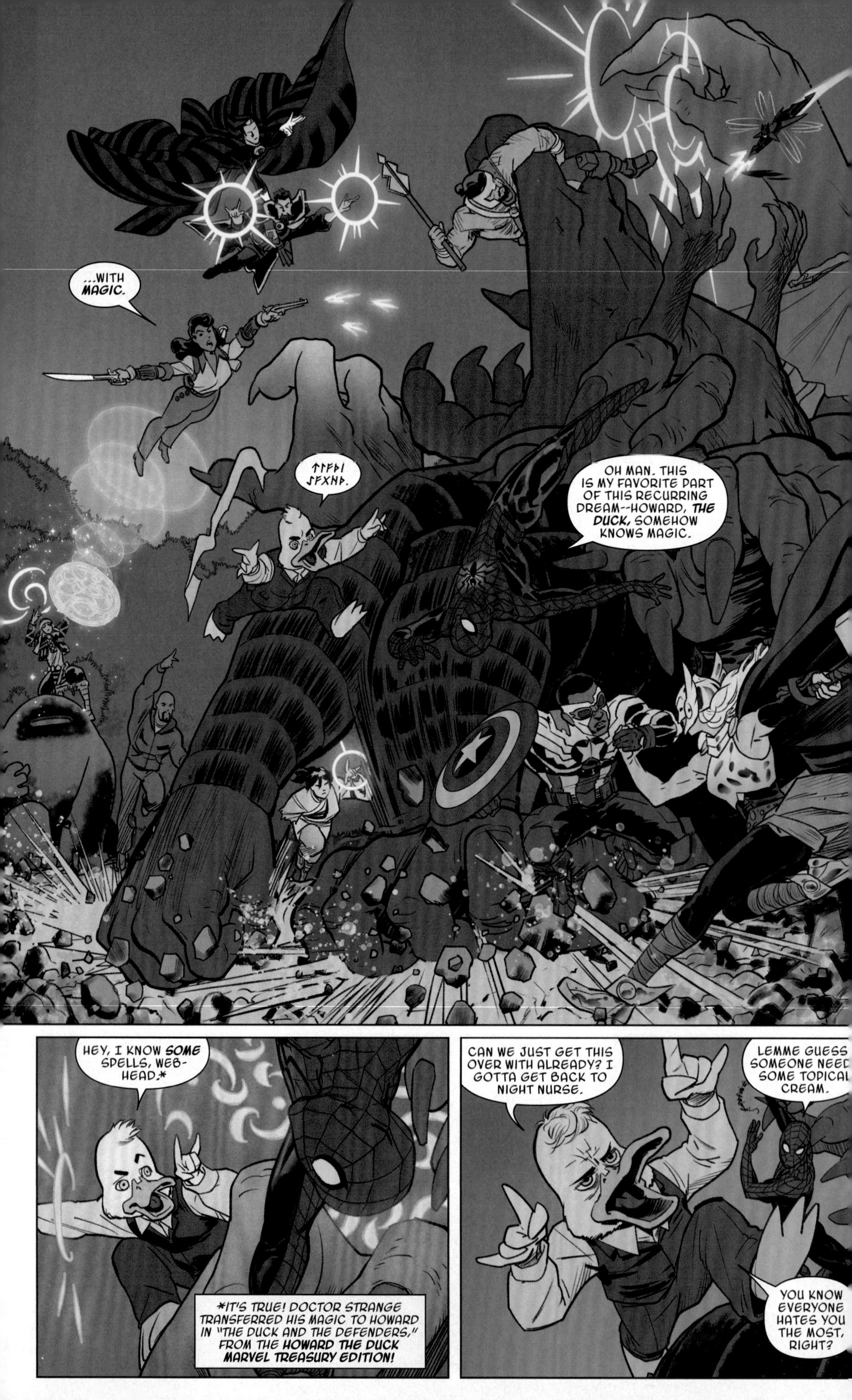
...WITH MAGIC.
OH MAN. THIS IS MY FAVORITE PART OF THIS RECURRING DREAM--HOWARD, THE DUCK, SOMEHOW KNOWS MAGIC.
HEY, I KNOW SOME SPELLS, WEB-HEAD.*
*IT'S TRUE! DOCTOR STRANGE TRANSFERRED HIS MAGIC TO HOWARD IN "THE DUCK AND THE DEFENDERS," FROM THE HOWARD THE DUCK MARVEL TREASURY EDITION!
CAN WE JUST GET THIS OVER WITH ALREADY? I GOTTA GET BACK TO NIGHT NURSE.
LEMME GUESS SOMEONE NEED SOME TOPICAL CREAM.
YOU KNOW EVERYONE HATES YOU THE MOST, RIGHT?

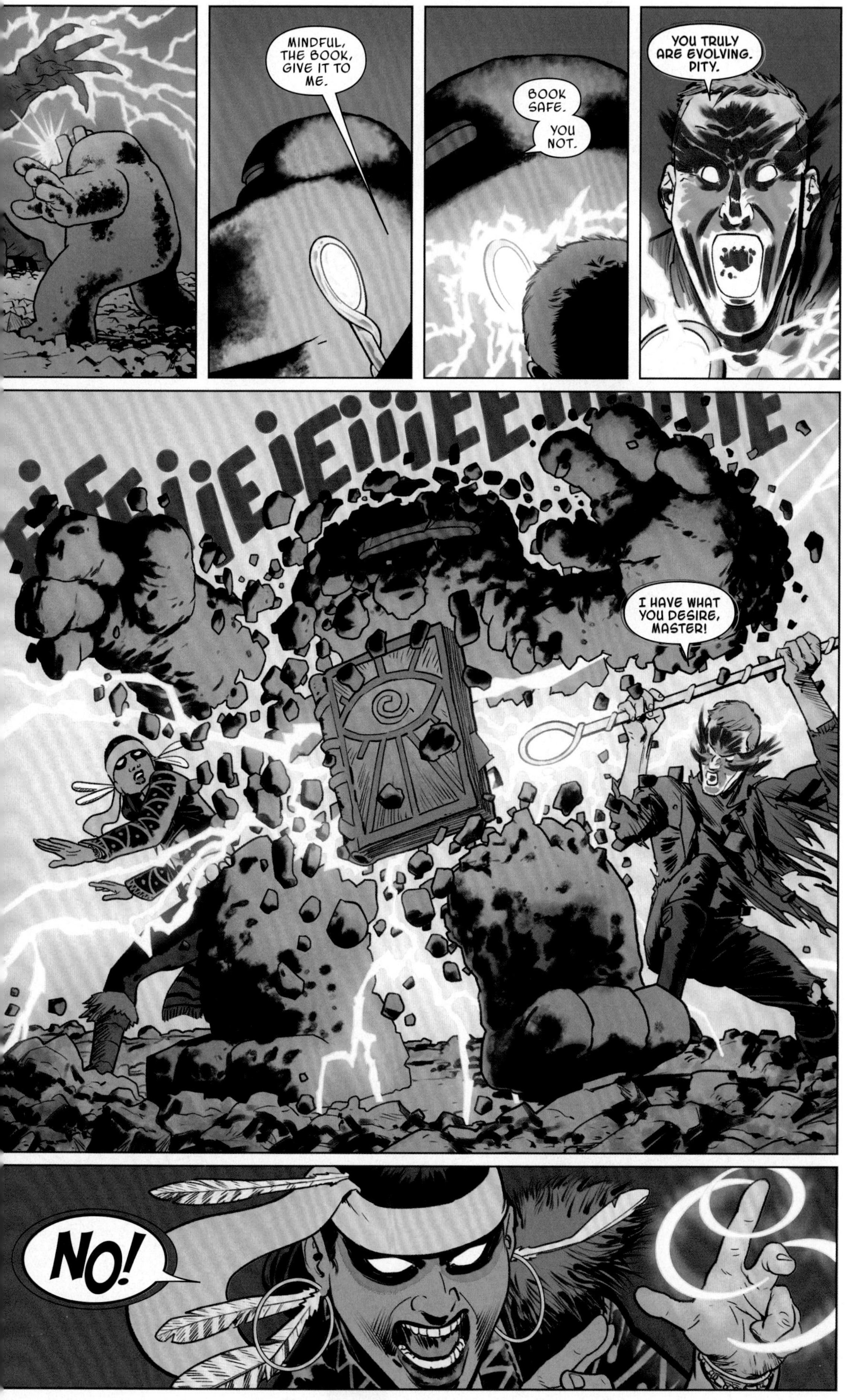
MINDFUL, THE BOOK, GIVE IT TO ME.
BOOK SAFE.
YOU NOT.
YOU TRULY ARE EVOLVING. PITY.
I HAVE WHAT YOU DESIRE, MASTER!
NO!

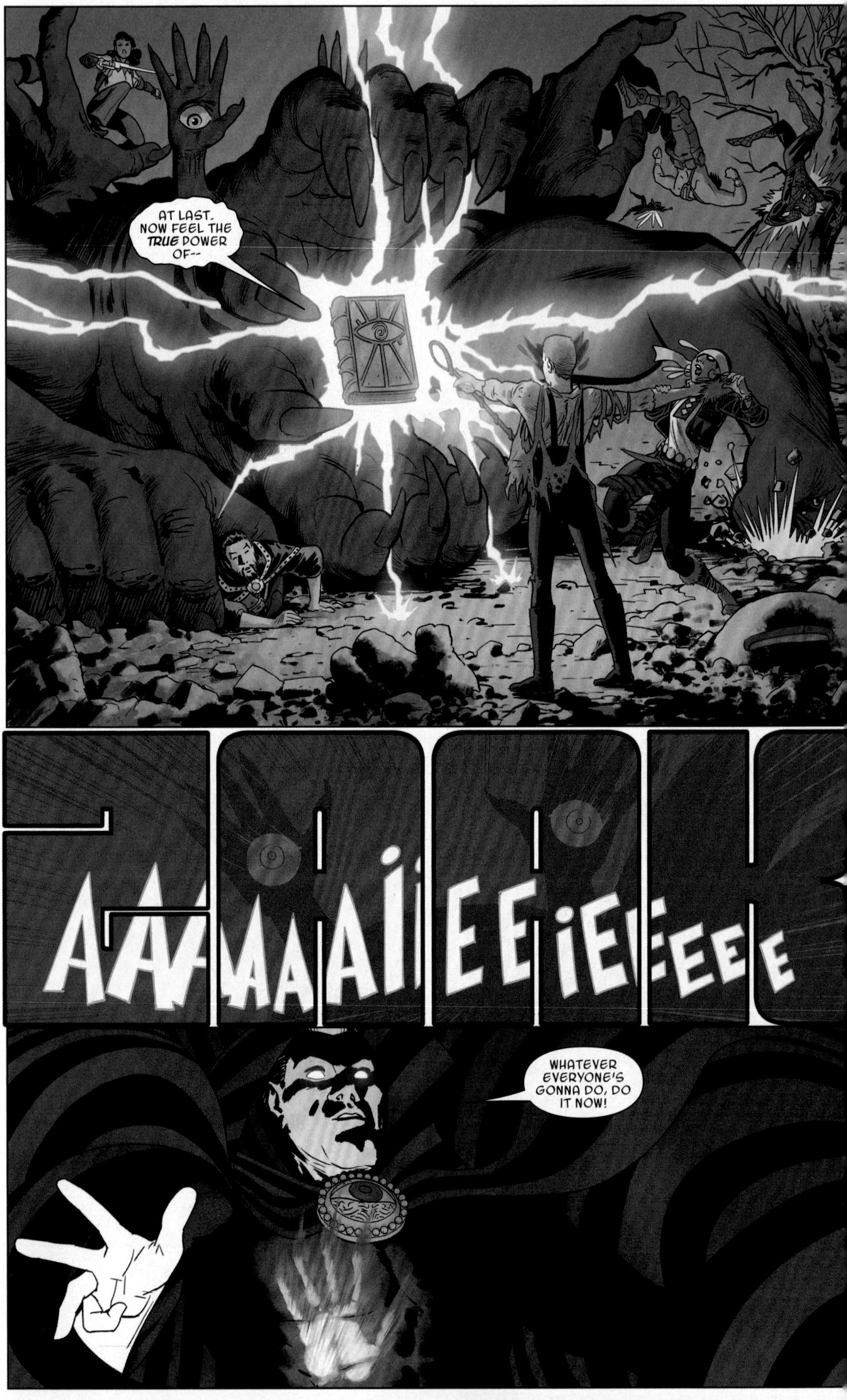
AT LAST. NOW FEEL THE TRUE POWER OF--
AAAAAIIEEiEEEE
WHATEVER EVERYONE'S GONNA DO, DO IT NOW!

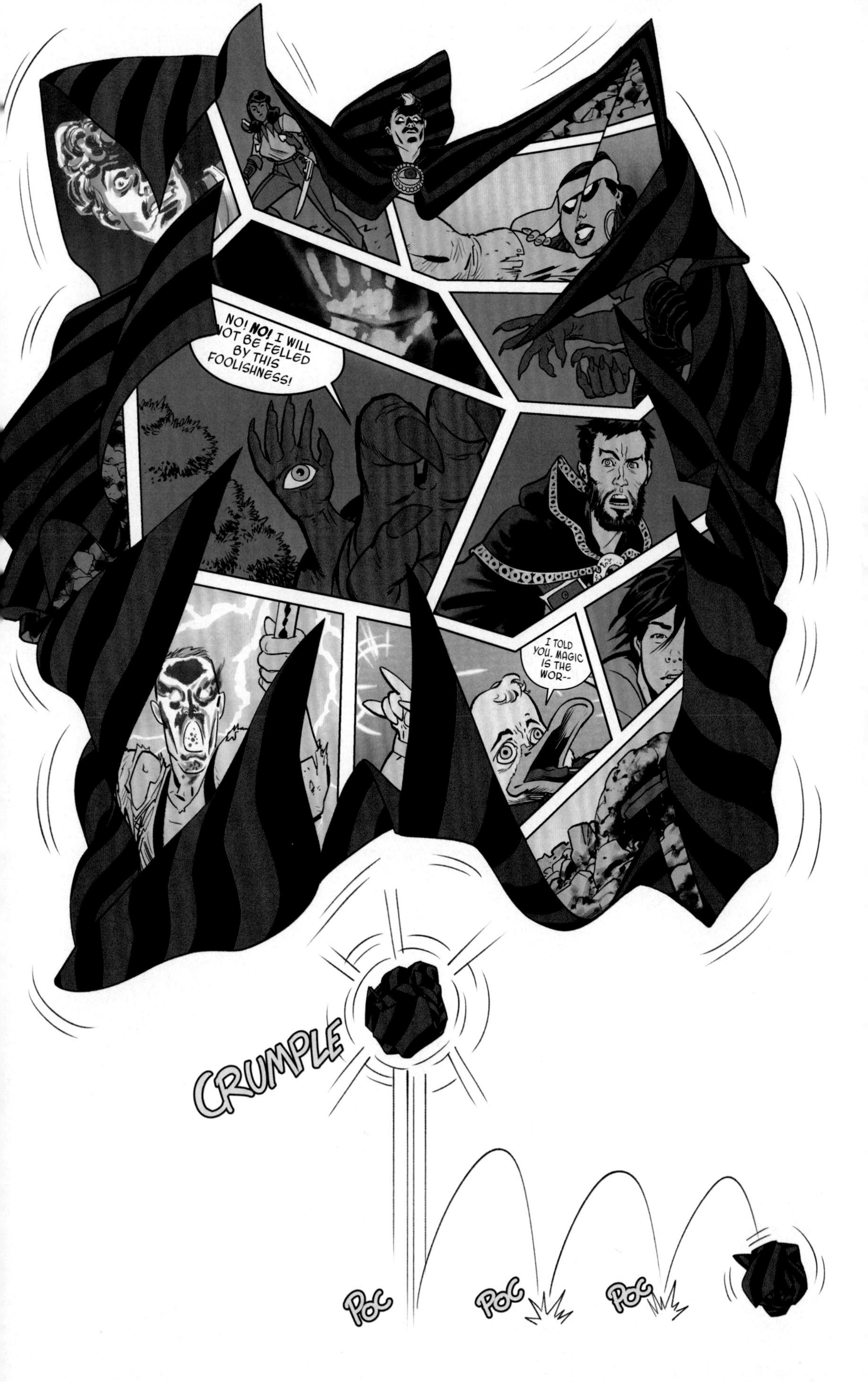

NO! **NO!** I WILL NOT BE FELLED BY THIS FOOLISHNESS!
I TOLD YOU. MAGIC IS THE WOR--
CRUMPLE
POC
POC
POC

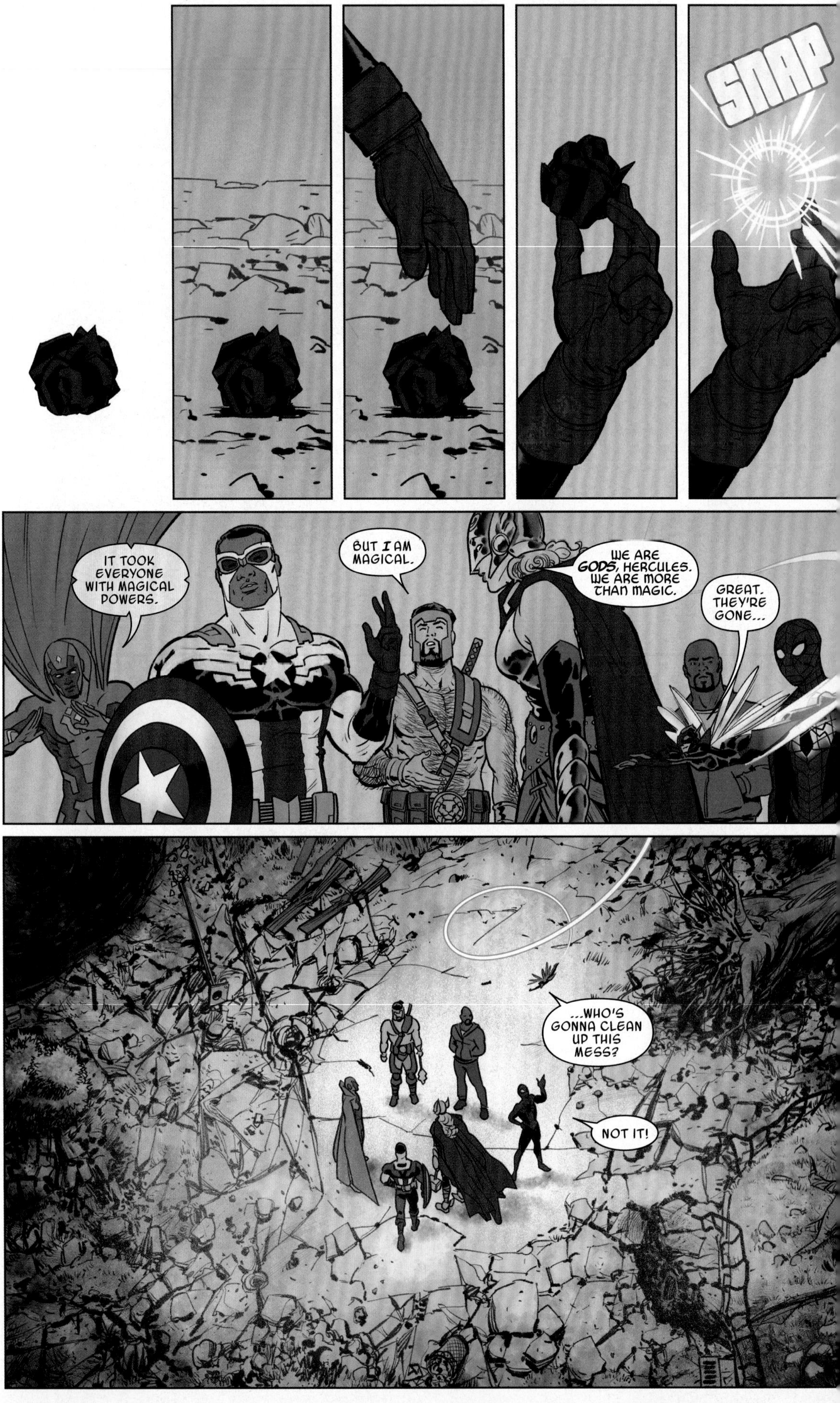
SNAP
IT TOOK EVERYONE WITH MAGICAL POWERS.
BUT I AM MAGICAL.
WE ARE GODS, HERCULES. WE ARE MORE THAN MAGIC.
GREAT. THEY'RE GONE...
...WHO'S GONNA CLEAN UP THIS MESS?
NOT IT!

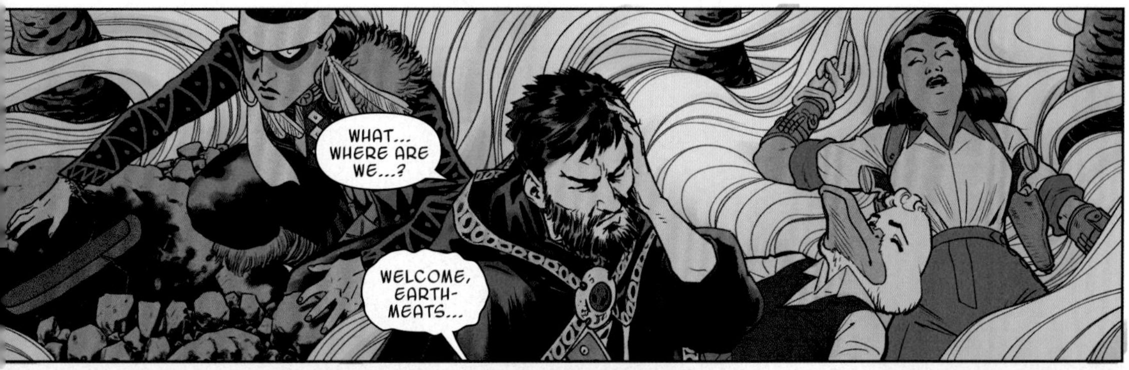
WHAT... WHERE ARE WE...?
WELCOME, EARTH-MEATS...

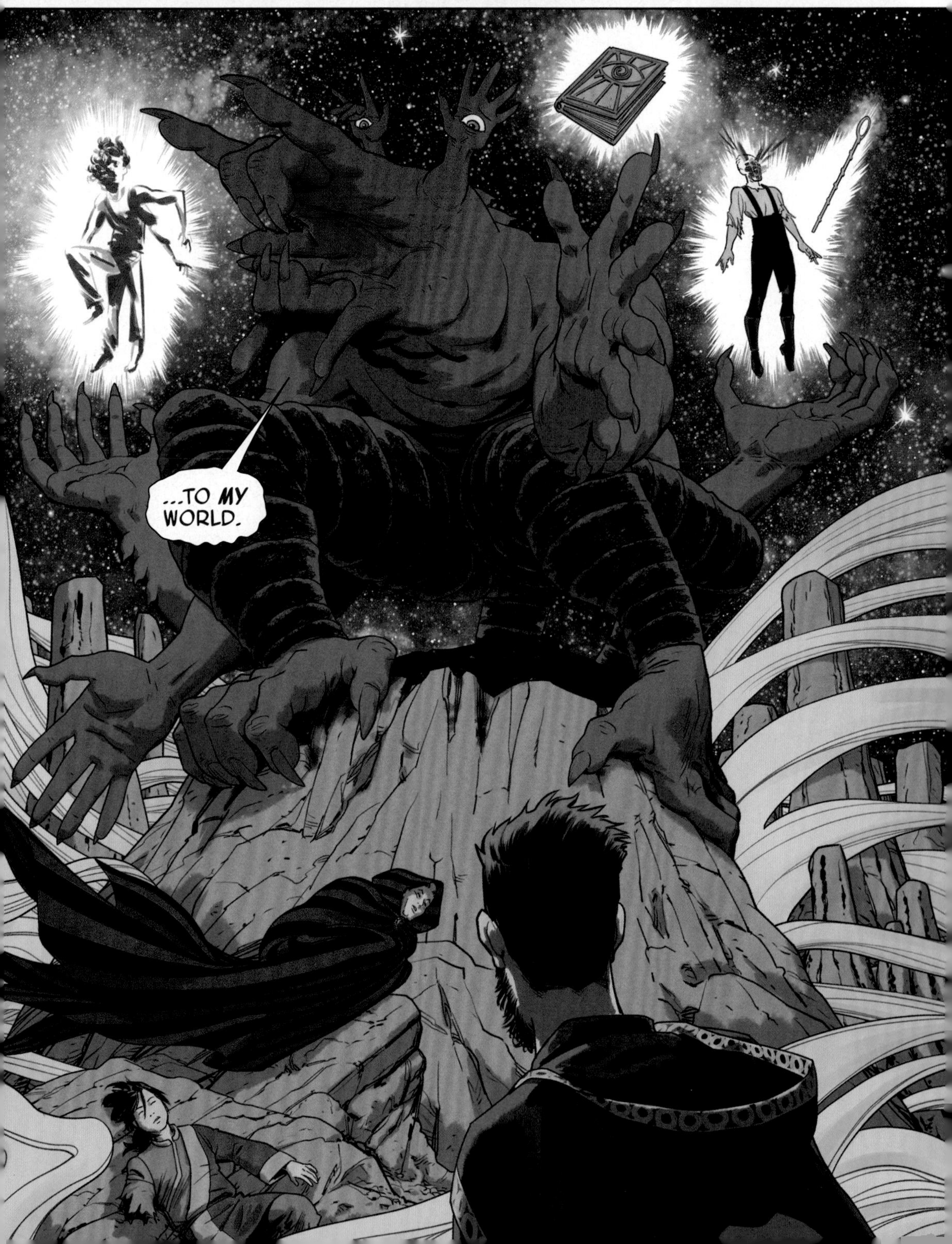
...TO MY WORLD.

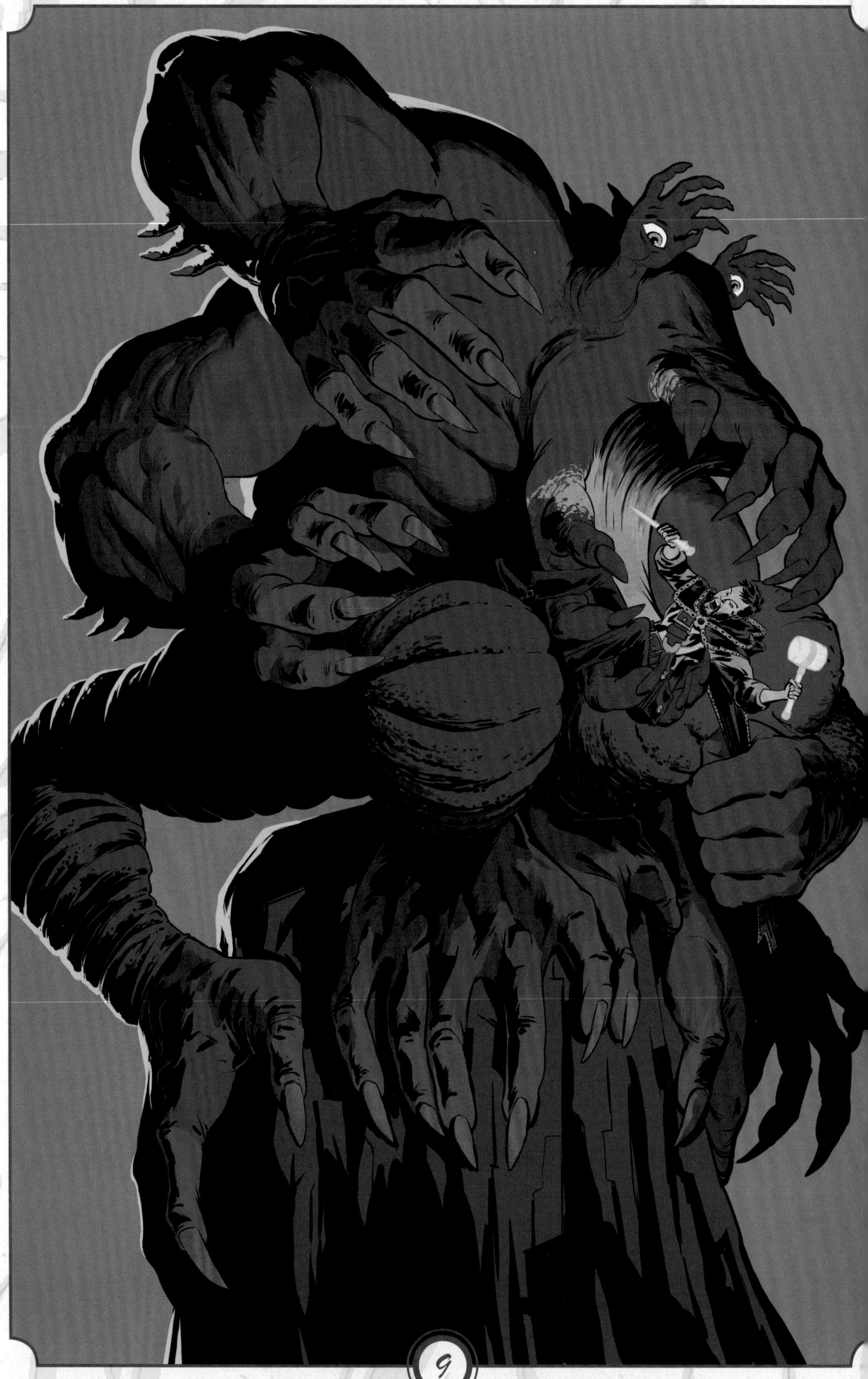

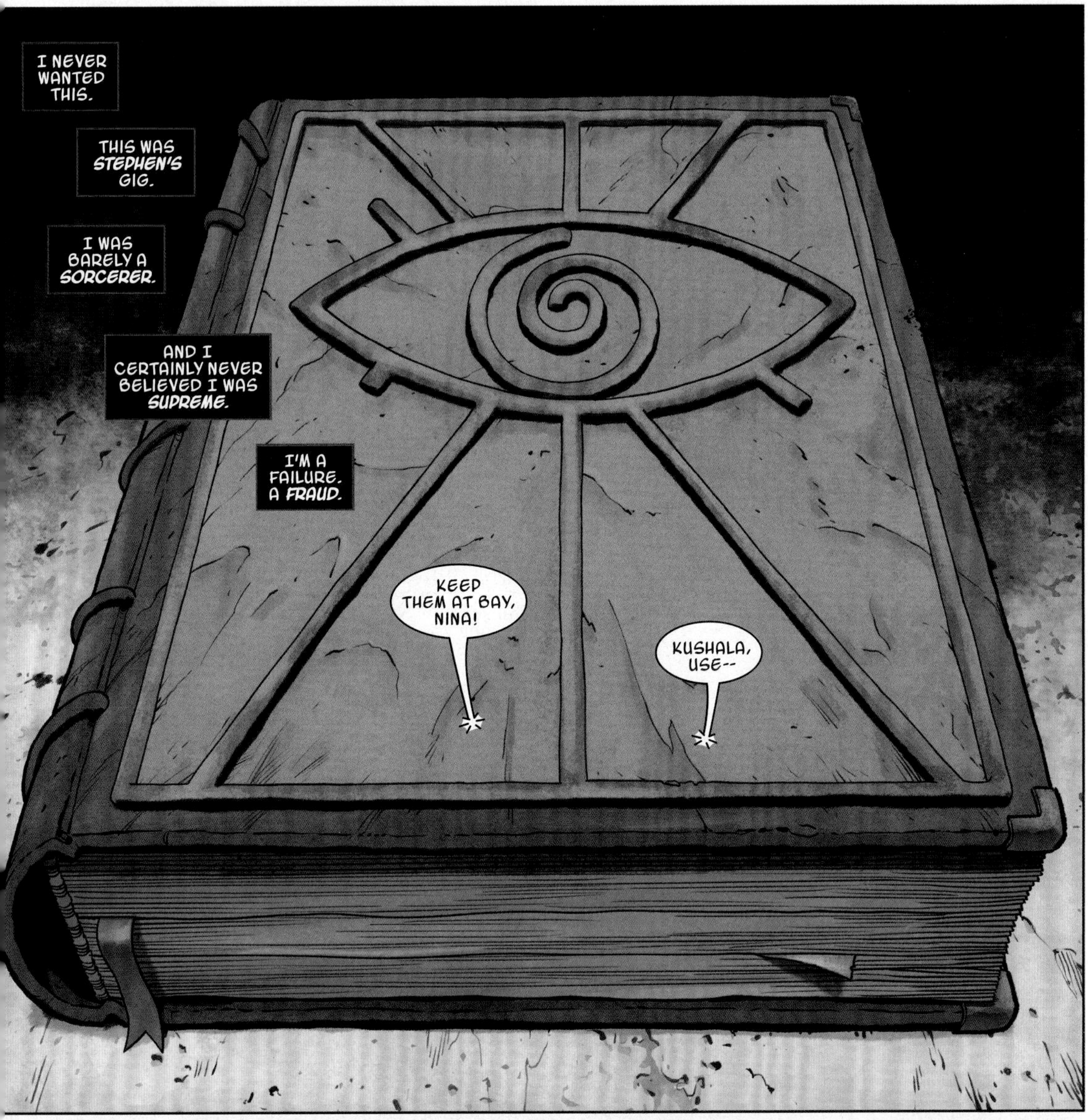
I NEVER WANTED THIS.
THIS WAS STEPHEN'S GIG.
I WAS BARELY A SORCERER.
AND I CERTAINLY NEVER BELIEVED I WAS SUPREME.
I'M A FAILURE. A FRAUD.
KEEP THEM AT BAY, NINA!
KUSHALA, USE--

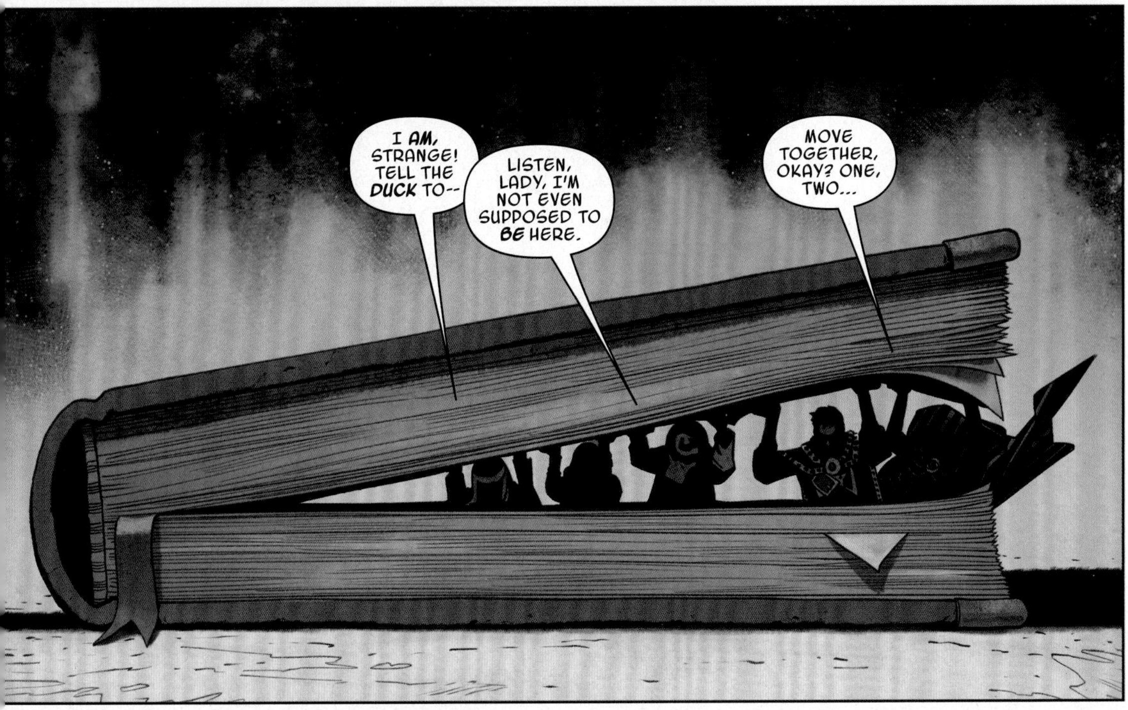
I AM, STRANGE! TELL THE DUCK TO--
LISTEN, LADY, I'M NOT EVEN SUPPOSED TO BE HERE.
MOVE TOGETHER, OKAY? ONE, TWO...

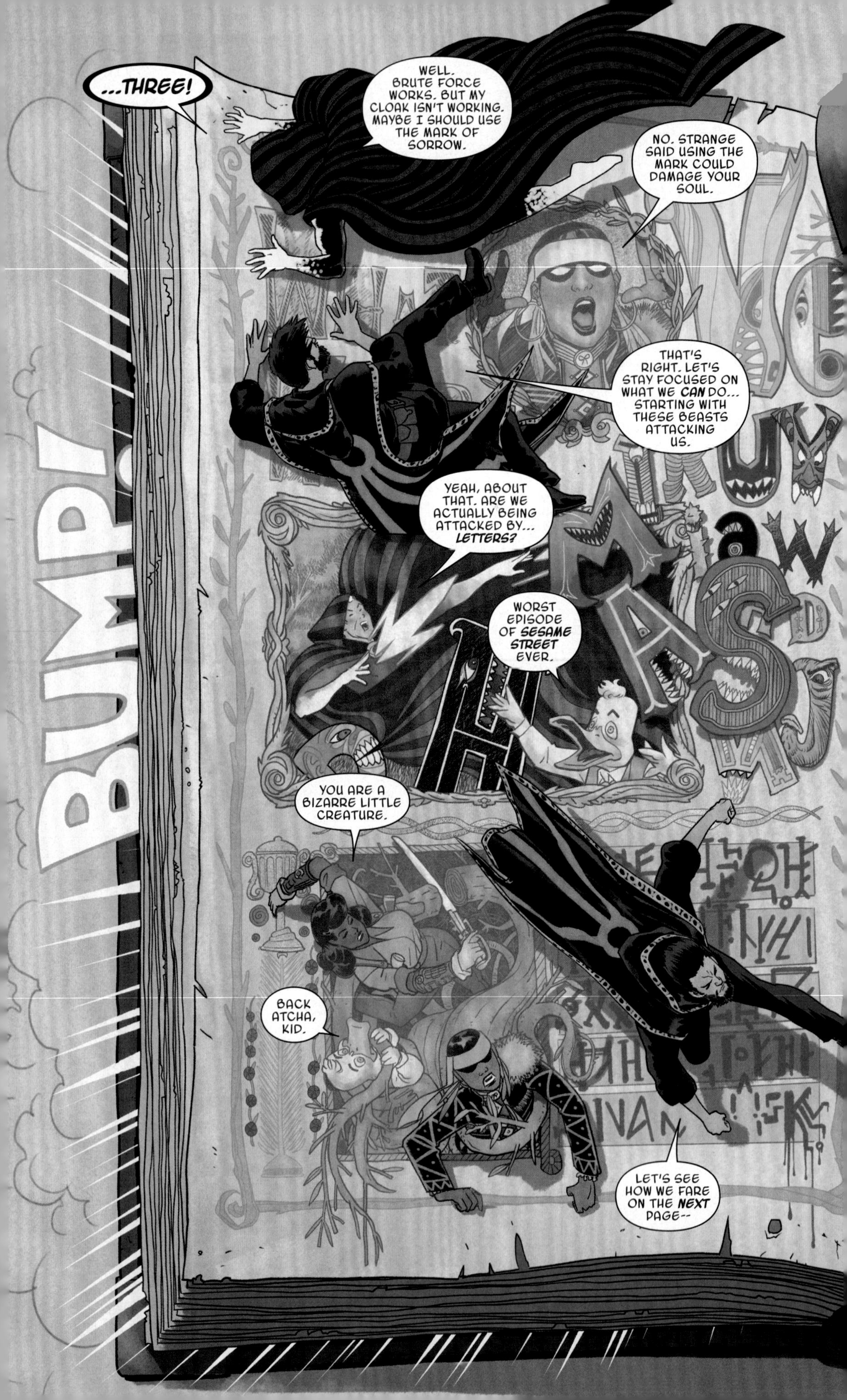

...THREE!
BUMP!
WELL. BRUTE FORCE WORKS. BUT MY CLOAK ISN'T WORKING. MAYBE I SHOULD USE THE MARK OF SORROW.
NO. STRANGE SAID USING THE MARK COULD DAMAGE YOUR SOUL.
THAT'S RIGHT. LET'S STAY FOCUSED ON WHAT WE **CAN** DO... STARTING WITH THESE BEASTS ATTACKING US.
YEAH, ABOUT THAT. ARE WE ACTUALLY BEING ATTACKED BY... ***LETTERS?***
WORST EPISODE OF ***SESAME STREET*** EVER.
YOU ARE A BIZARRE LITTLE CREATURE.
BACK ATCHA, KID.
LET'S SEE HOW WE FARE ON THE ***NEXT*** PAGE--

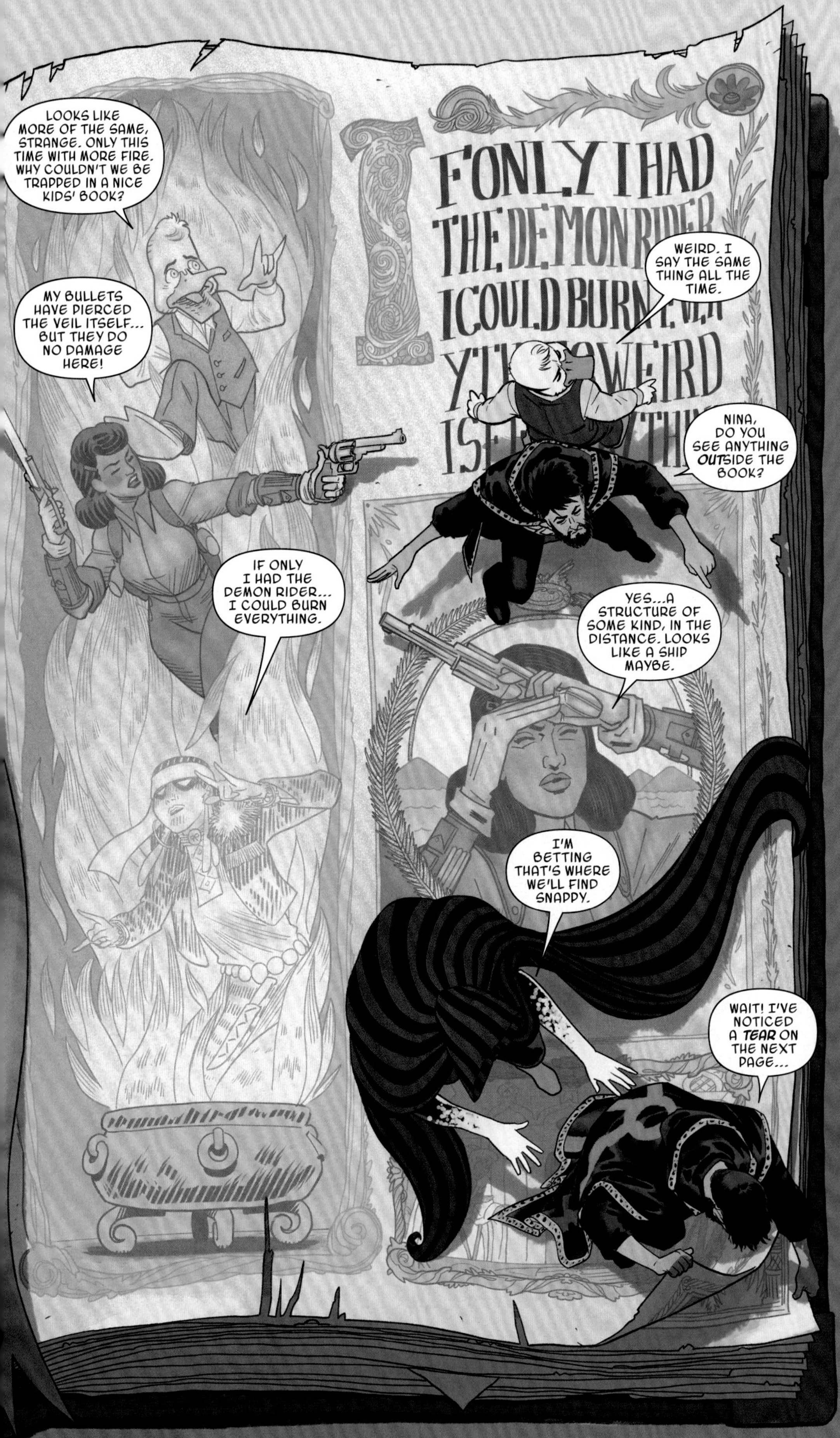
LOOKS LIKE MORE OF THE SAME, STRANGE. ONLY THIS TIME WITH MORE FIRE. WHY COULDN'T WE BE TRAPPED IN A NICE KIDS' BOOK?
IF ONLY I HAD
WEIRD. I SAY THE SAME THING ALL THE TIME.
MY BULLETS HAVE PIERCED THE VEIL ITSELF... BUT THEY DO NO DAMAGE HERE!
NINA, DO YOU SEE ANYTHING OUTSIDE THE BOOK?
IF ONLY I HAD THE DEMON RIDER... I COULD BURN EVERYTHING.
YES...A STRUCTURE OF SOME KIND, IN THE DISTANCE. LOOKS LIKE A SHIP MAYBE.
I'M BETTING THAT'S WHERE WE'LL FIND SNAPPY.
WAIT! I'VE NOTICED A TEAR ON THE NEXT PAGE...

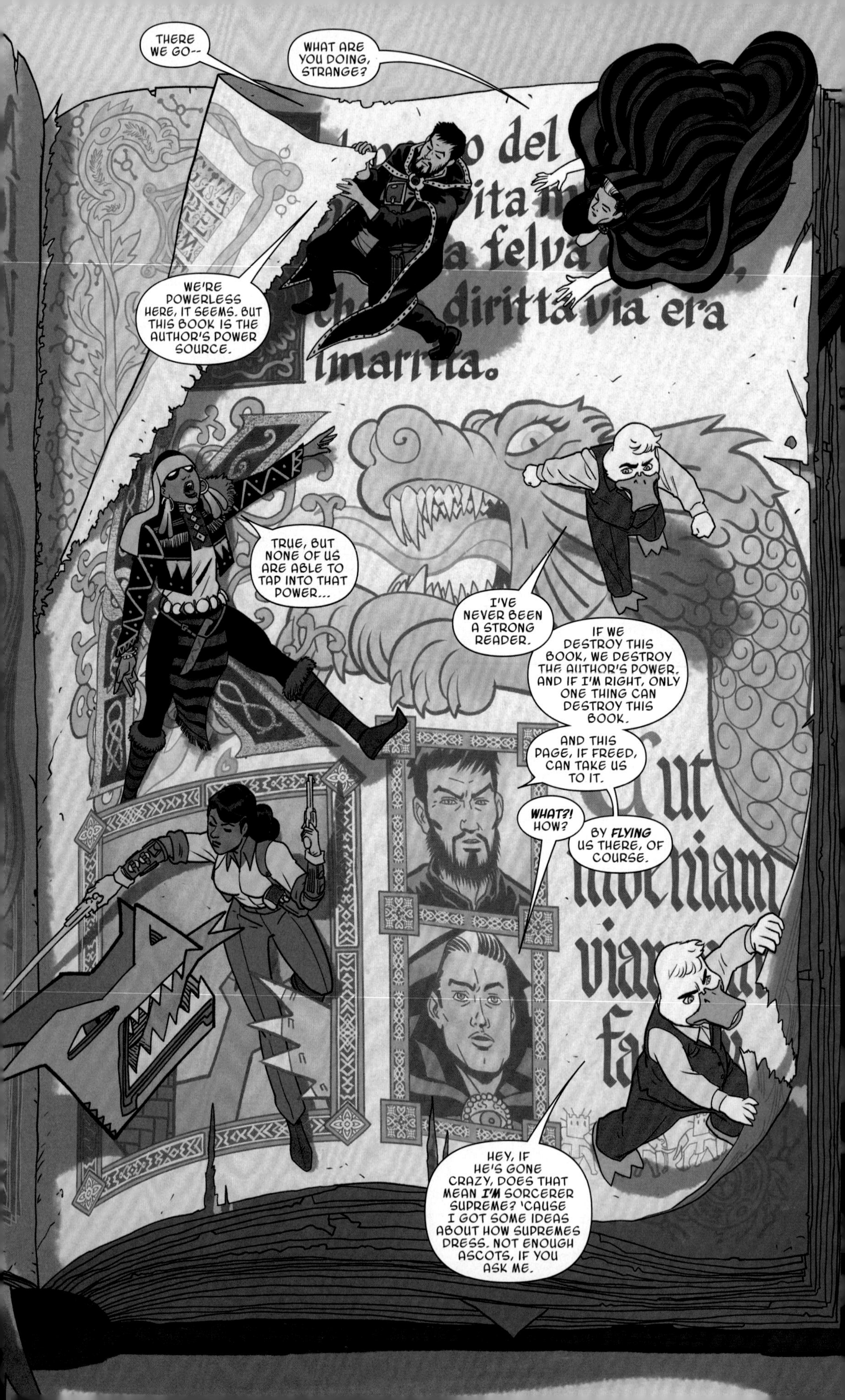
THERE WE GO--
WHAT ARE YOU DOING, STRANGE?
WE'RE POWERLESS HERE, IT SEEMS. BUT THIS BOOK IS THE AUTHOR'S POWER SOURCE.
TRUE, BUT NONE OF US ARE ABLE TO TAP INTO THAT POWER...
I'VE NEVER BEEN A STRONG READER.
IF WE DESTROY THIS BOOK, WE DESTROY THE AUTHOR'S POWER. AND IF I'M RIGHT, ONLY ONE THING CAN DESTROY THIS BOOK.
AND THIS PAGE, IF FREED, CAN TAKE US TO IT.
WHAT?! HOW?
BY ***FLYING*** US THERE, OF COURSE.
HEY, IF HE'S GONE CRAZY, DOES THAT MEAN ***I'M*** SORCERER SUPREME? 'CAUSE I GOT SOME IDEAS ABOUT HOW SUPREMES DRESS. NOT ENOUGH ASCOTS, IF YOU ASK ME.

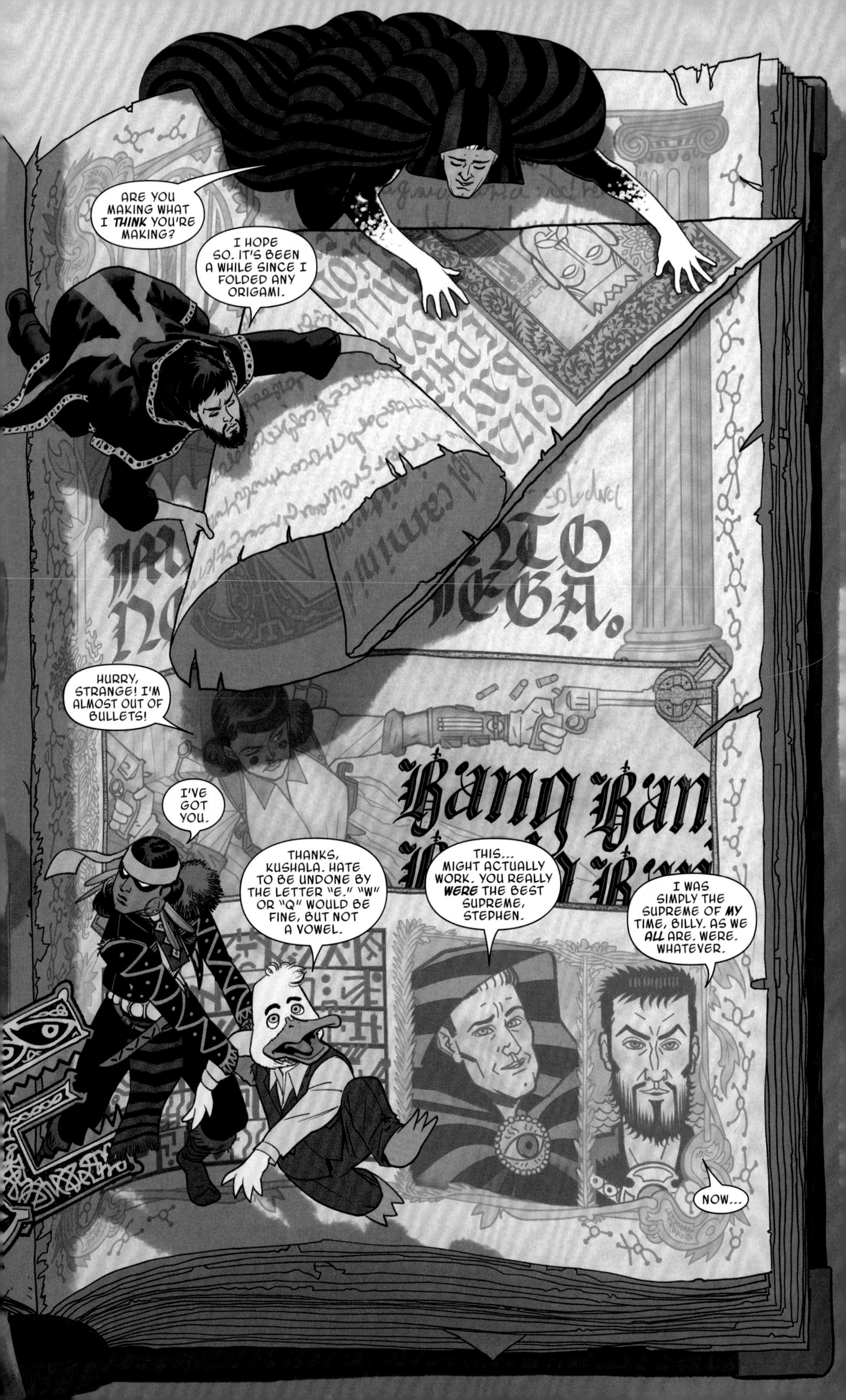
ARE YOU MAKING WHAT I *THINK* YOU'RE MAKING?
I HOPE SO. IT'S BEEN A WHILE SINCE I FOLDED ANY ORIGAMI.
HURRY, STRANGE! I'M ALMOST OUT OF BULLETS!
I'VE GOT YOU.
THANKS, KUSHALA. HATE TO BE UNDONE BY THE LETTER "E." "W" OR "Q" WOULD BE FINE, BUT NOT A VOWEL.
THIS... MIGHT ACTUALLY WORK. YOU REALLY *WERE* THE BEST SUPREME, STEPHEN.
I WAS SIMPLY THE SUPREME OF *MY* TIME, BILLY. AS WE *ALL* ARE. WERE. WHATEVER.
NOW...

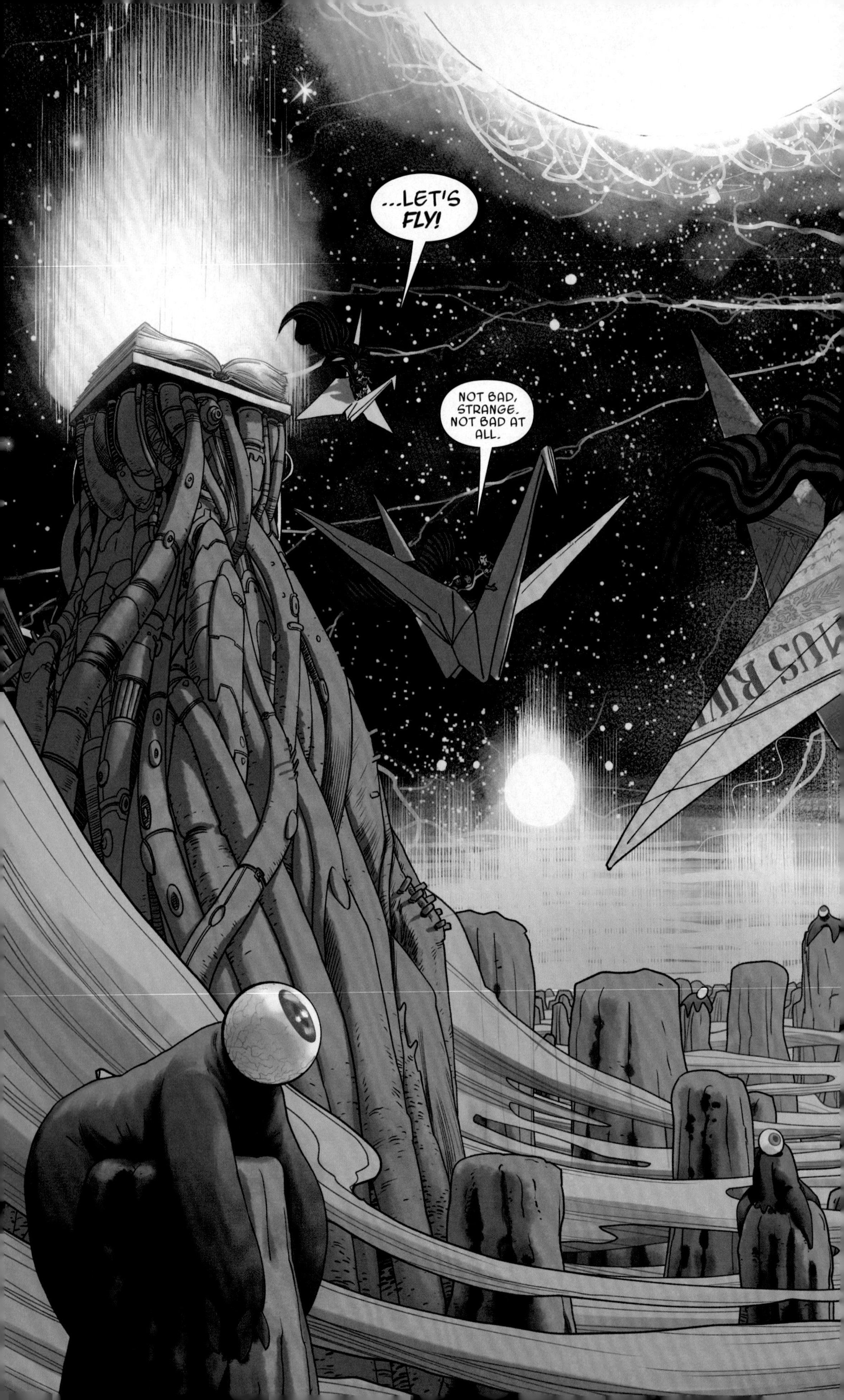
...LET'S FLY!
NOT BAD, STRANGE. NOT BAD AT ALL.

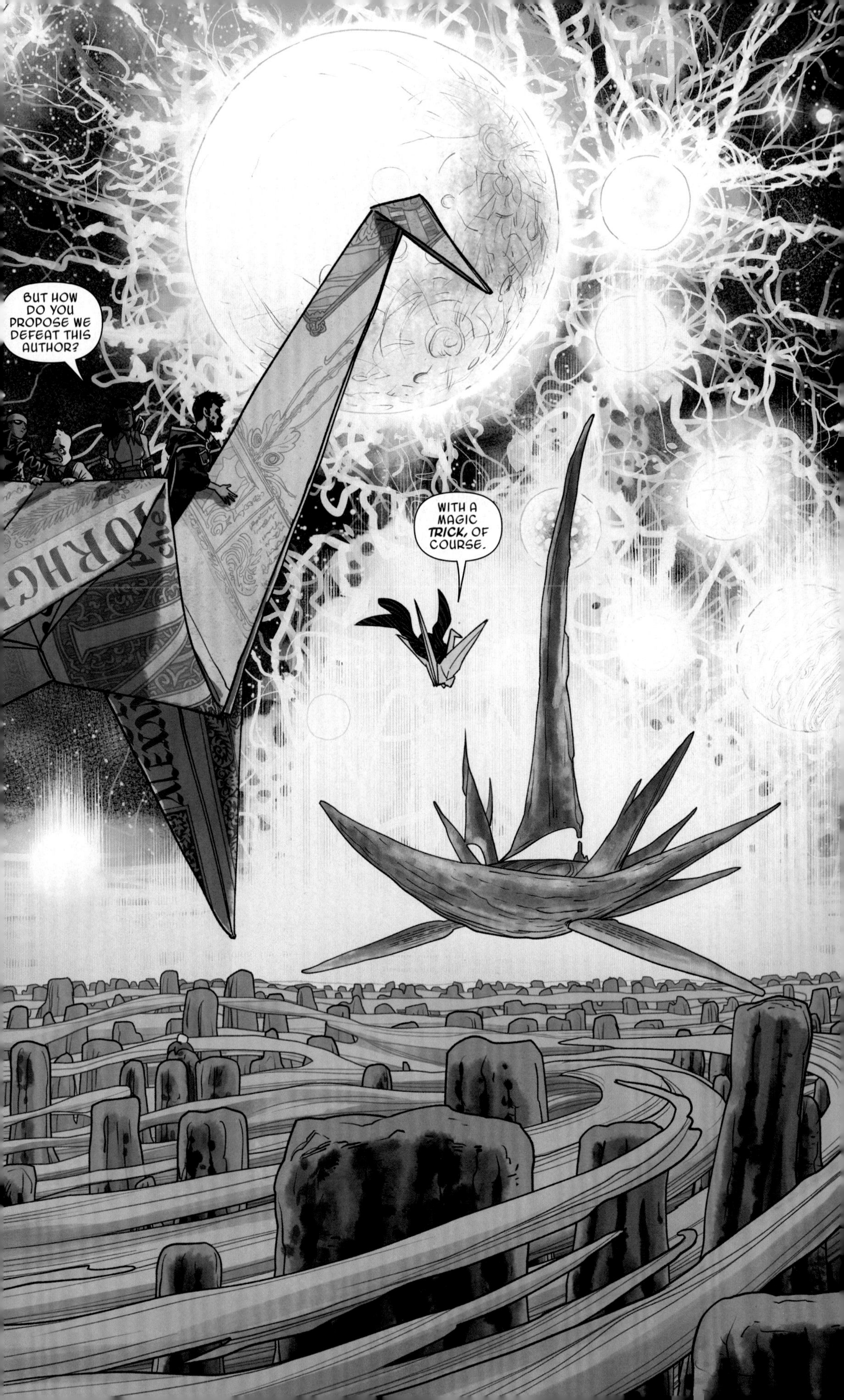
BUT HOW DO YOU PROPOSE WE DEFEAT THIS AUTHOR?
WITH A MAGIC **TRICK,** OF COURSE.

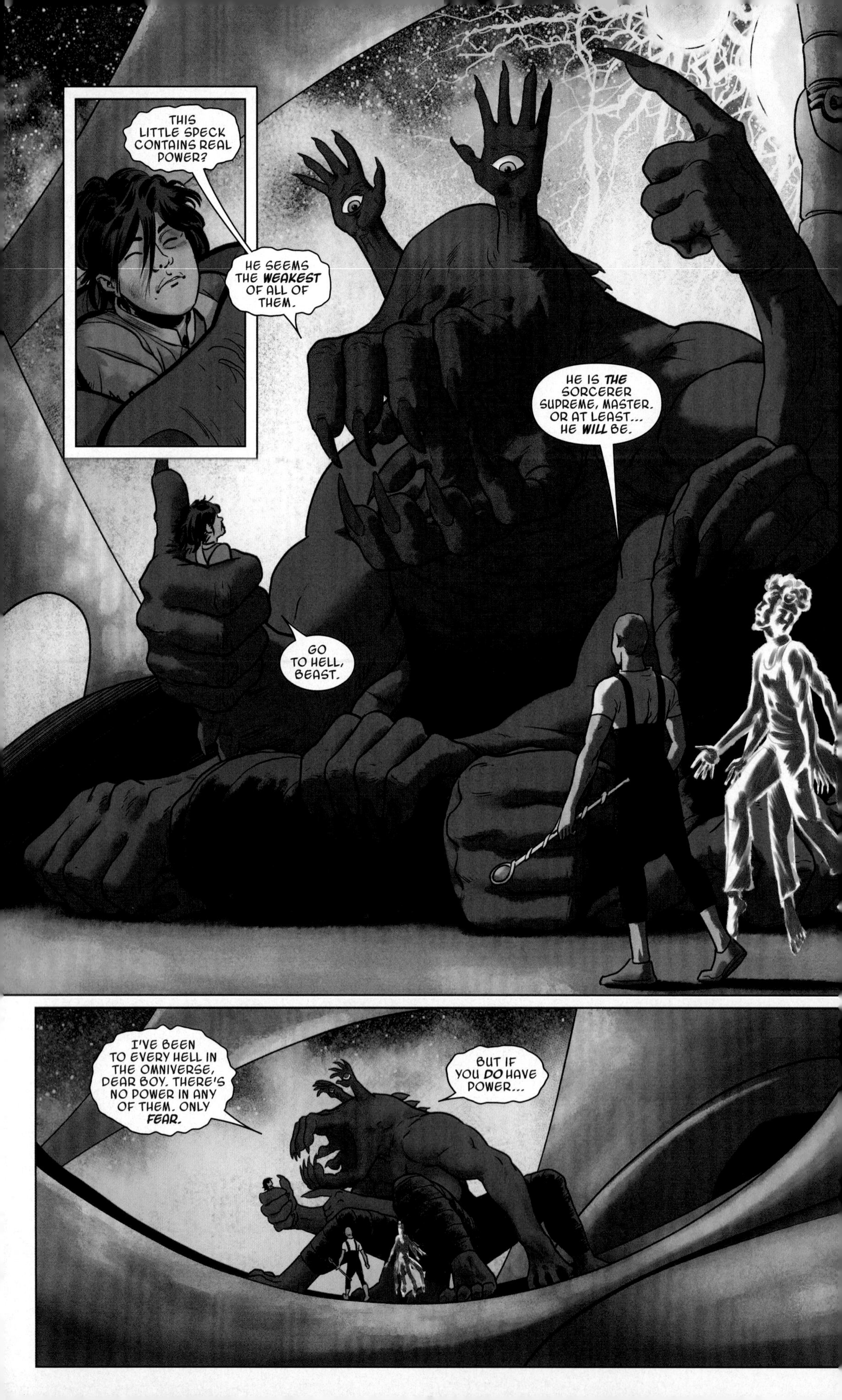
THIS LITTLE SPECK CONTAINS REAL POWER?
HE SEEMS THE **WEAKEST** OF ALL OF THEM.
HE IS **THE** SORCERER SUPREME, MASTER. OR AT LEAST... HE **WILL** BE.
GO TO HELL, BEAST.
I'VE BEEN TO EVERY HELL IN THE OMNIVERSE, DEAR BOY. THERE'S NO POWER IN ANY OF THEM. ONLY **FEAR.**
BUT IF YOU **DO** HAVE POWER...

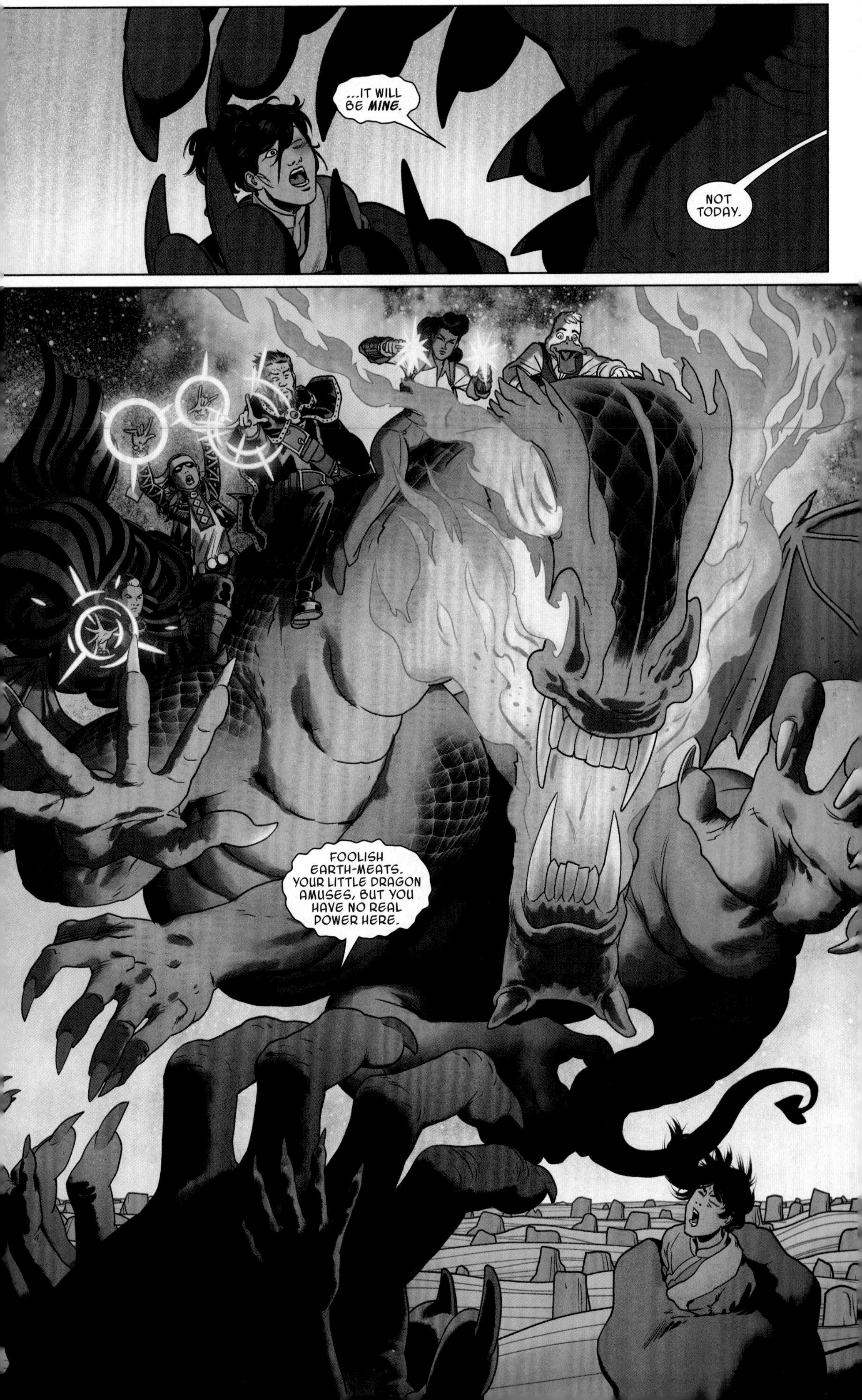
...IT WILL BE *MINE*.
NOT TODAY.
FOOLISH EARTH-MEATS. YOUR LITTLE DRAGON AMUSES, BUT YOU HAVE NO REAL POWER HERE.

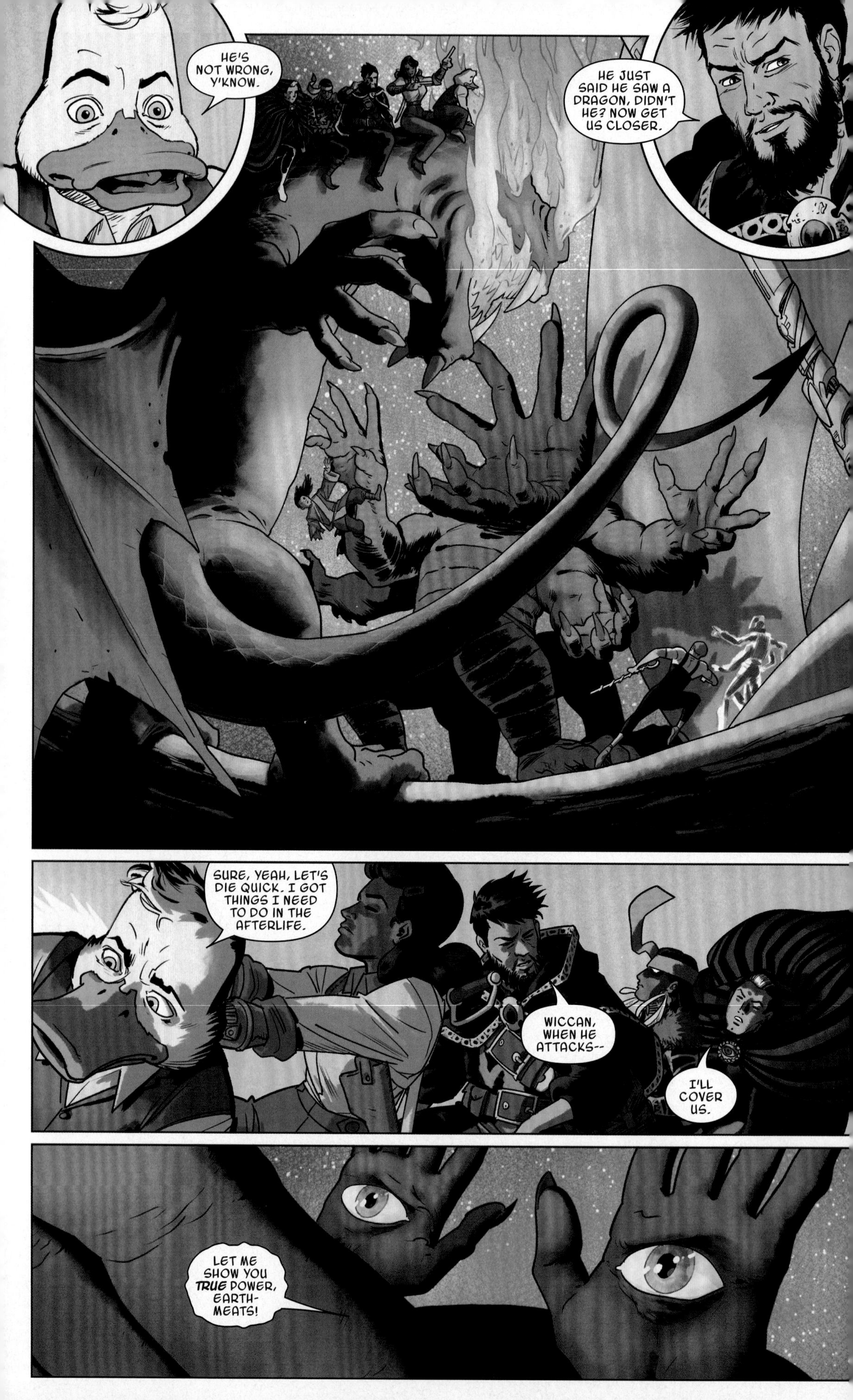
HE'S NOT WRONG, Y'KNOW.
HE JUST SAID HE SAW A DRAGON, DIDN'T HE? NOW GET US CLOSER.
SURE, YEAH, LET'S DIE QUICK. I GOT THINGS I NEED TO DO IN THE AFTERLIFE.
WICCAN, WHEN HE ATTACKS--
I'LL COVER US.
LET ME SHOW YOU TRUE POWER, EARTH-MEATS!

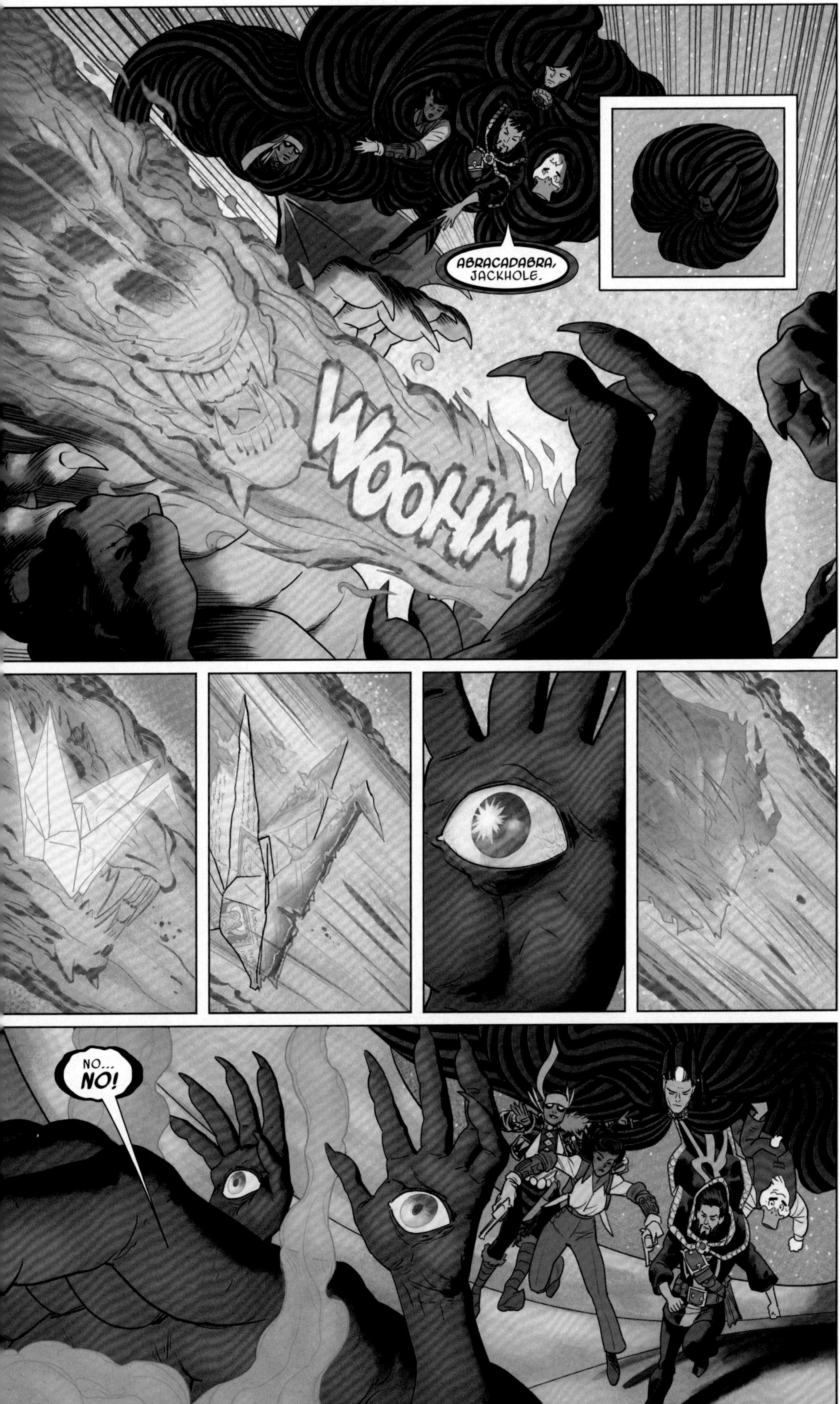
ABRACADABRA, JACKHOLE.
WOOHM
NO... NO!

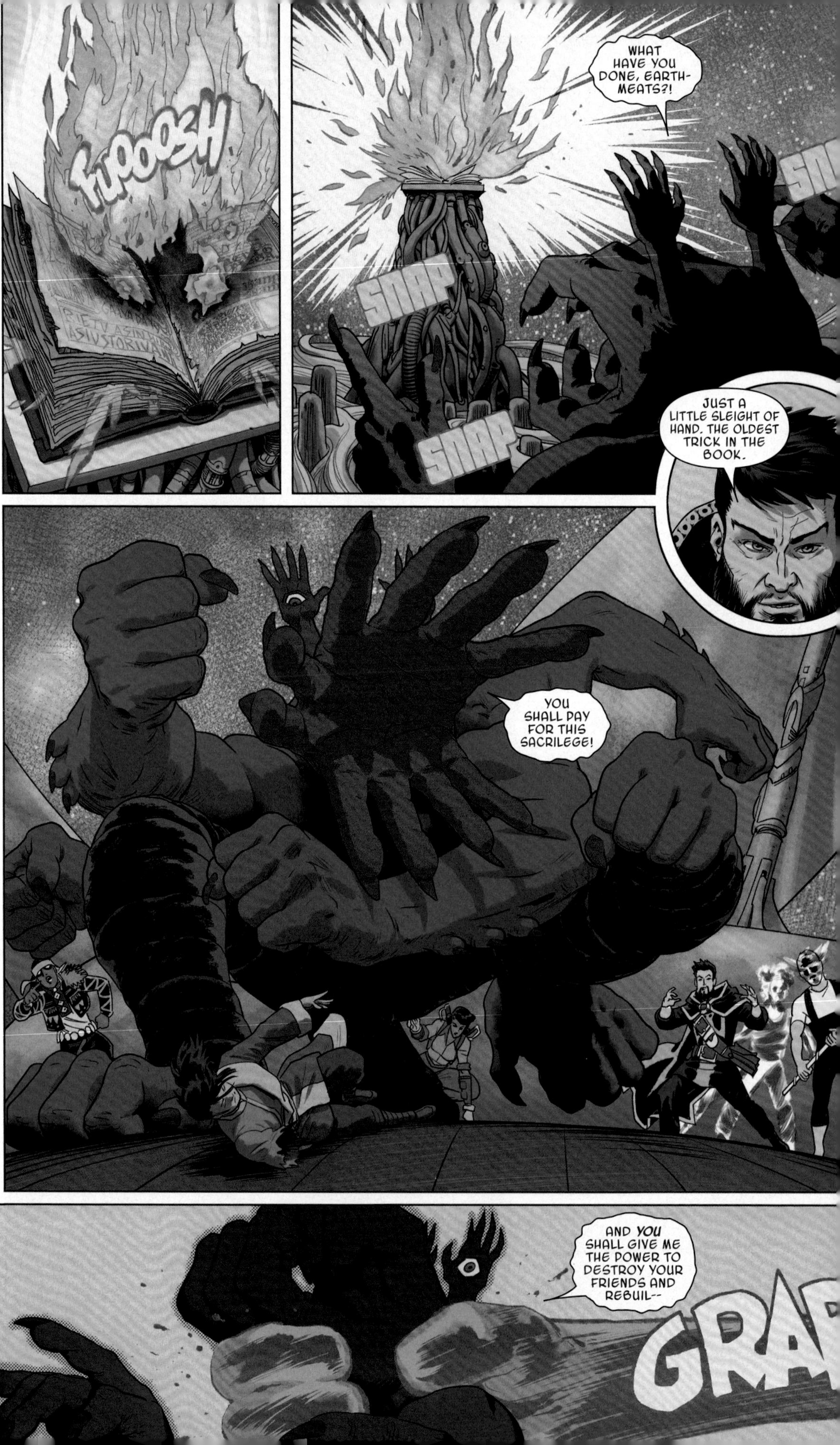
FWOOSH
WHAT HAVE YOU DONE, EARTH-MEATS?!
SNAP
SNAP
JUST A LITTLE SLEIGHT OF HAND. THE OLDEST TRICK IN THE BOOK.
YOU SHALL PAY FOR THIS SACRILEGE!
AND YOU SHALL GIVE ME THE POWER TO DESTROY YOUR FRIENDS AND REBUIL--

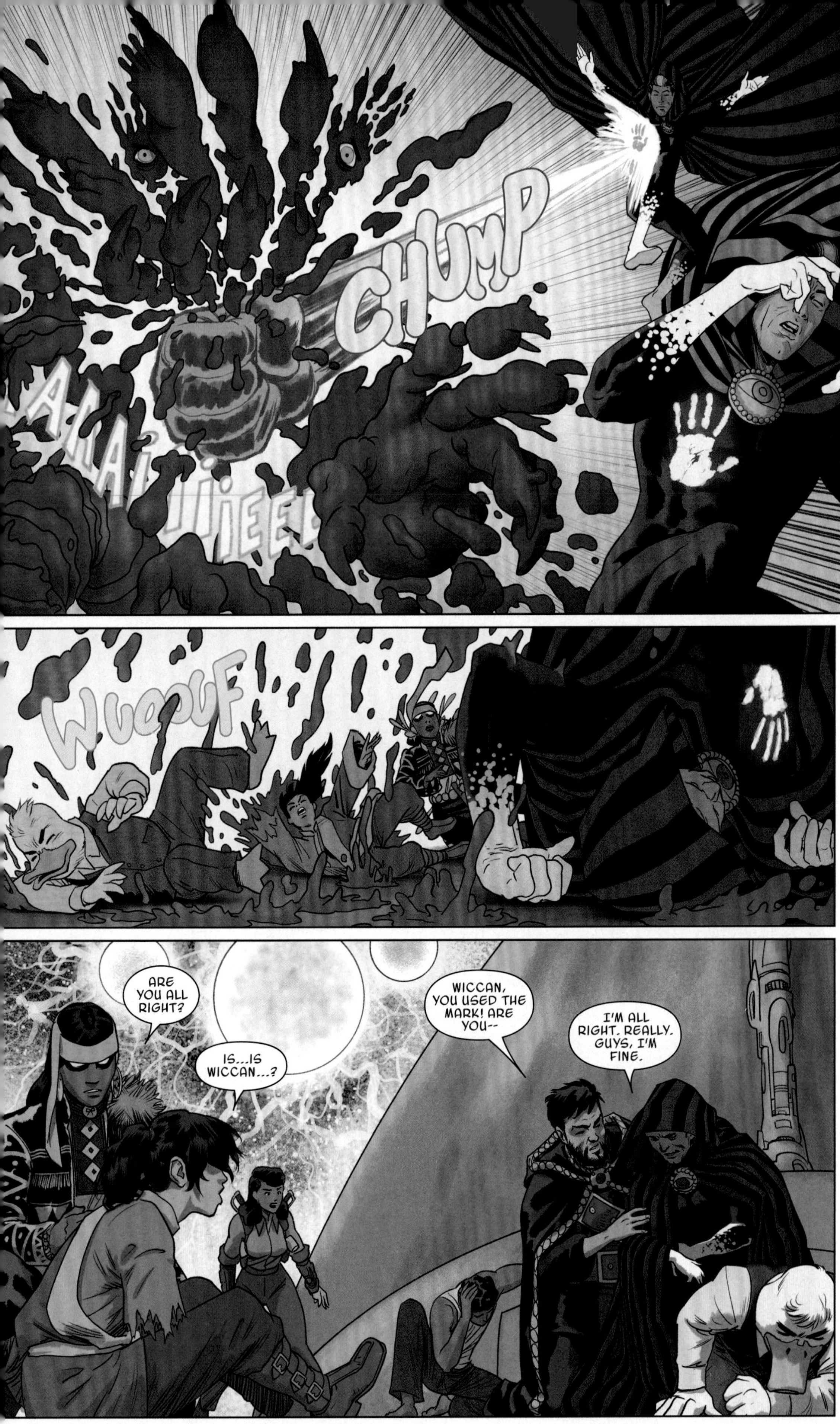
CHUMP
AAAIIIEEE
WUOOUF
ARE YOU ALL RIGHT?
IS...IS WICCAN...?
WICCAN, YOU USED THE MARK! ARE YOU--
I'M ALL RIGHT. REALLY. GUYS, I'M FINE.

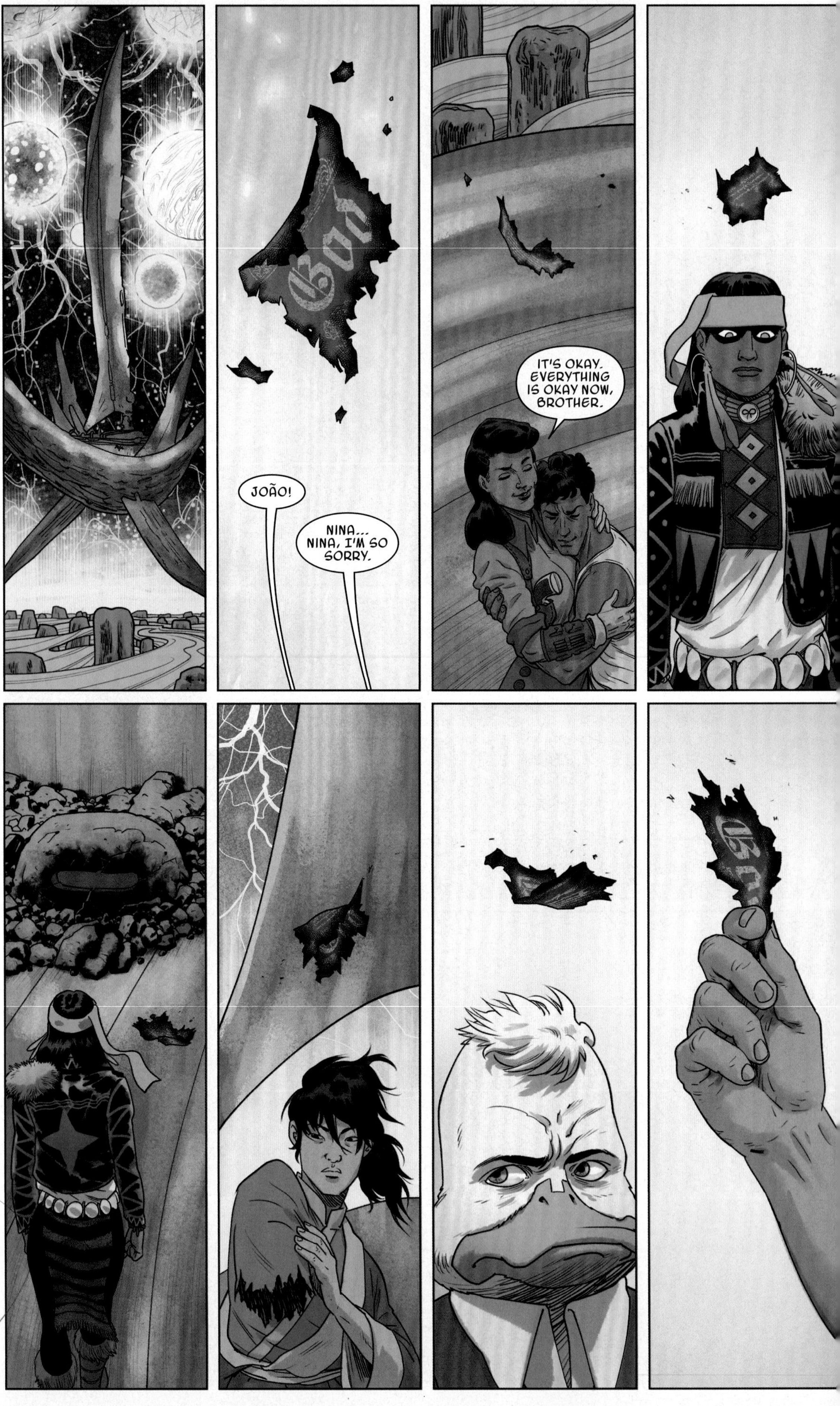
JOÃO!
NINA... NINA, I'M SO SORRY.
IT'S OKAY. EVERYTHING IS OKAY NOW, BROTHER.

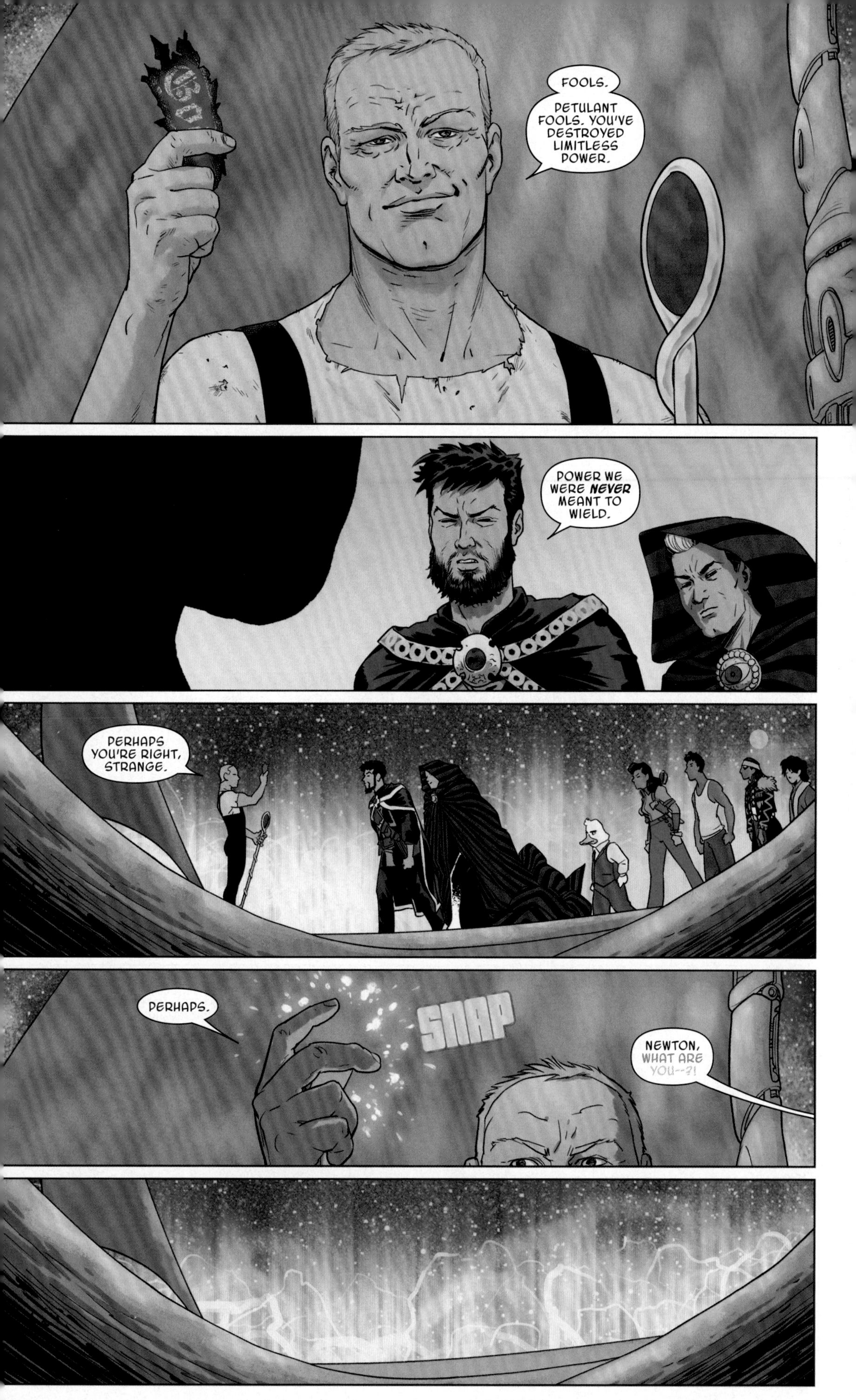
FOOLS.
PETULANT FOOLS. YOU'VE DESTROYED LIMITLESS POWER.
POWER WE WERE **NEVER** MEANT TO WIELD.
PERHAPS YOU'RE RIGHT, STRANGE.
PERHAPS.
SNAP
NEWTON, WHAT ARE YOU--?!

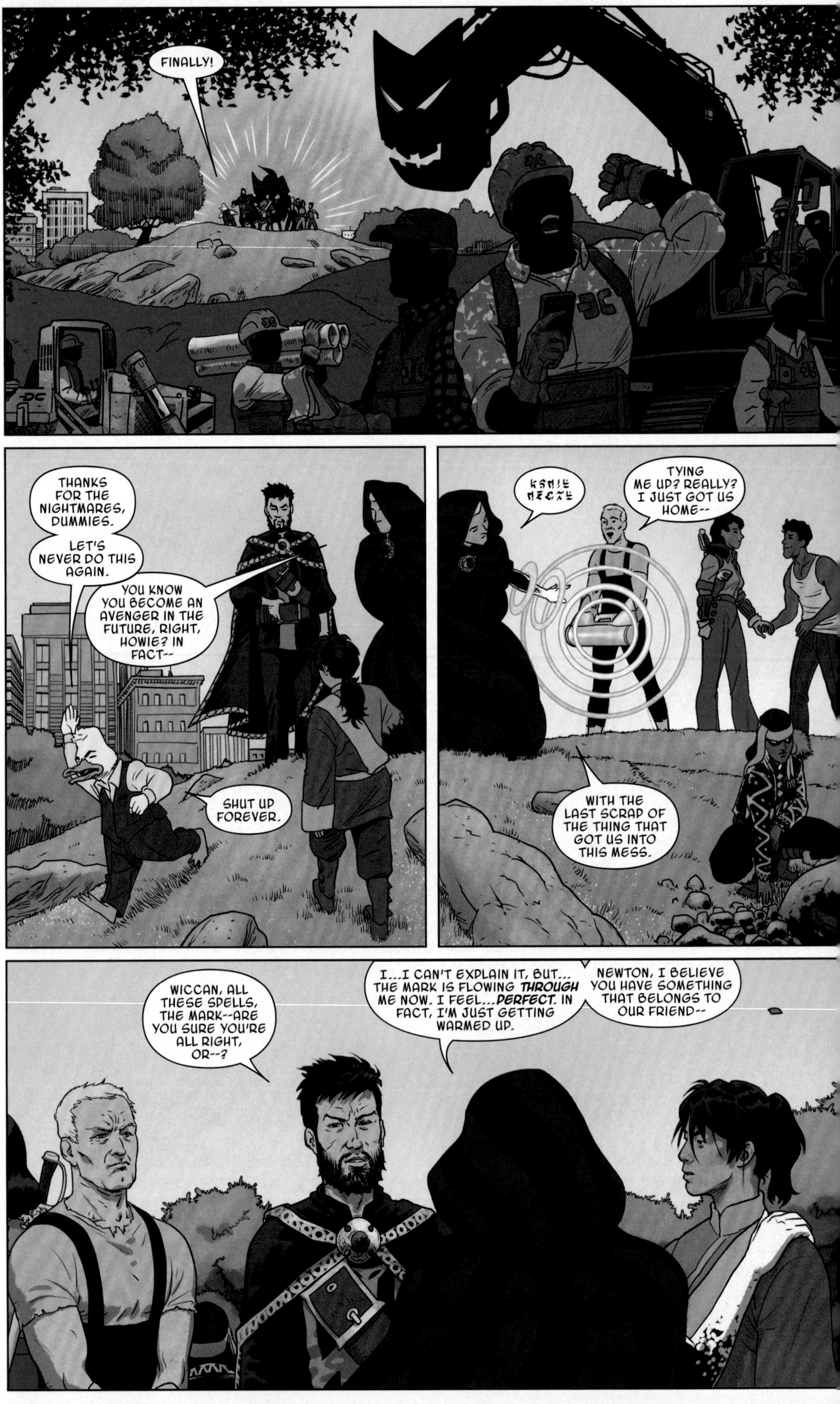
FINALLY!
THANKS FOR THE NIGHTMARES, DUMMIES.
LET'S NEVER DO THIS AGAIN.
YOU KNOW YOU BECOME AN AVENGER IN THE FUTURE, RIGHT, HOWIE? IN FACT--
SHUT UP FOREVER.
TYING ME UP? REALLY? I JUST GOT US HOME--
WITH THE LAST SCRAP OF THE THING THAT GOT US INTO THIS MESS.
WICCAN, ALL THESE SPELLS, THE MARK--ARE YOU SURE YOU'RE ALL RIGHT, OR--?
I...I CAN'T EXPLAIN IT, BUT... THE MARK IS FLOWING THROUGH ME NOW. I FEEL...PERFECT. IN FACT, I'M JUST GETTING WARMED UP.
NEWTON, I BELIEVE YOU HAVE SOMETHING THAT BELONGS TO OUR FRIEND--

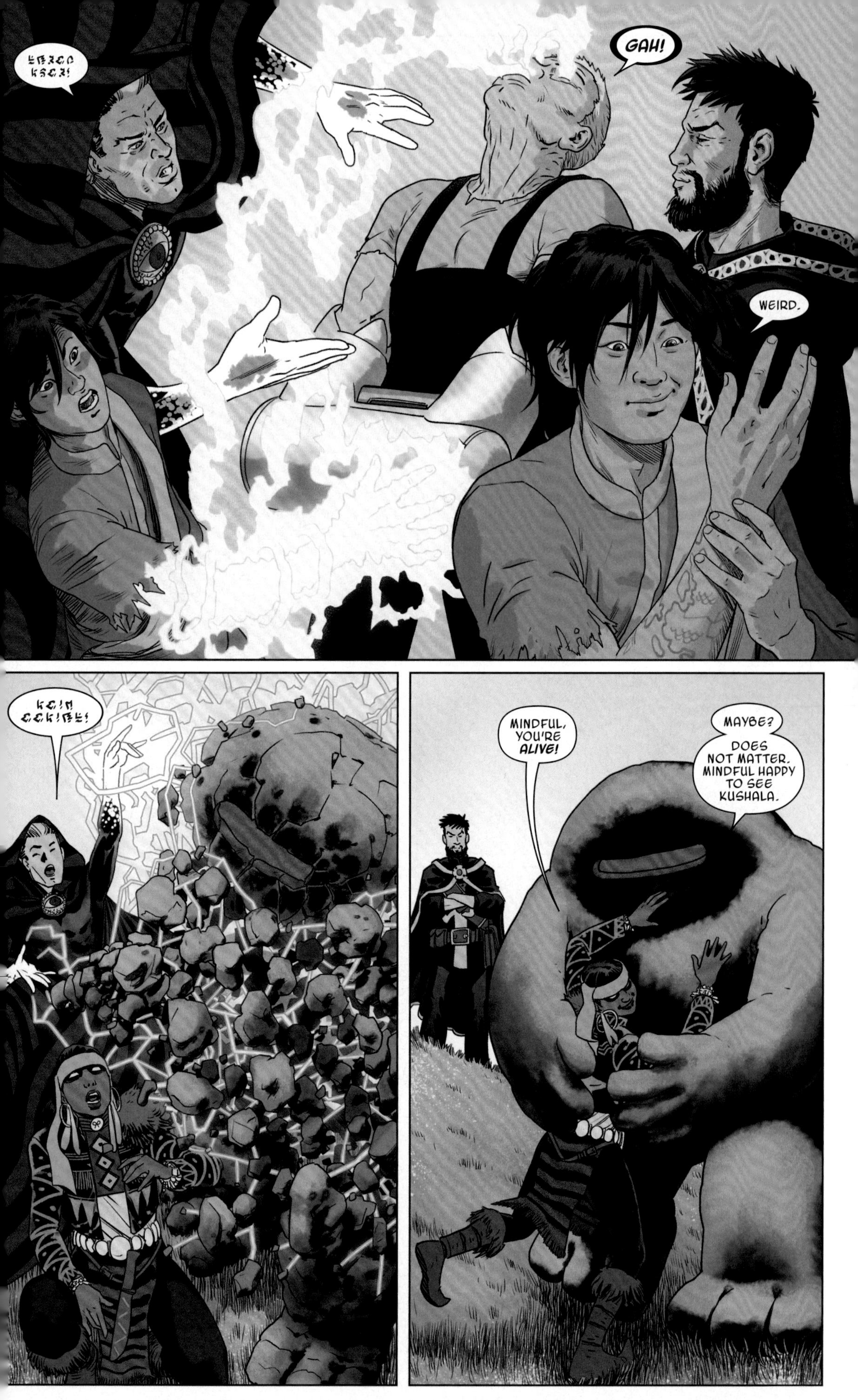

GAH!
WEIRD.
MINDFUL, YOU'RE **ALIVE!**
MAYBE?
DOES NOT MATTER. MINDFUL HAPPY TO SEE KUSHALA.

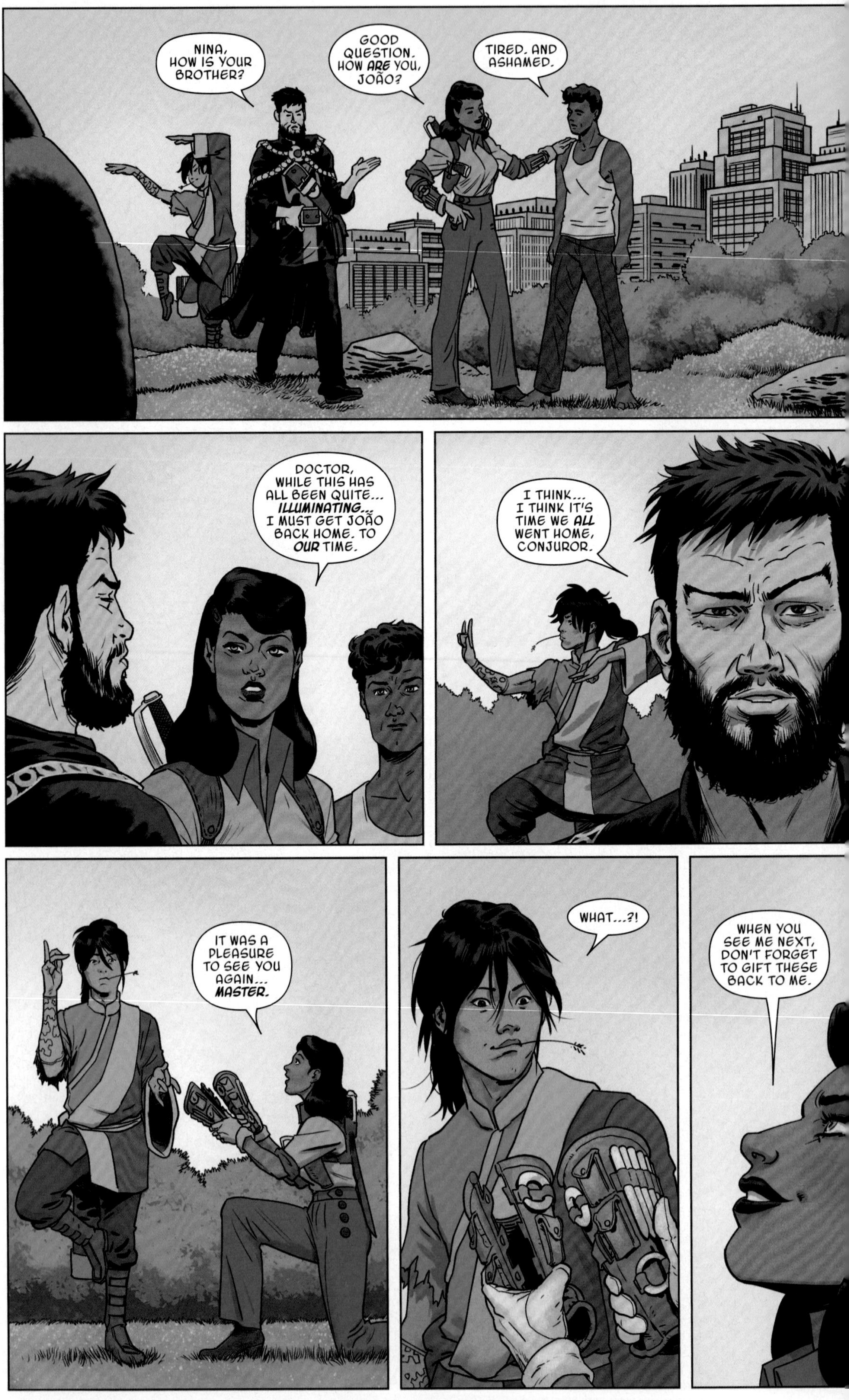

NINA, HOW IS YOUR BROTHER?
GOOD QUESTION. HOW ARE YOU, JOÃO?
TIRED. AND ASHAMED.
DOCTOR, WHILE THIS HAS ALL BEEN QUITE... ILLUMINATING... I MUST GET JOÃO BACK HOME. TO OUR TIME.
I THINK... I THINK IT'S TIME WE ALL WENT HOME, CONJUROR.
IT WAS A PLEASURE TO SEE YOU AGAIN... MASTER.
WHAT...?!
WHEN YOU SEE ME NEXT, DON'T FORGET TO GIFT THESE BACK TO ME.

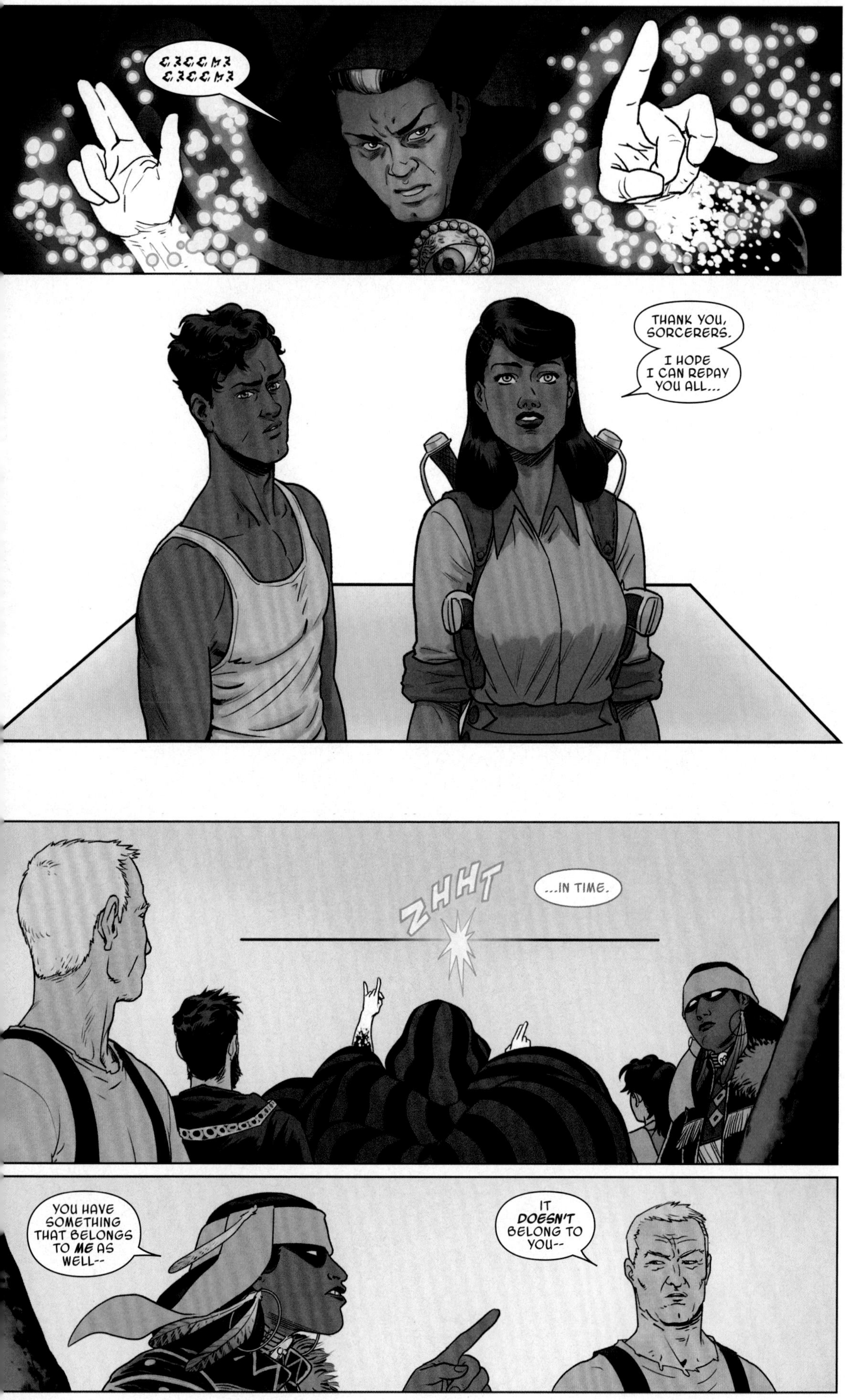
THANK YOU, SORCERERS.
I HOPE I CAN REPAY YOU ALL...
ZHHT
...IN TIME.
YOU HAVE SOMETHING THAT BELONGS TO *ME* AS WELL--
IT *DOESN'T* BELONG TO YOU--

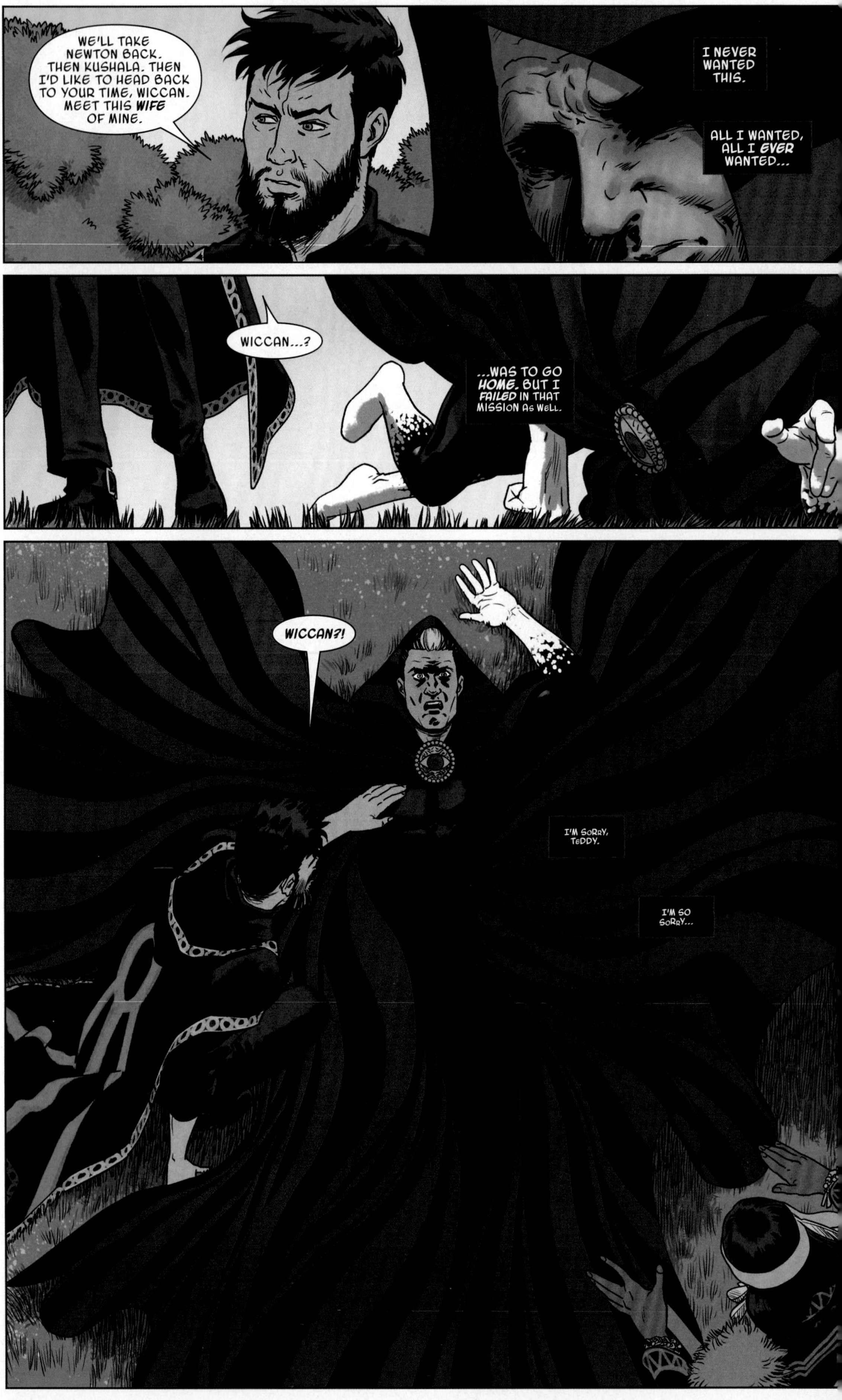
WE'LL TAKE NEWTON BACK. THEN KUSHALA. THEN I'D LIKE TO HEAD BACK TO YOUR TIME, WICCAN. MEET THIS WIFE OF MINE.
I NEVER WANTED THIS.
ALL I WANTED, ALL I EVER WANTED...
WICCAN...?
...WAS TO GO HOME. BUT I FAILED IN THAT MISSION AS WELL.
WICCAN?!
I'M SORRY, TEDDY.
I'M SO SORRY...

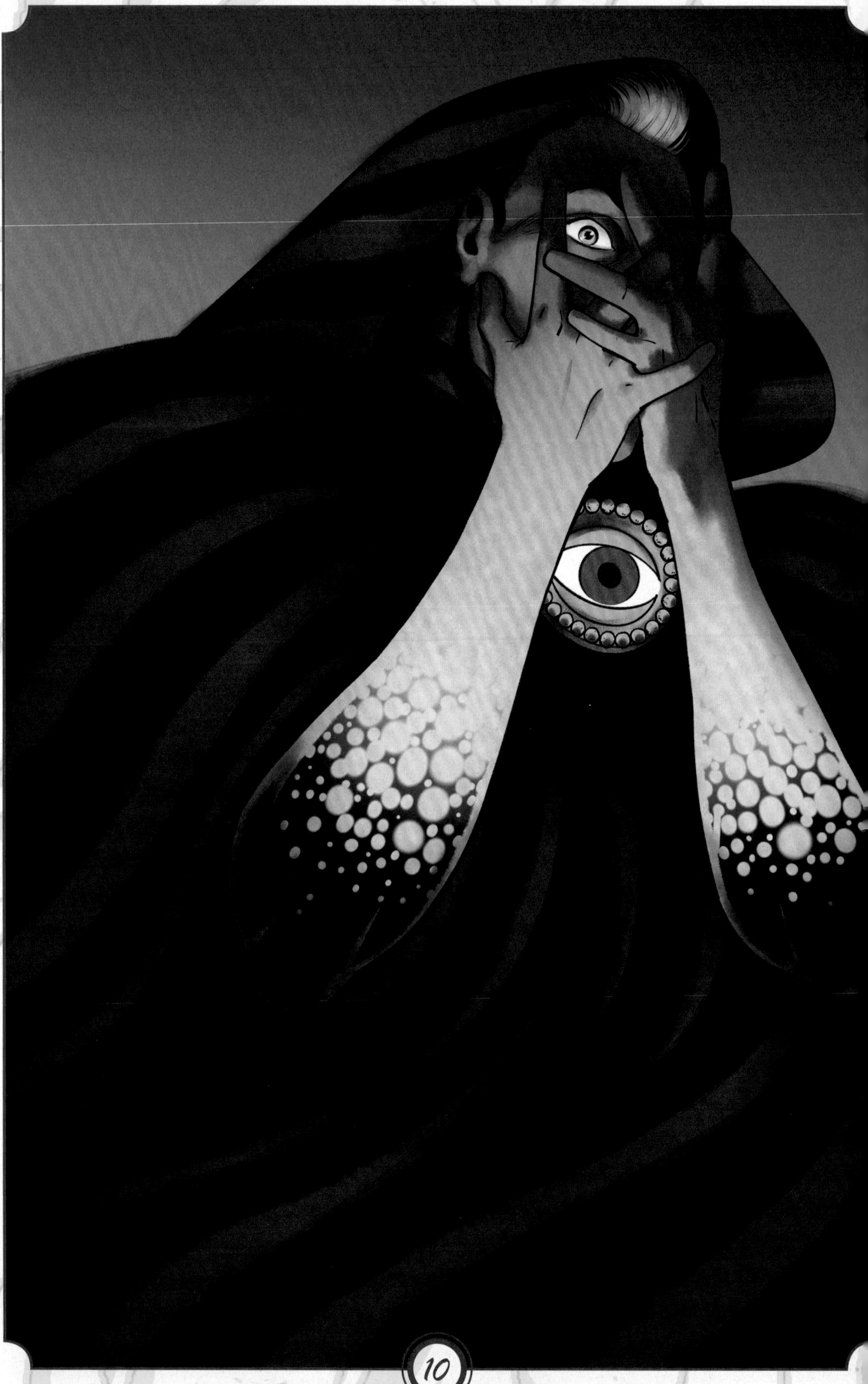

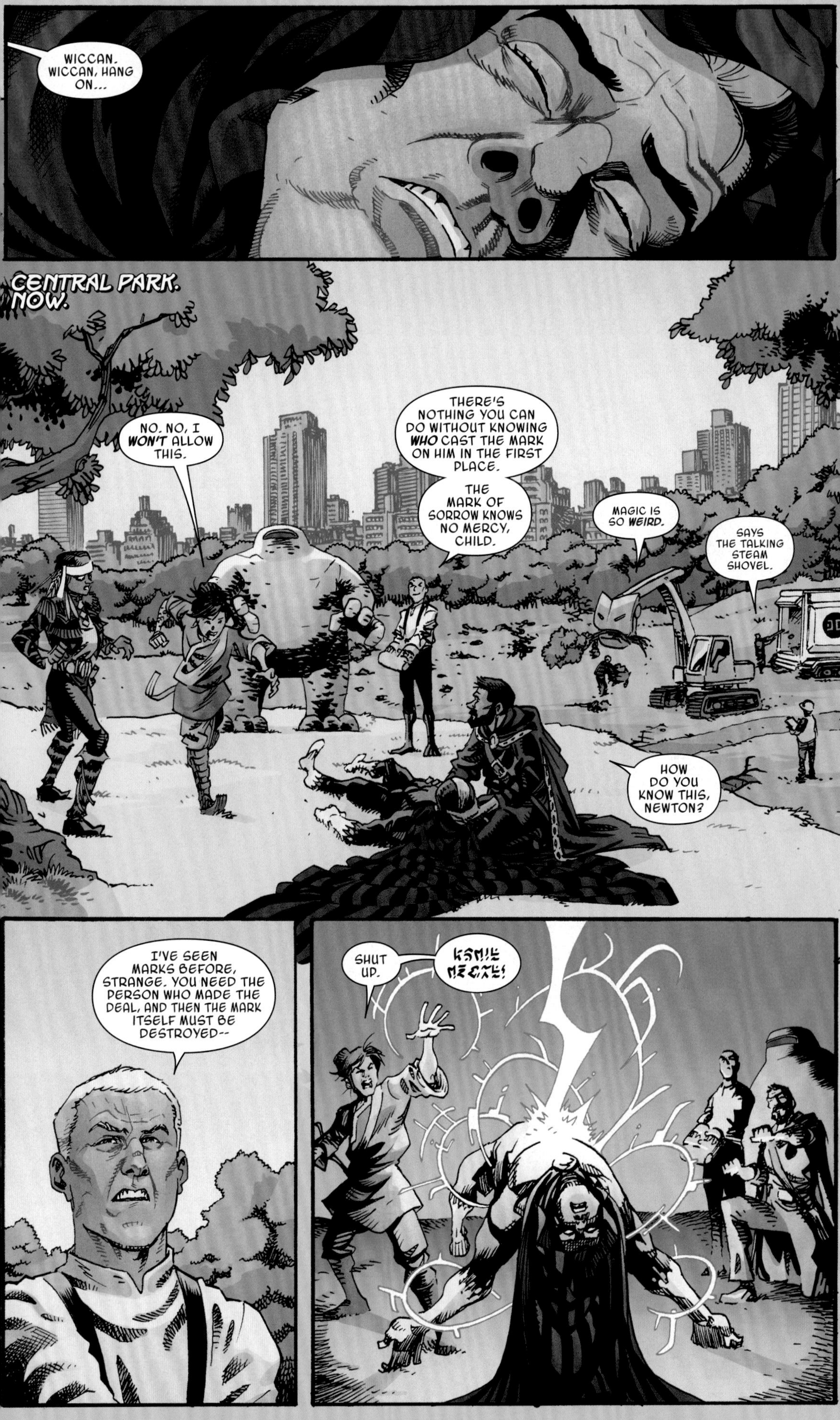
WICCAN. WICCAN, HANG ON...
CENTRAL PARK. NOW.
NO. NO, I WON'T ALLOW THIS.
THERE'S NOTHING YOU CAN DO WITHOUT KNOWING WHO CAST THE MARK ON HIM IN THE FIRST PLACE.
THE MARK OF SORROW KNOWS NO MERCY, CHILD.
MAGIC IS SO WEIRD.
SAYS THE TALKING STEAM SHOVEL.
HOW DO YOU KNOW THIS, NEWTON?
I'VE SEEN MARKS BEFORE, STRANGE. YOU NEED THE PERSON WHO MADE THE DEAL, AND THEN THE MARK ITSELF MUST BE DESTROYED--
SHUT UP.

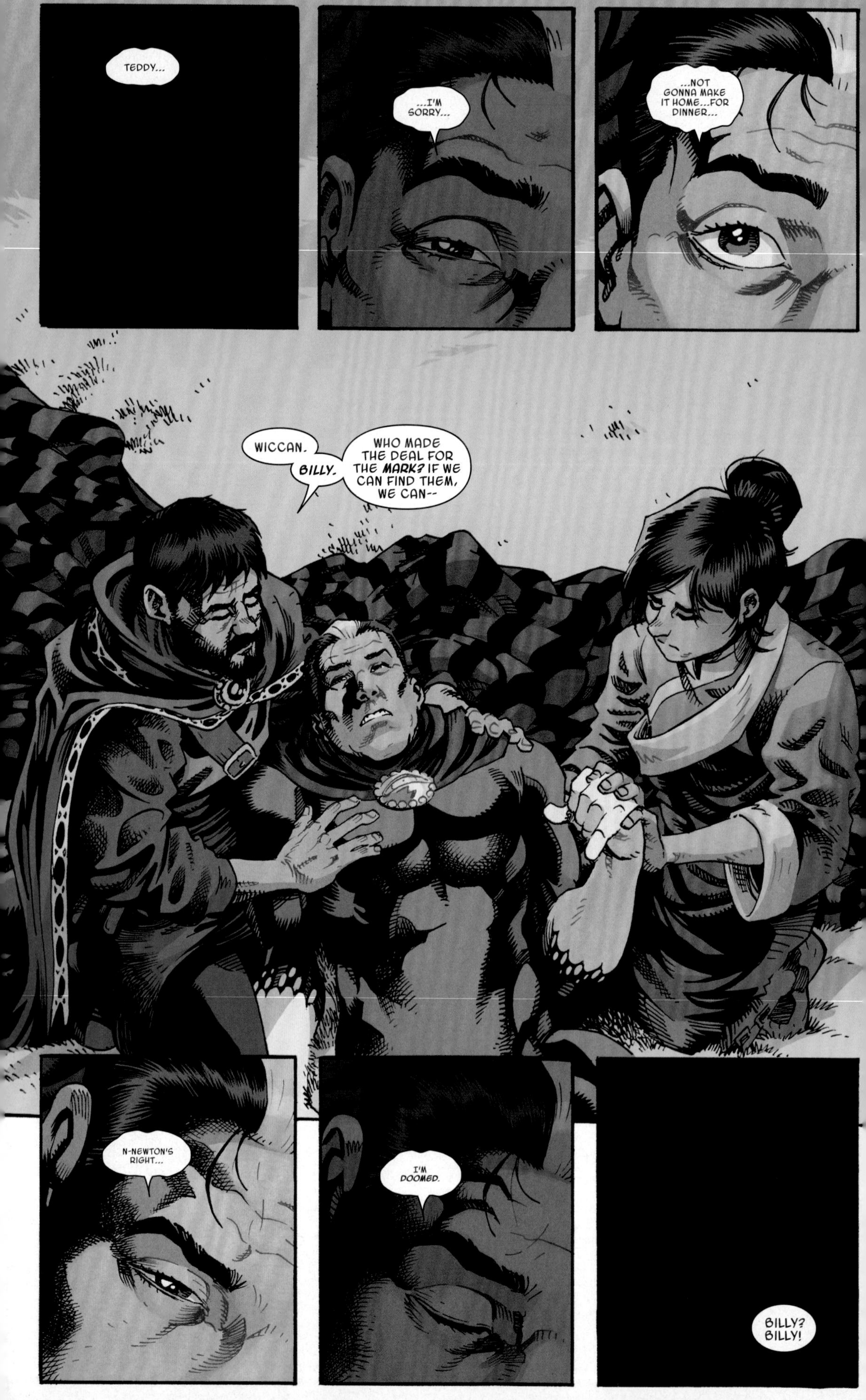
TEDDY...
...I'M SORRY...
...NOT GONNA MAKE IT HOME...FOR DINNER...
WICCAN.
BILLY.
WHO MADE THE DEAL FOR THE MARK? IF WE CAN FIND THEM, WE CAN--
N-NEWTON'S RIGHT...
I'M DOOMED.
BILLY? BILLY!

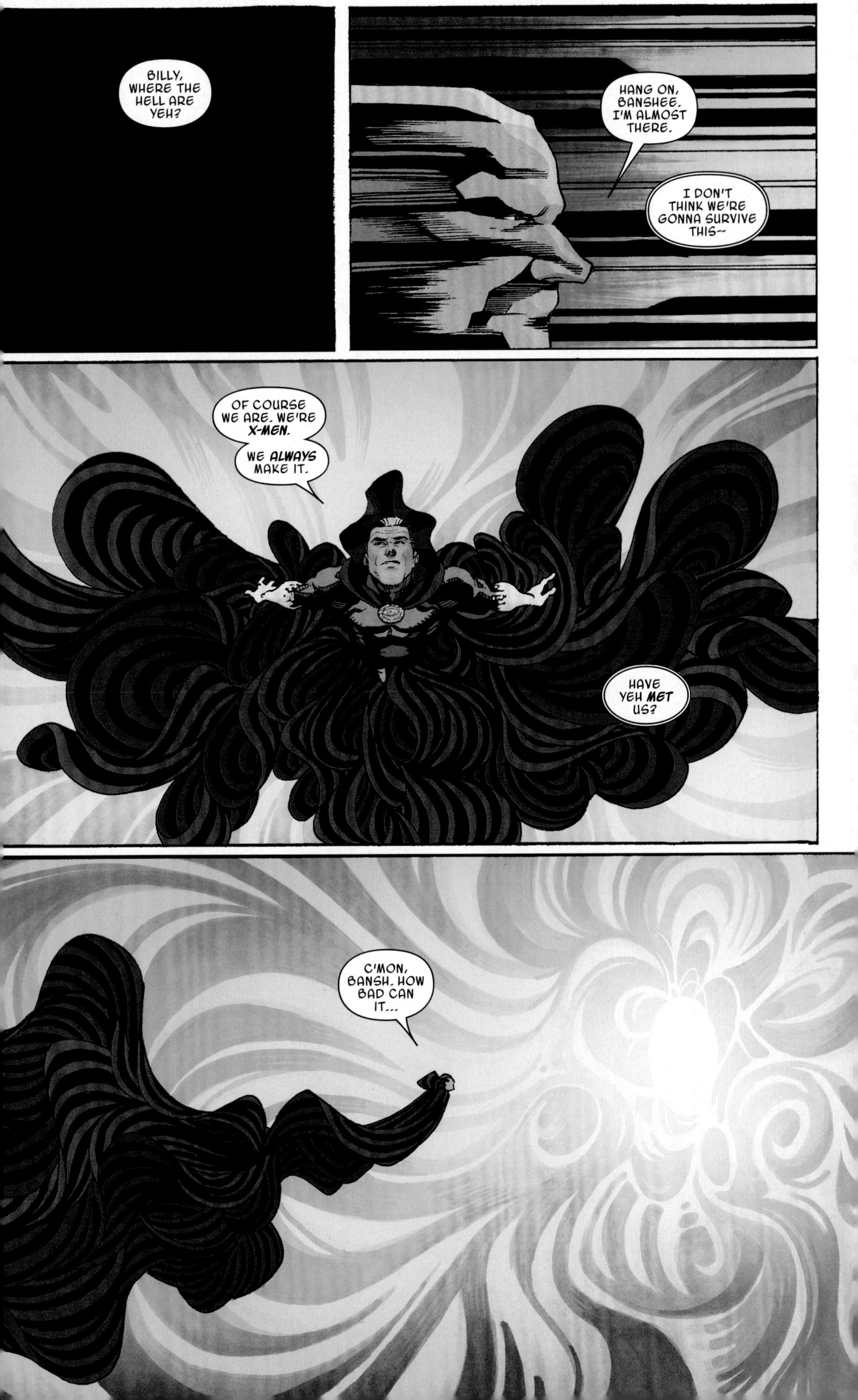

BILLY, WHERE THE HELL ARE YEH?
HANG ON, BANSHEE. I'M ALMOST THERE.
I DON'T THINK WE'RE GONNA SURVIVE THIS--
OF COURSE WE ARE. WE'RE X-MEN.
WE ALWAYS MAKE IT.
HAVE YEH MET US?
C'MON, BANSH. HOW BAD CAN IT...

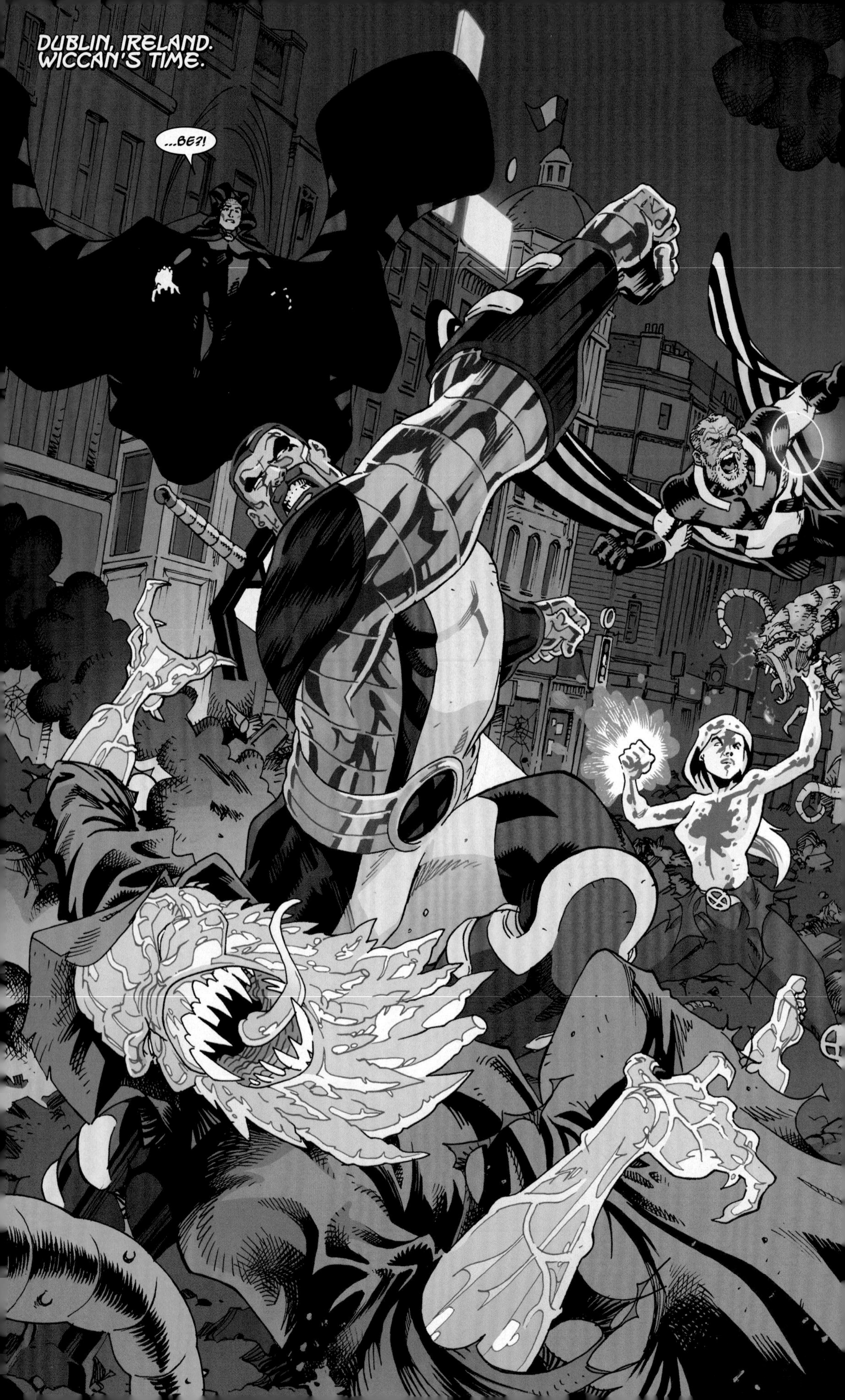
DUBLIN, IRELAND. WICCAN'S TIME.
...BE?!

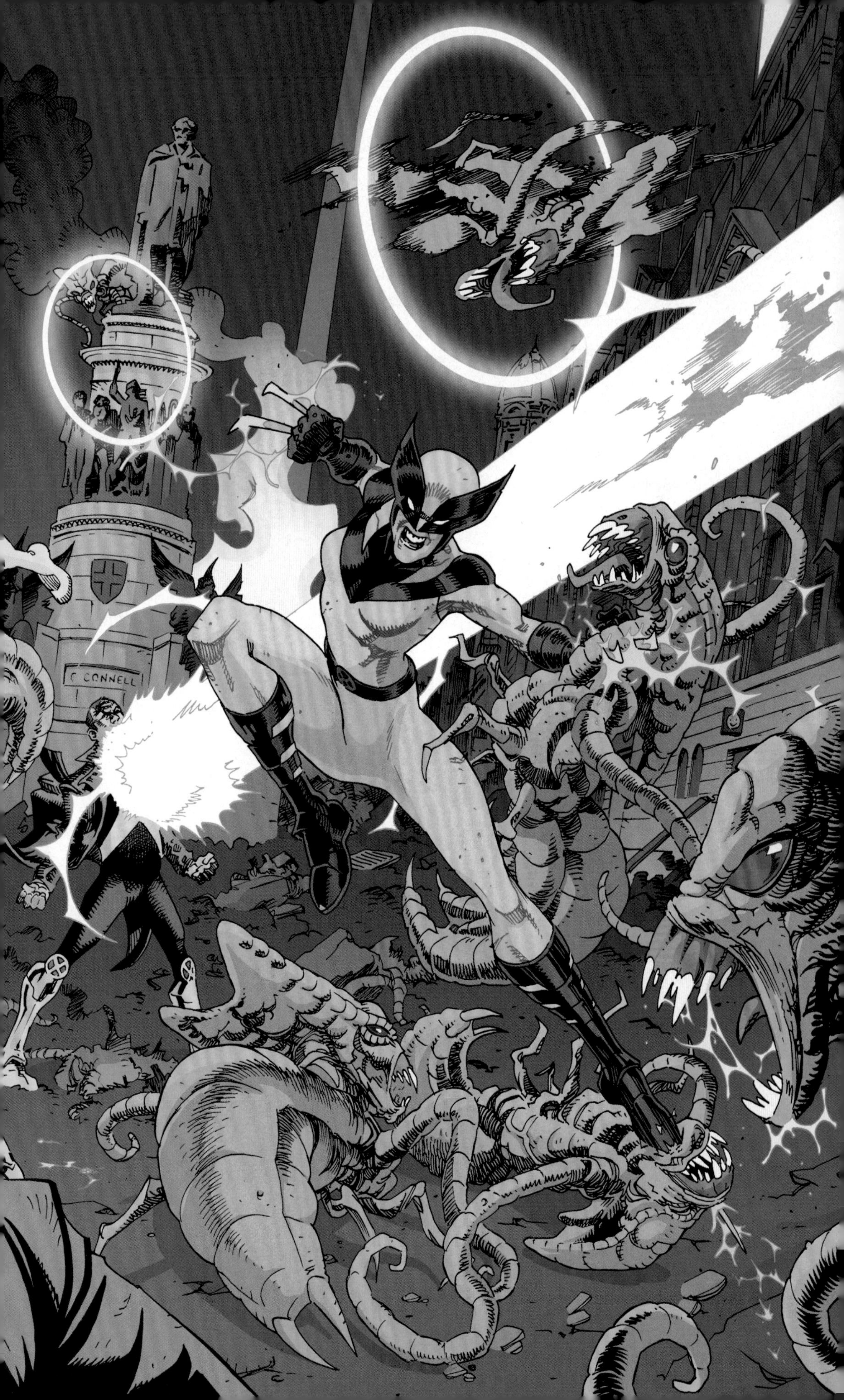

CONNELL

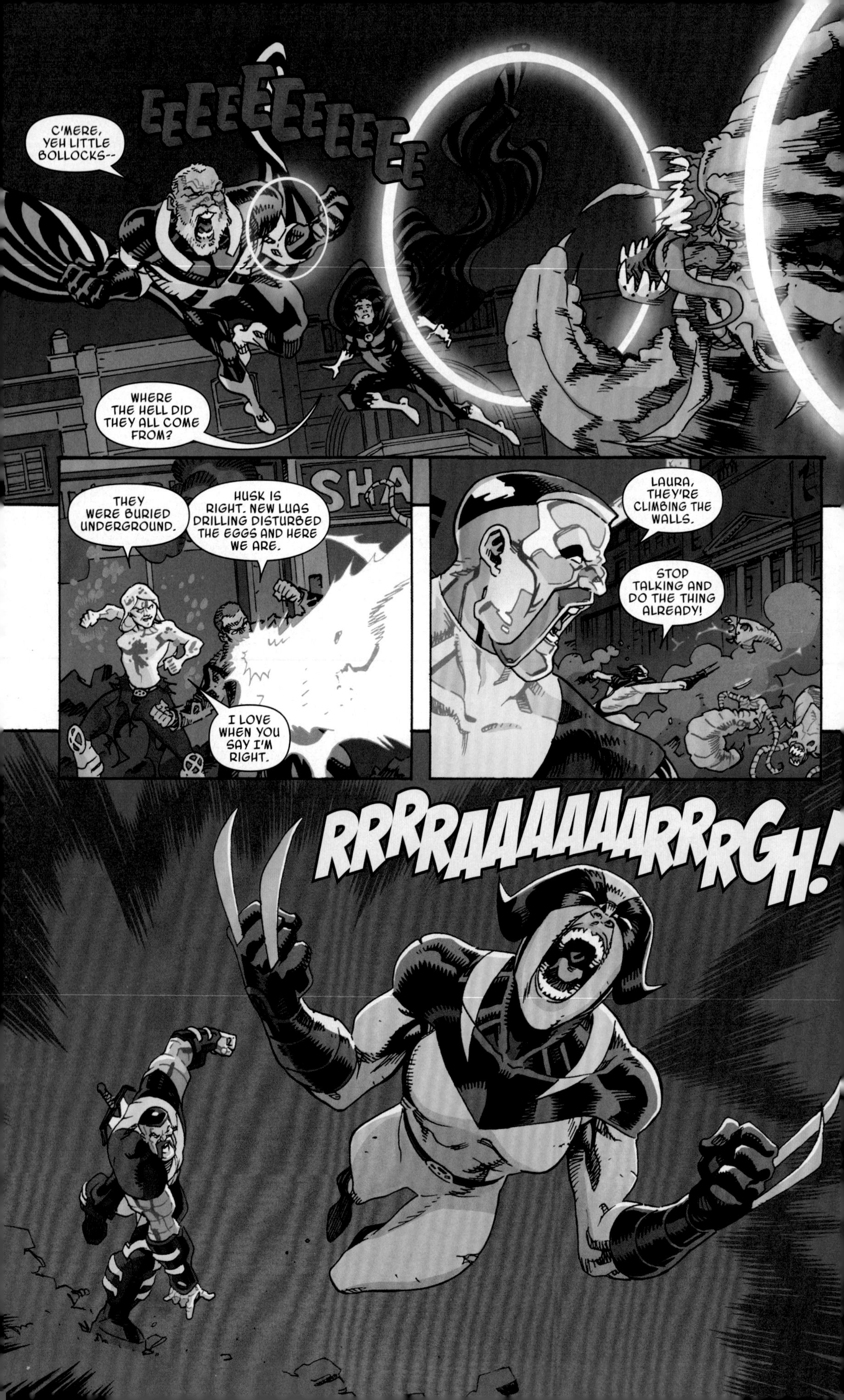
EEEEEEEEEEEEE
C'MERE, YEH LITTLE BOLLOCKS--
WHERE THE HELL DID THEY ALL COME FROM?
THEY WERE BURIED UNDERGROUND.
HUSK IS RIGHT. NEW LUAS DRILLING DISTURBED THE EGGS AND HERE WE ARE.
I LOVE WHEN YOU SAY I'M RIGHT.
LAURA, THEY'RE CLIMBING THE WALLS.
STOP TALKING AND DO THE THING ALREADY!
RRRRAAAAAAARRRGH!

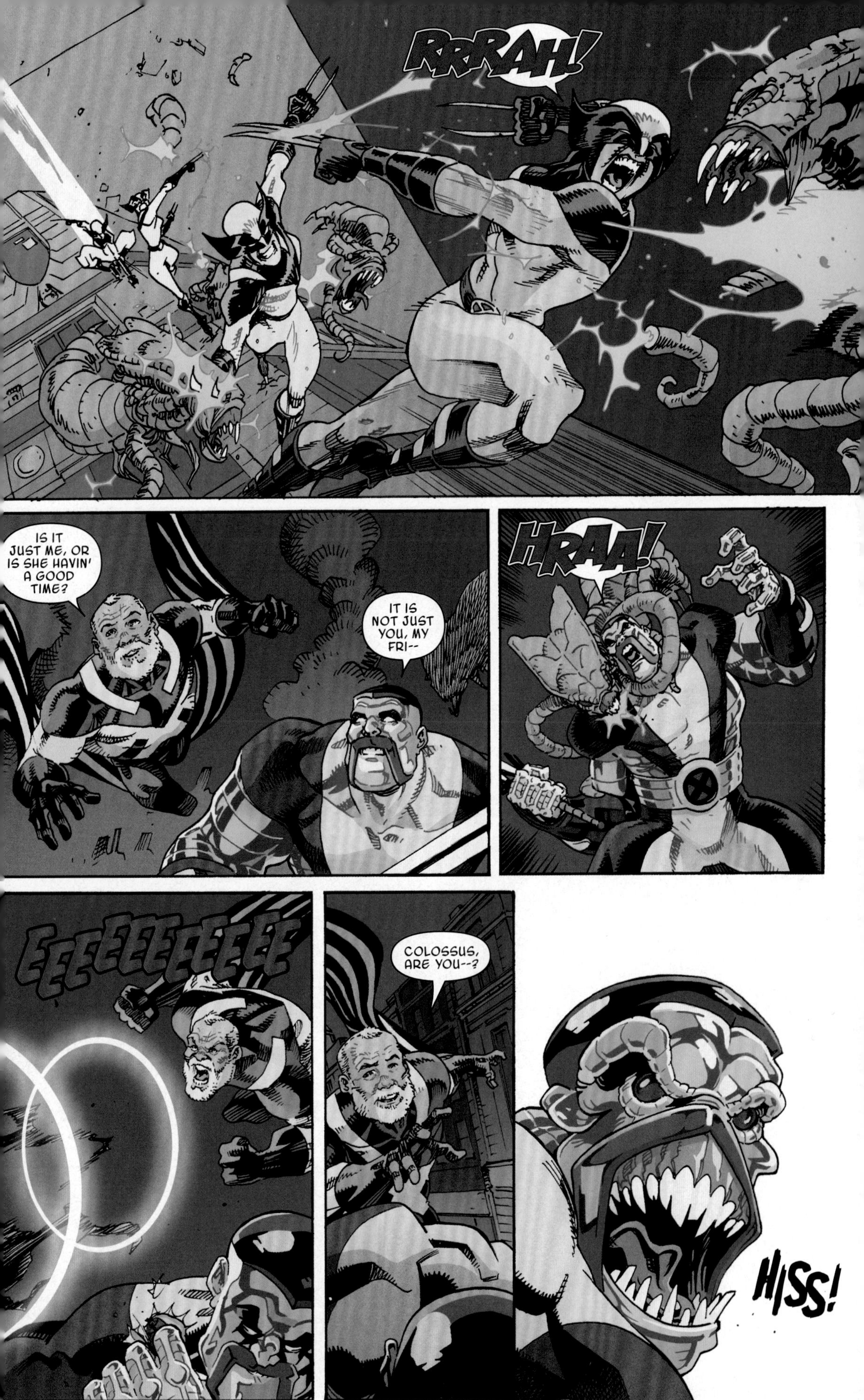
RRRAH!
IS IT JUST ME, OR IS SHE HAVIN' A GOOD TIME?
IT IS NOT JUST YOU, MY FRI--
HRAA!
EEEEEEEEEEE
COLOSSUS, ARE YOU--?
HISS!

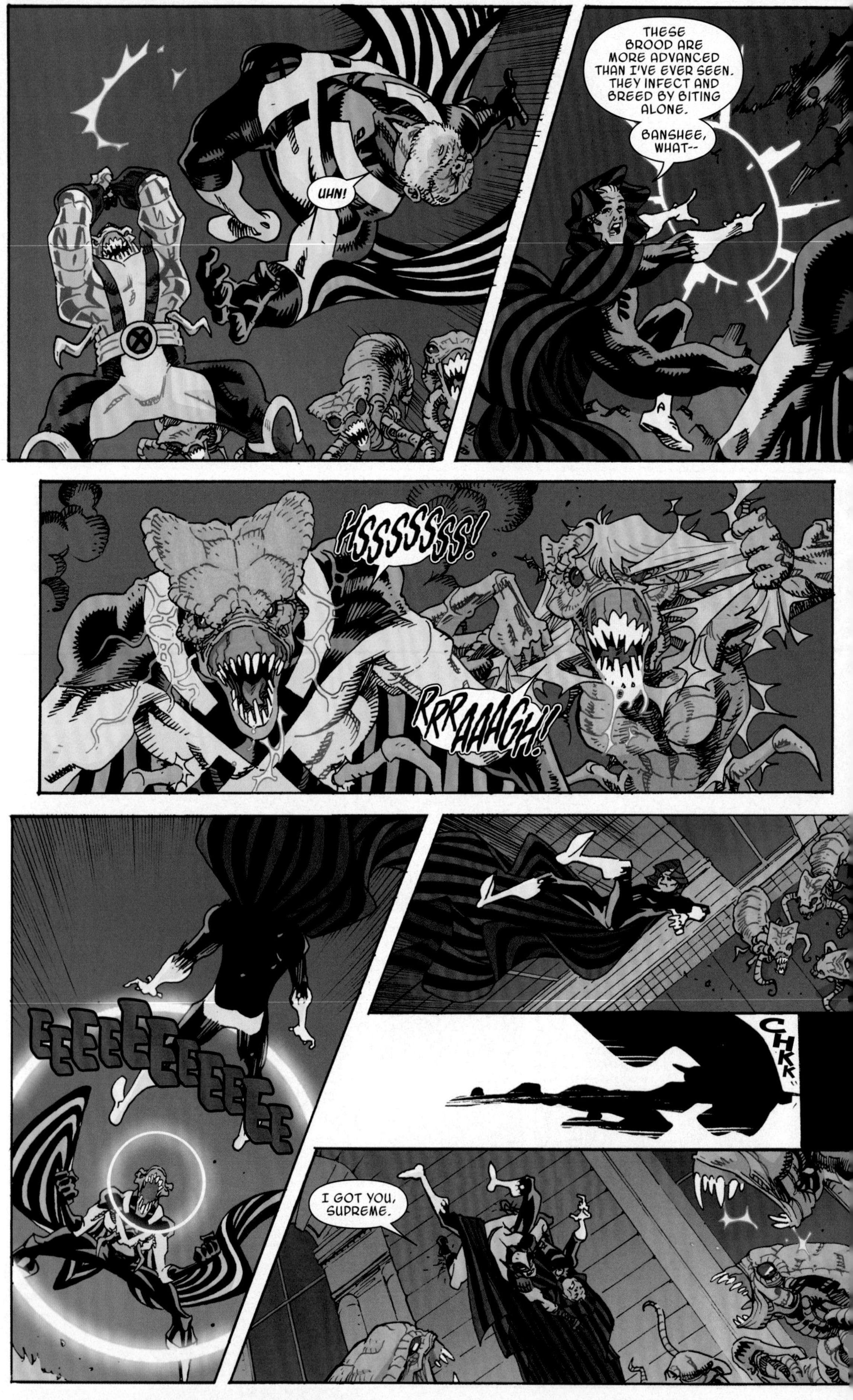
UHN!
THESE BROOD ARE MORE ADVANCED THAN I'VE EVER SEEN. THEY INFECT AND BREED BY BITING ALONE.
BANSHEE, WHAT--
HSSSSSSSS!
RRRAAAGH!
EEEEEEEEEEEE
CHKK
I GOT YOU, SUPREME.

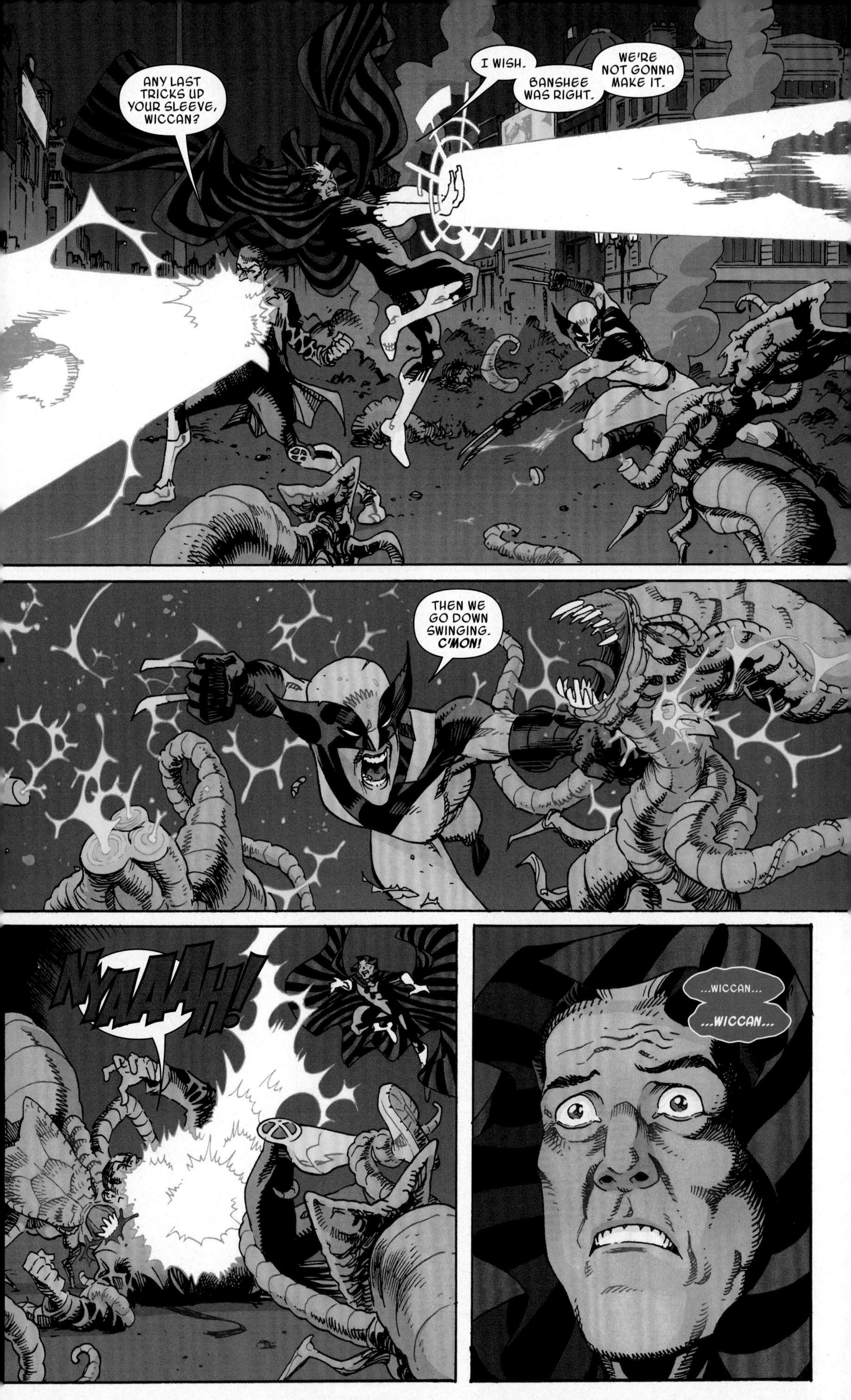
ANY LAST TRICKS UP YOUR SLEEVE, WICCAN?
I WISH.
BANSHEE WAS RIGHT.
WE'RE NOT GONNA MAKE IT.
THEN WE GO DOWN SWINGING. C'MON!
NYAAAH!
...WICCAN...
...WICCAN...

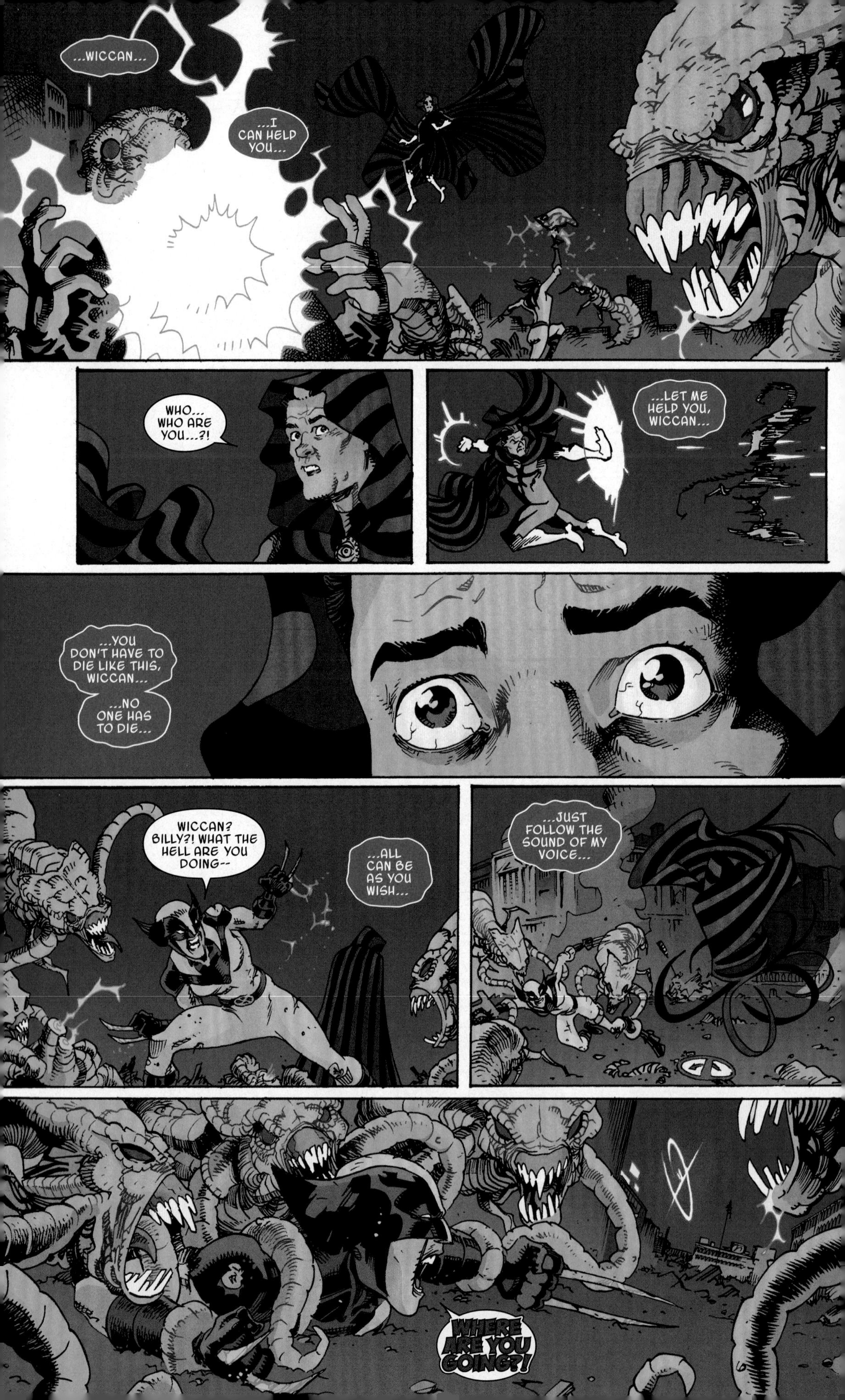
...WICCAN...
...I CAN HELP YOU...
WHO... WHO ARE YOU...?!
...LET ME HELP YOU, WICCAN...
...YOU DON'T HAVE TO DIE LIKE THIS, WICCAN...
...NO ONE HAS TO DIE...
WICCAN? BILLY?! WHAT THE HELL ARE YOU DOING--
...ALL CAN BE AS YOU WISH...
...JUST FOLLOW THE SOUND OF MY VOICE...
WHERE ARE YOU GOING?!

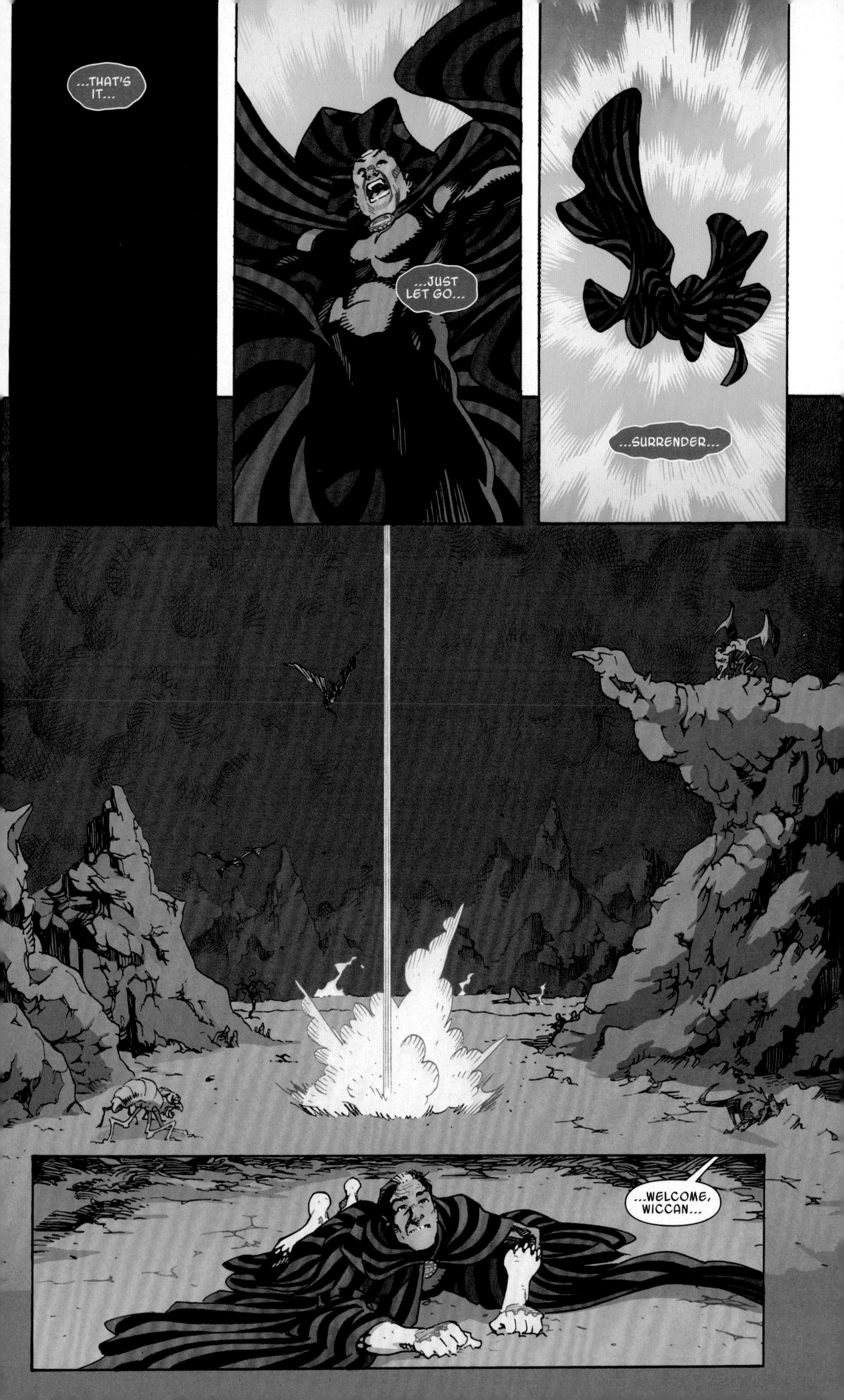
...THAT'S IT...
...JUST LET GO...
...SURRENDER...
...WELCOME, WICCAN...

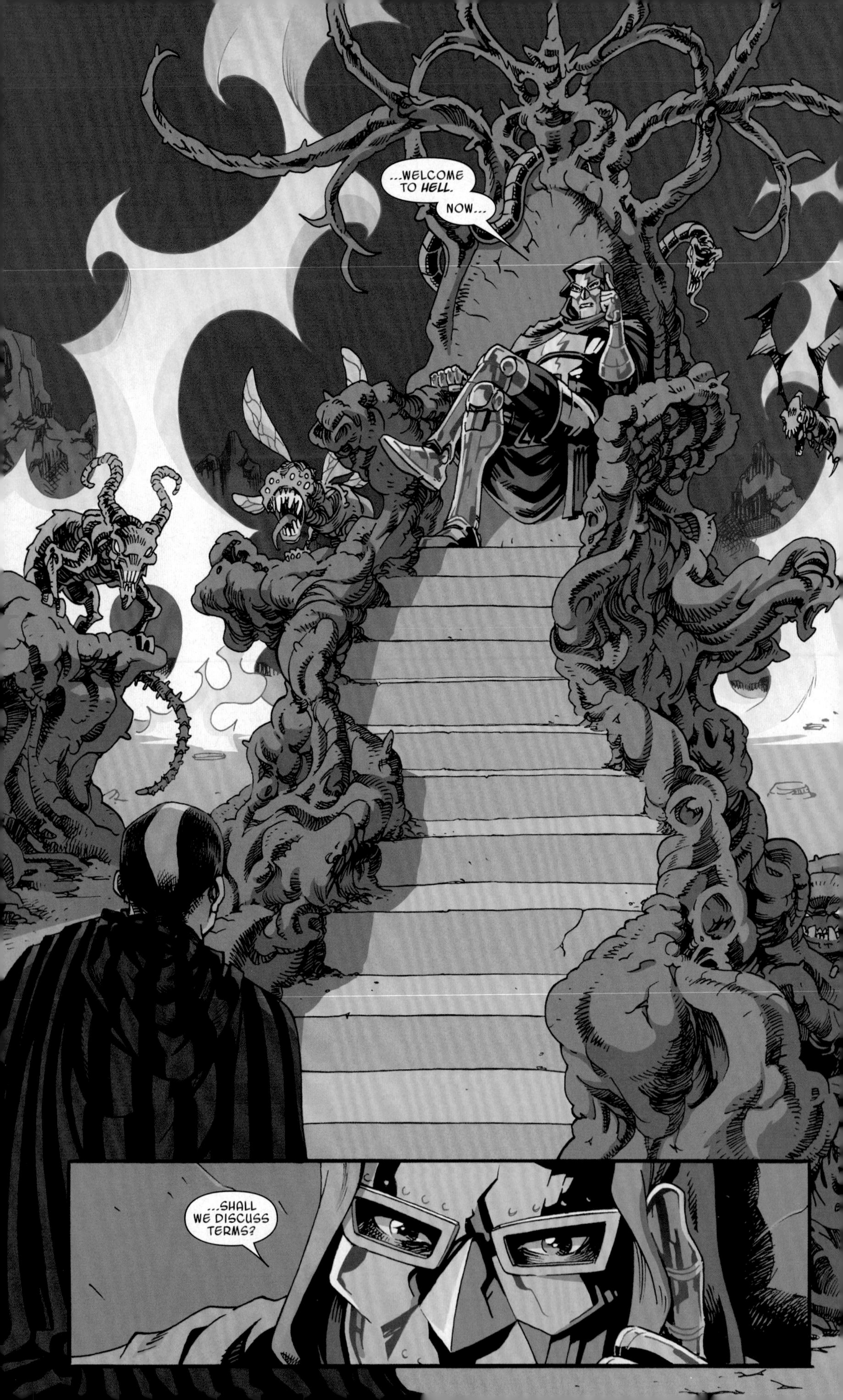
...WELCOME TO HELL.
NOW...
...SHALL WE DISCUSS TERMS?

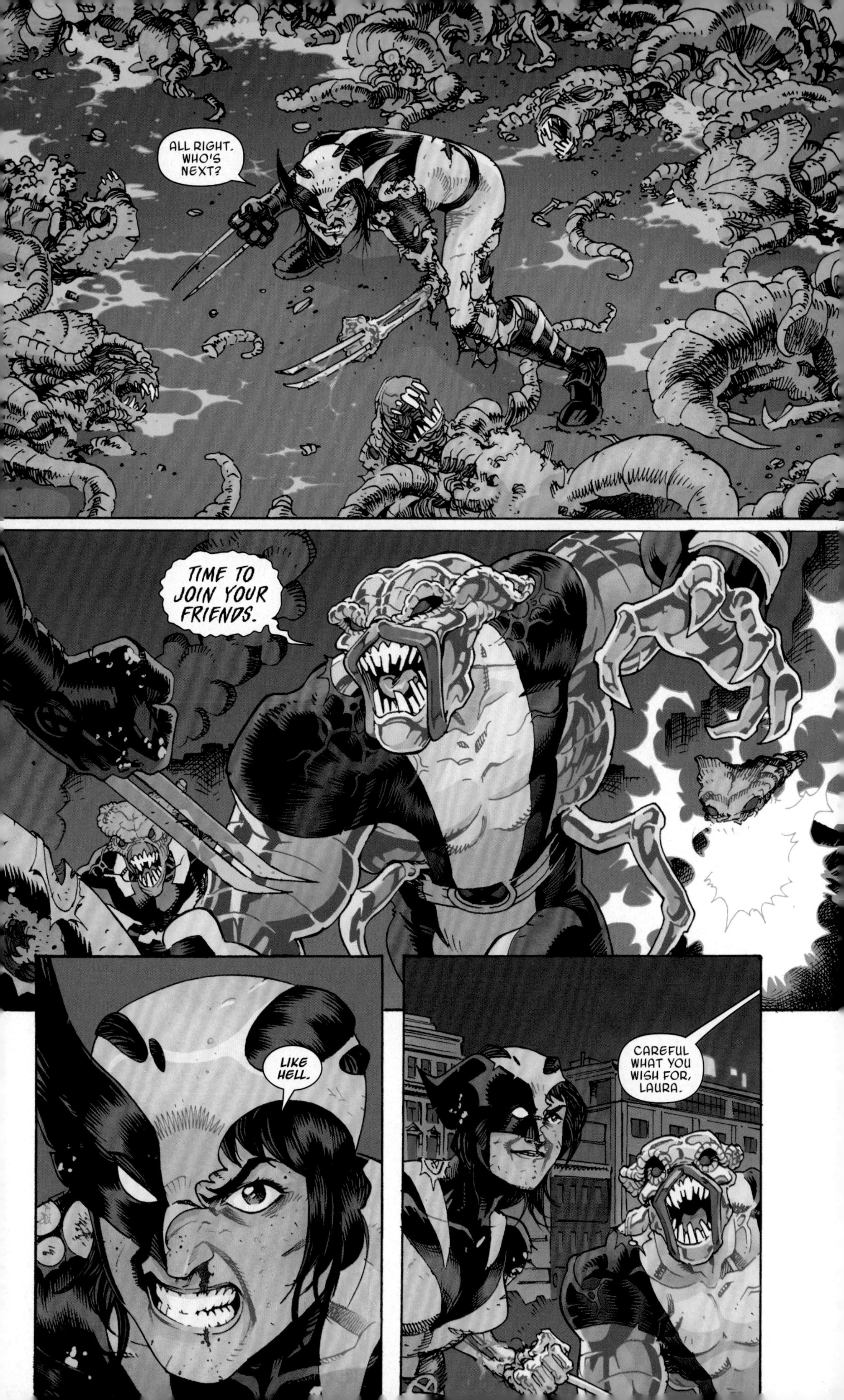
ALL RIGHT. WHO'S NEXT?
TIME TO JOIN YOUR FRIENDS.
LIKE HELL.
CAREFUL WHAT YOU WISH FOR, LAURA.

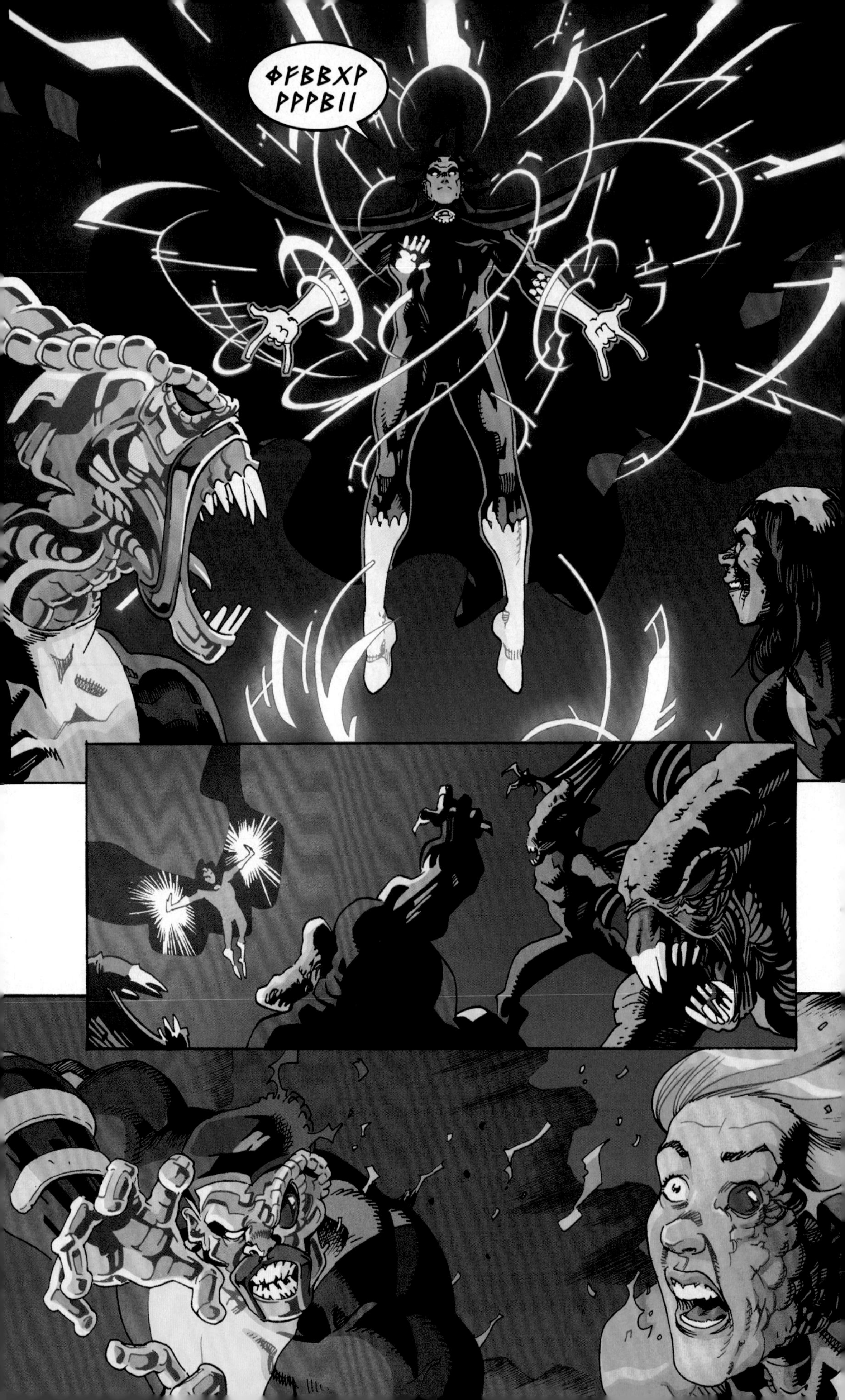

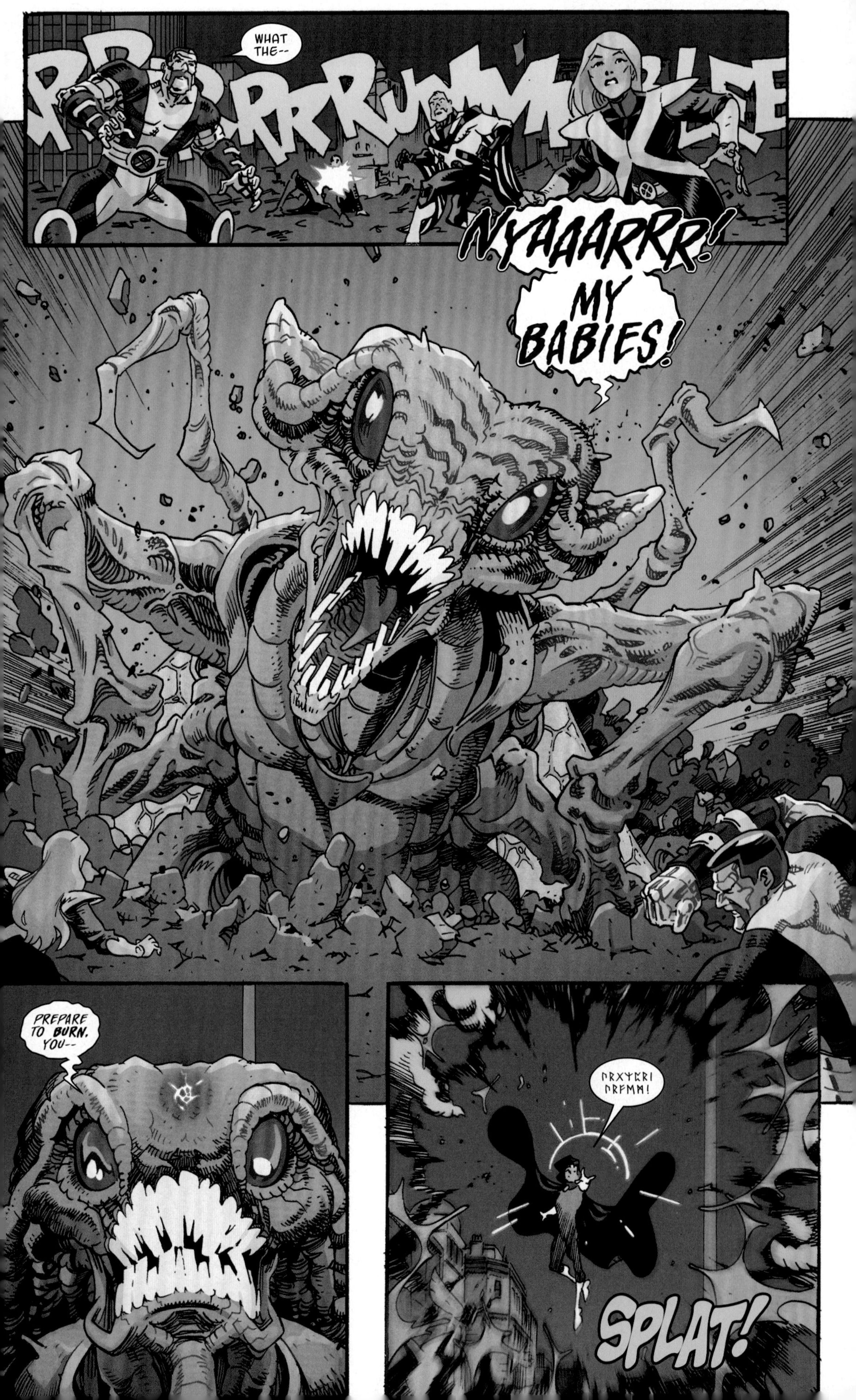
WHAT THE--
RRRRRRRUMMBLE
NYAAARRR!
MY BABIES!
PREPARE TO BURN, YOU--
ᚢᚱᚷᛉᚴᚱᛁ ᚢᚠᛖᛗᛗ!
SPLAT!

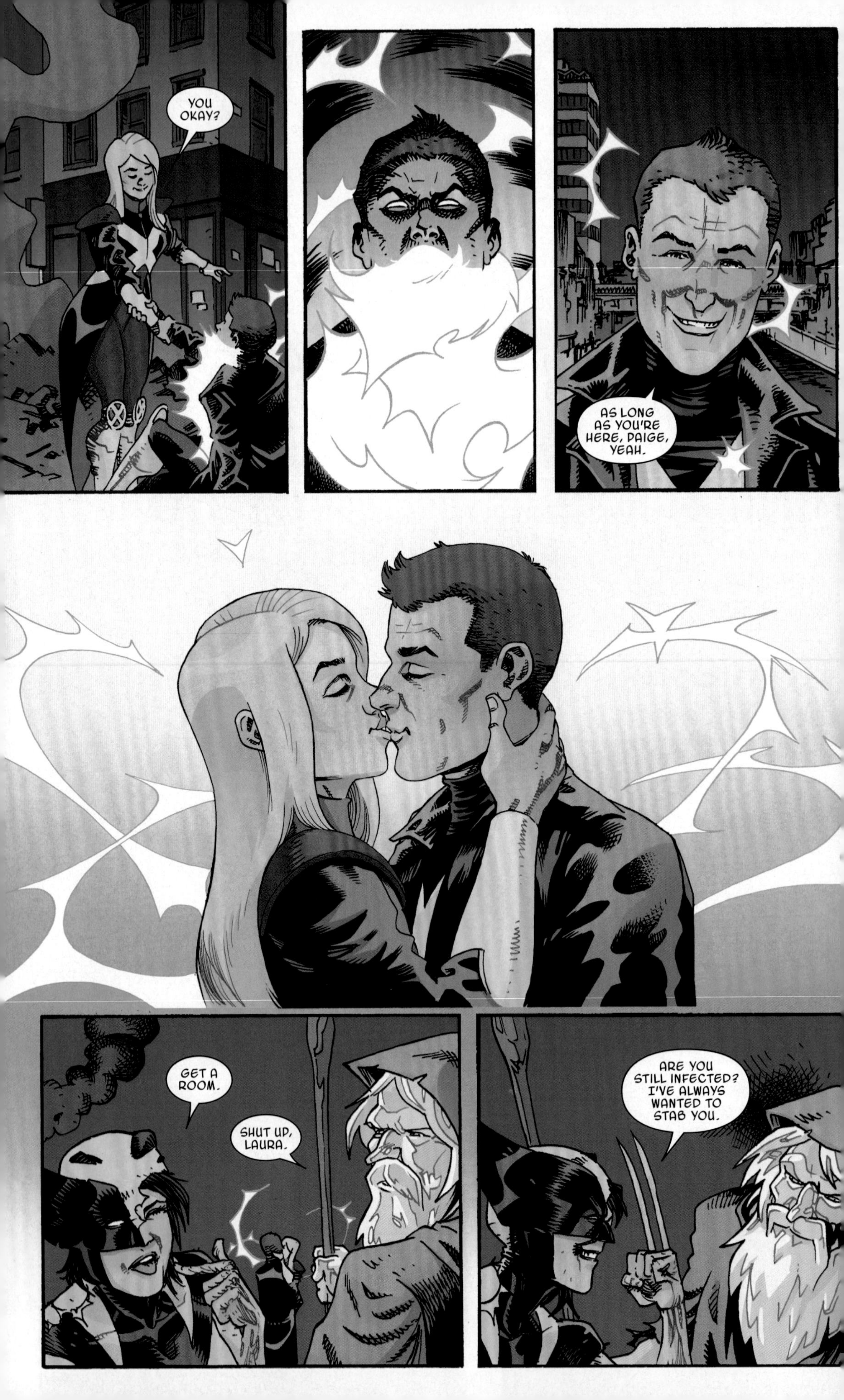
YOU OKAY?
AS LONG AS YOU'RE HERE, PAIGE, YEAH.
GET A ROOM.
SHUT UP, LAURA.
ARE YOU STILL INFECTED? I'VE ALWAYS WANTED TO STAB YOU.

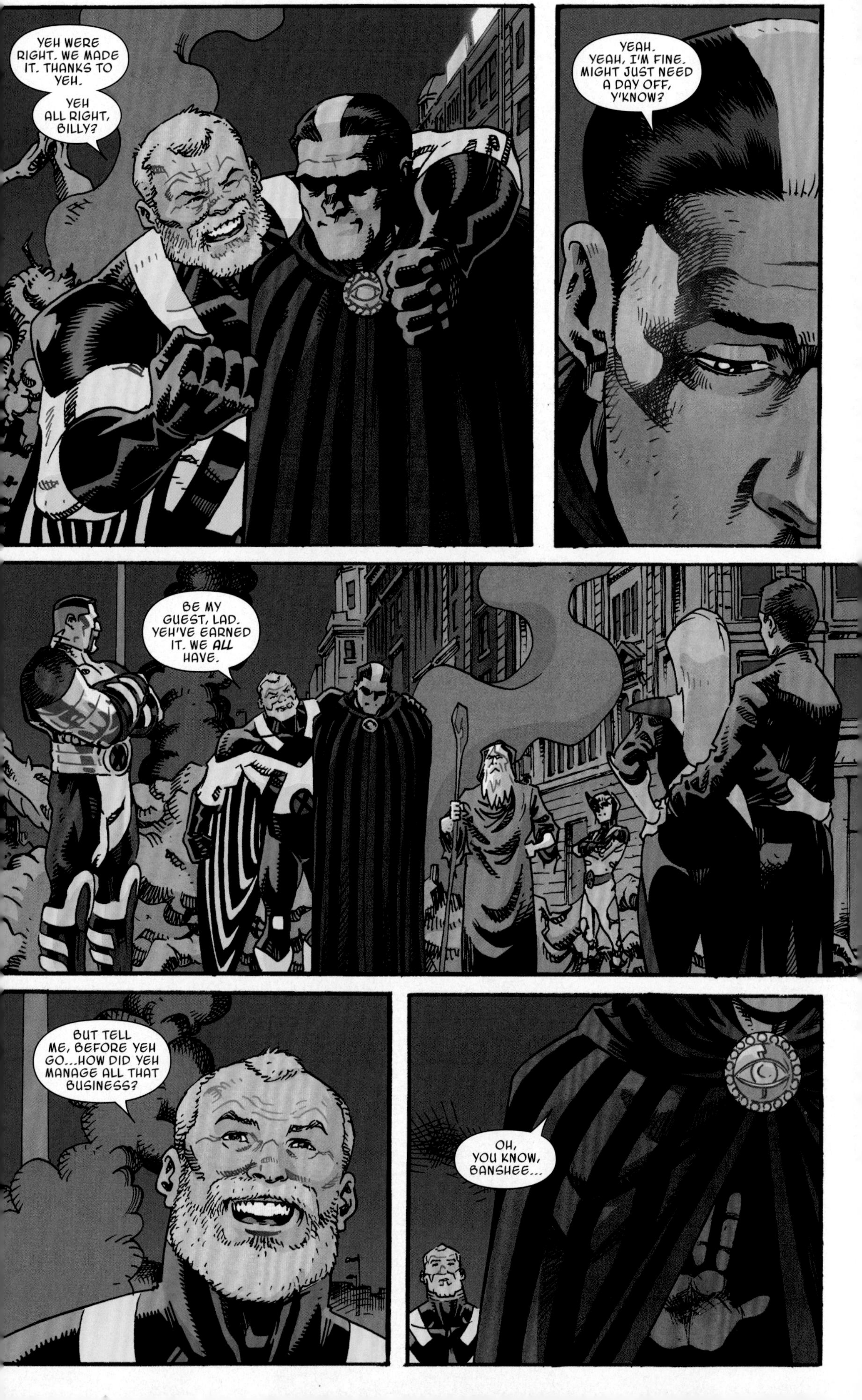
YEH WERE RIGHT. WE MADE IT. THANKS TO YEH.
YEH ALL RIGHT, BILLY?
YEAH. YEAH, I'M FINE. MIGHT JUST NEED A DAY OFF, Y'KNOW?
BE MY GUEST, LAD. YEH'VE EARNED IT. WE ALL HAVE.
BUT TELL ME, BEFORE YEH GO...HOW DID YEH MANAGE ALL THAT BUSINESS?
OH, YOU KNOW, BANSHEE...

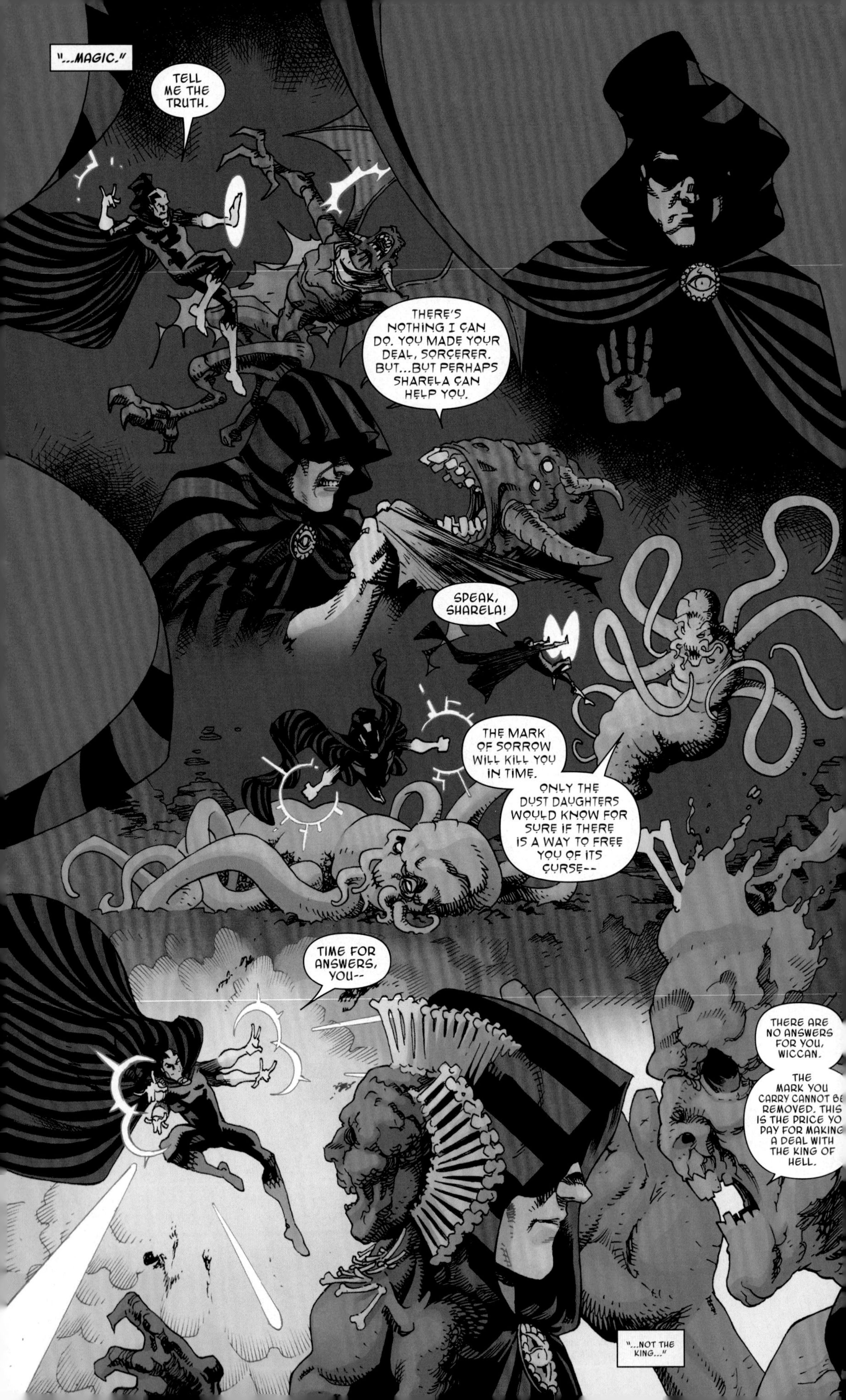
"...MAGIC."
TELL ME THE TRUTH.
THERE'S NOTHING I CAN DO. YOU MADE YOUR DEAL, SORCERER. BUT...BUT PERHAPS SHARELA CAN HELP YOU.
SPEAK, SHARELA!
THE MARK OF SORROW WILL KILL YOU IN TIME.
ONLY THE DUST DAUGHTERS WOULD KNOW FOR SURE IF THERE IS A WAY TO FREE YOU OF ITS CURSE--
TIME FOR ANSWERS, YOU--
THERE ARE NO ANSWERS FOR YOU, WICCAN.
THE MARK YOU CARRY CANNOT BE REMOVED. THIS IS THE PRICE YOU PAY FOR MAKING A DEAL WITH THE KING OF HELL.
"...NOT THE KING..."

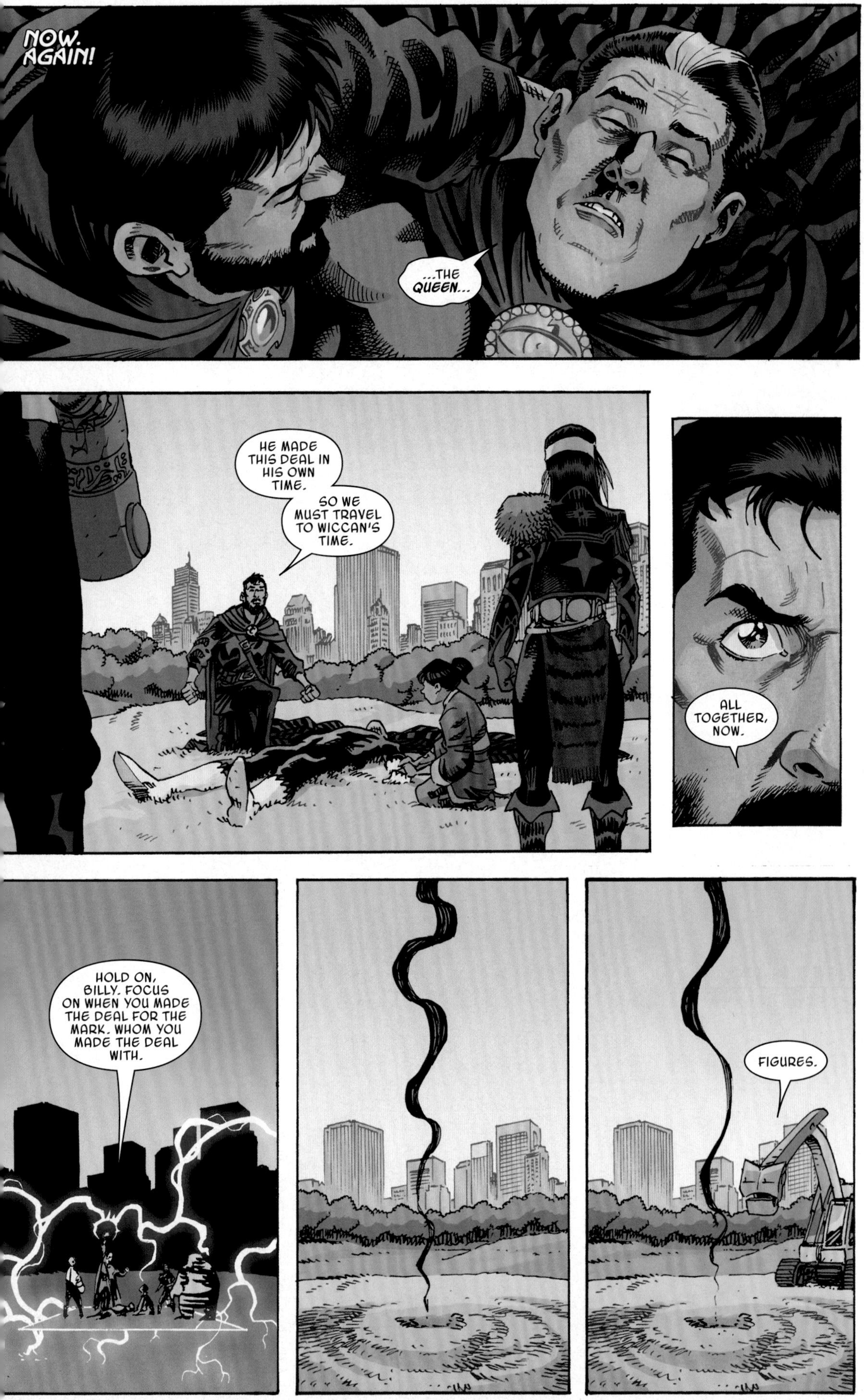
NOW. AGAIN!
...THE QUEEN...
HE MADE THIS DEAL IN HIS OWN TIME.
SO WE MUST TRAVEL TO WICCAN'S TIME.
ALL TOGETHER, NOW.
HOLD ON, BILLY. FOCUS ON WHEN YOU MADE THE DEAL FOR THE MARK. WHOM YOU MADE THE DEAL WITH.
FIGURES.

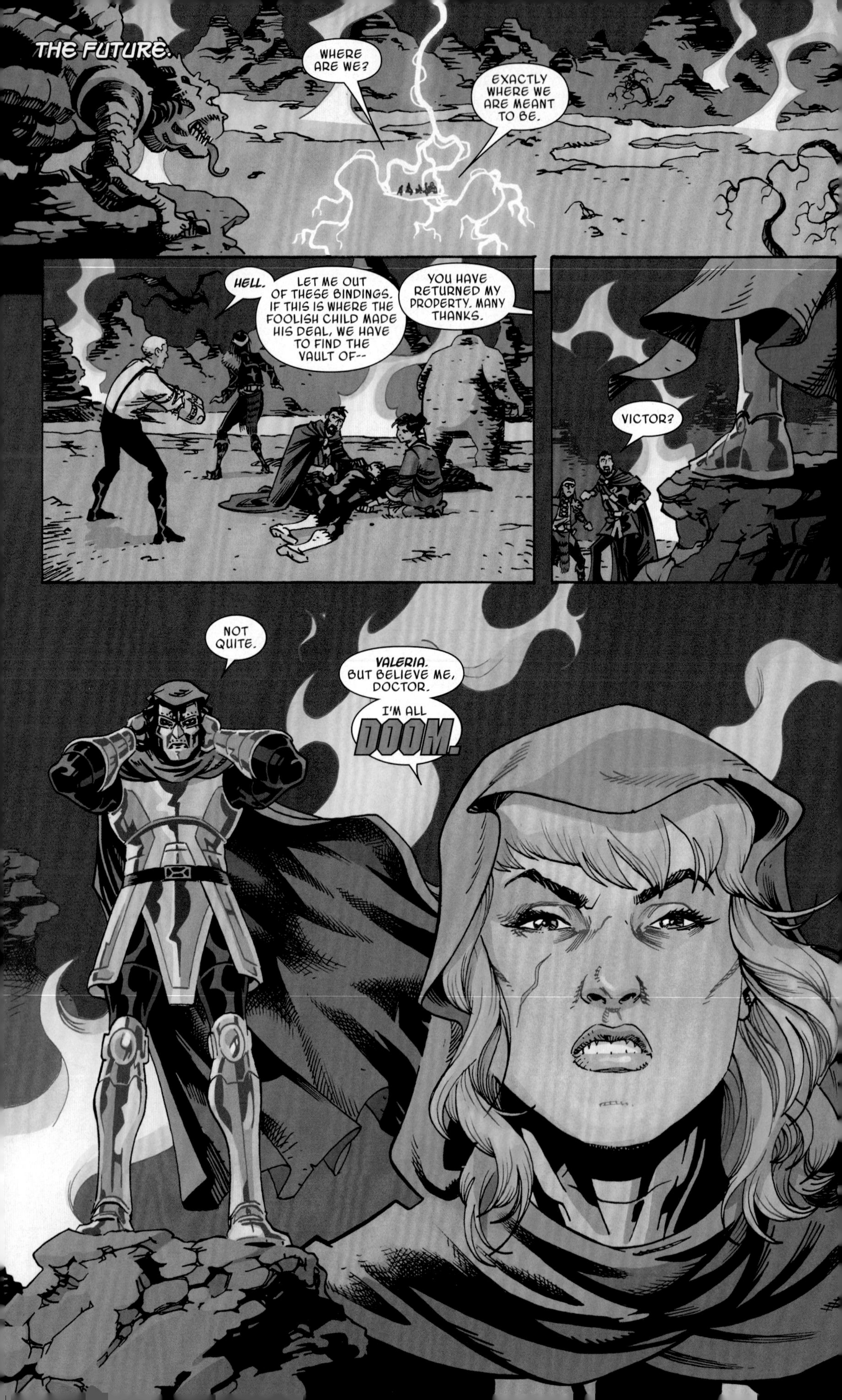
THE FUTURE.
WHERE ARE WE?
EXACTLY WHERE WE ARE MEANT TO BE.
HELL.
LET ME OUT OF THESE BINDINGS. IF THIS IS WHERE THE FOOLISH CHILD MADE HIS DEAL, WE HAVE TO FIND THE VAULT OF--
YOU HAVE RETURNED MY PROPERTY. MANY THANKS.
VICTOR?
NOT QUITE.
VALERIA. BUT BELIEVE ME, DOCTOR.
I'M ALL DOOM.

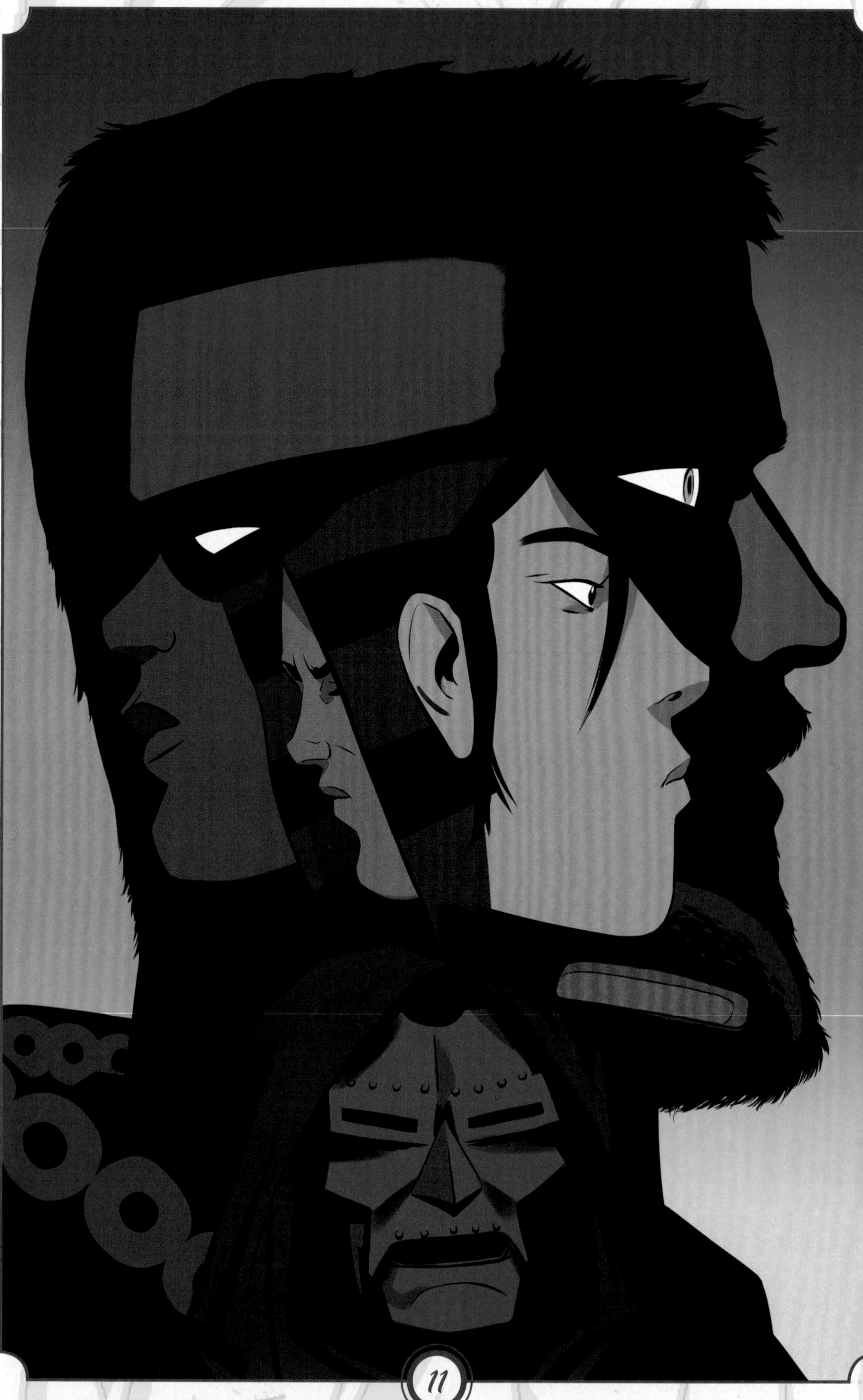

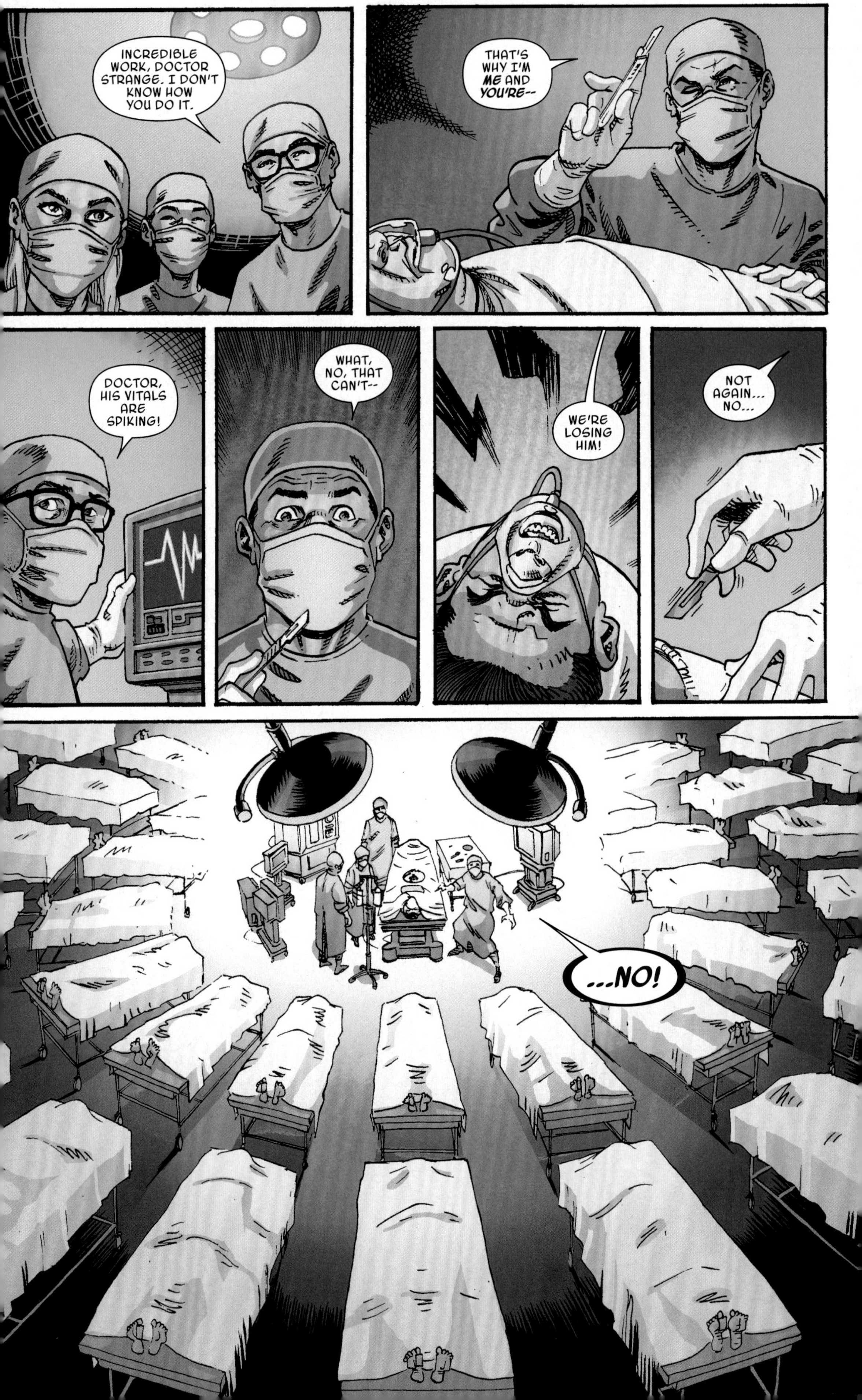

INCREDIBLE WORK, DOCTOR STRANGE. I DON'T KNOW HOW YOU DO IT.
THAT'S WHY I'M *ME* AND *YOU'RE*--
DOCTOR, HIS VITALS ARE SPIKING!
WHAT, NO, THAT CAN'T--
WE'RE LOSING HIM!
NOT AGAIN... NO...
...NO!

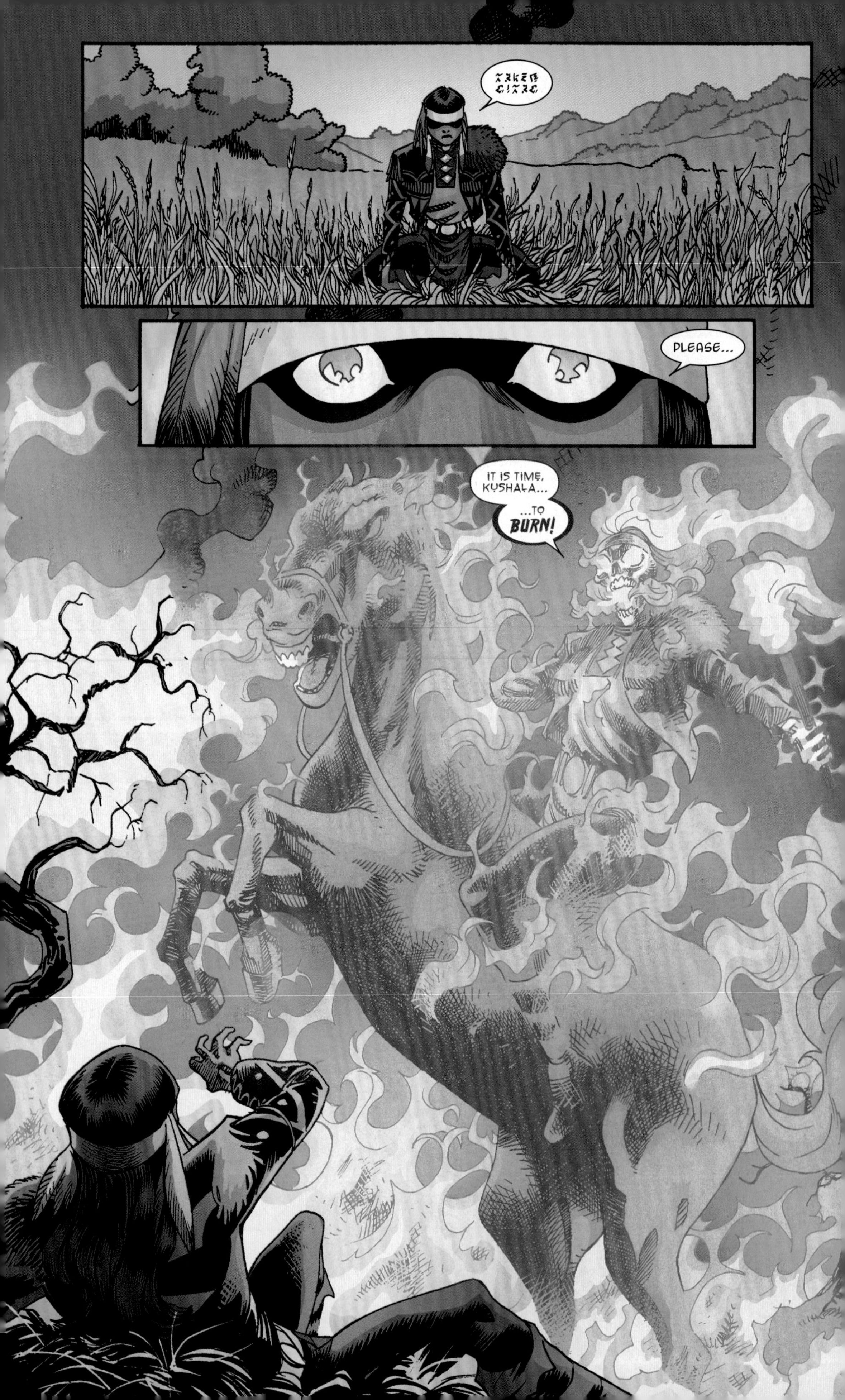
PLEASE...
IT IS TIME, KUSHALA...
...TO BURN!

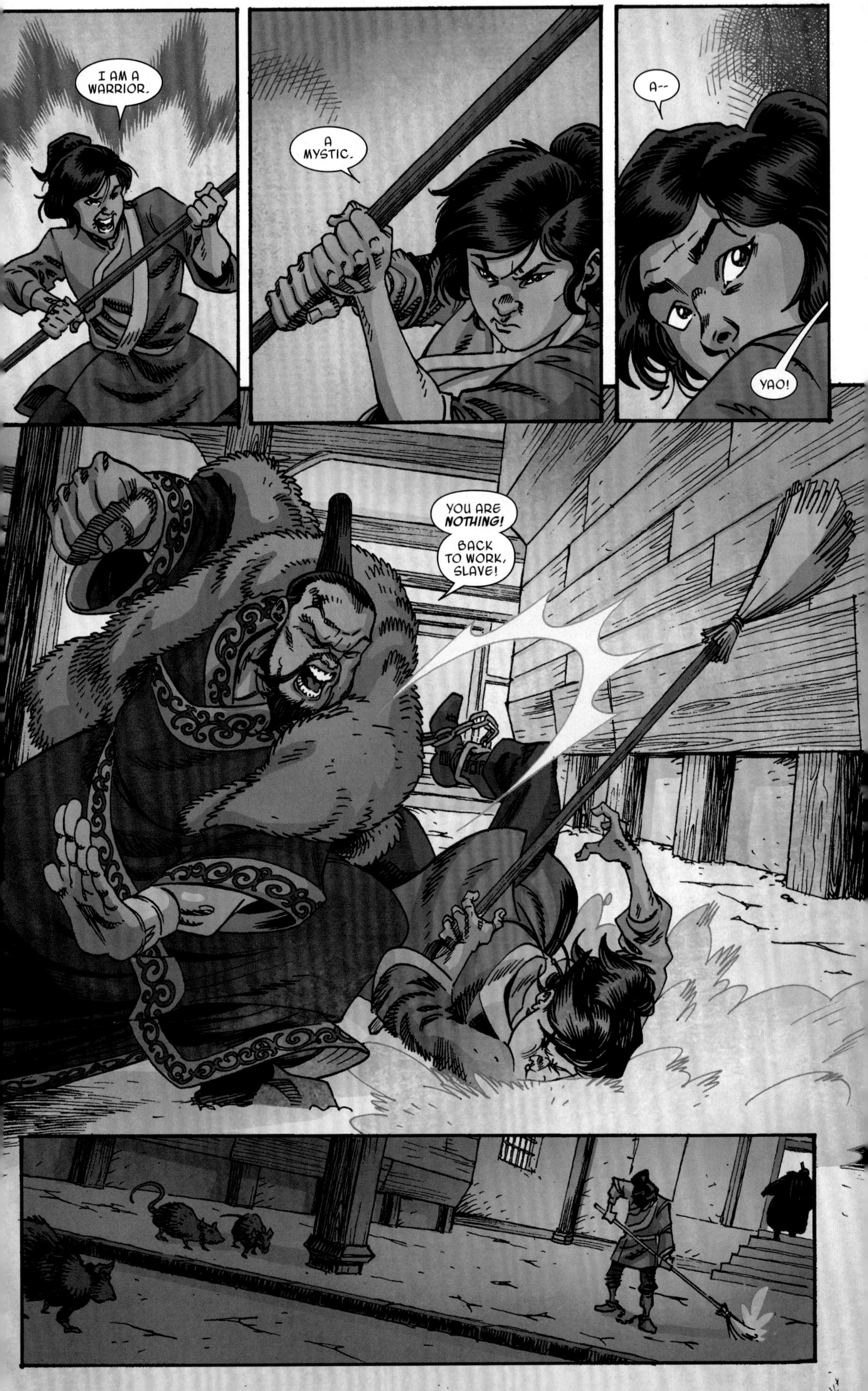

I AM A WARRIOR.
A MYSTIC.
A--
YAO!
YOU ARE **NOTHING!**
BACK TO WORK, SLAVE!

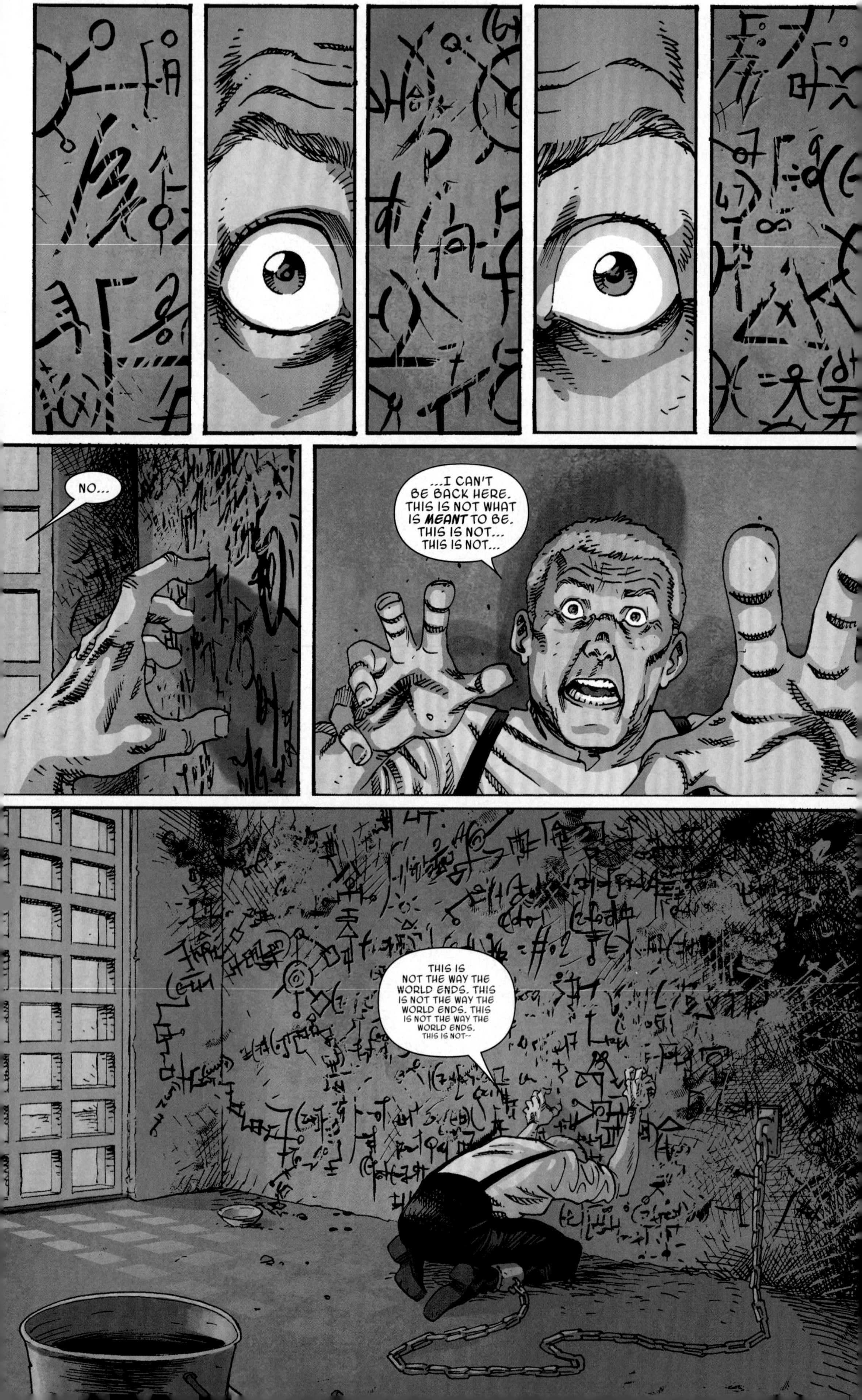
NO...
...I CAN'T BE BACK HERE. THIS IS NOT WHAT IS *MEANT* TO BE. THIS IS NOT... THIS IS NOT...
THIS IS NOT THE WAY THE WORLD ENDS. THIS IS NOT THE WAY THE WORLD ENDS. THIS IS NOT THE WAY THE WORLD ENDS. THIS IS NOT--

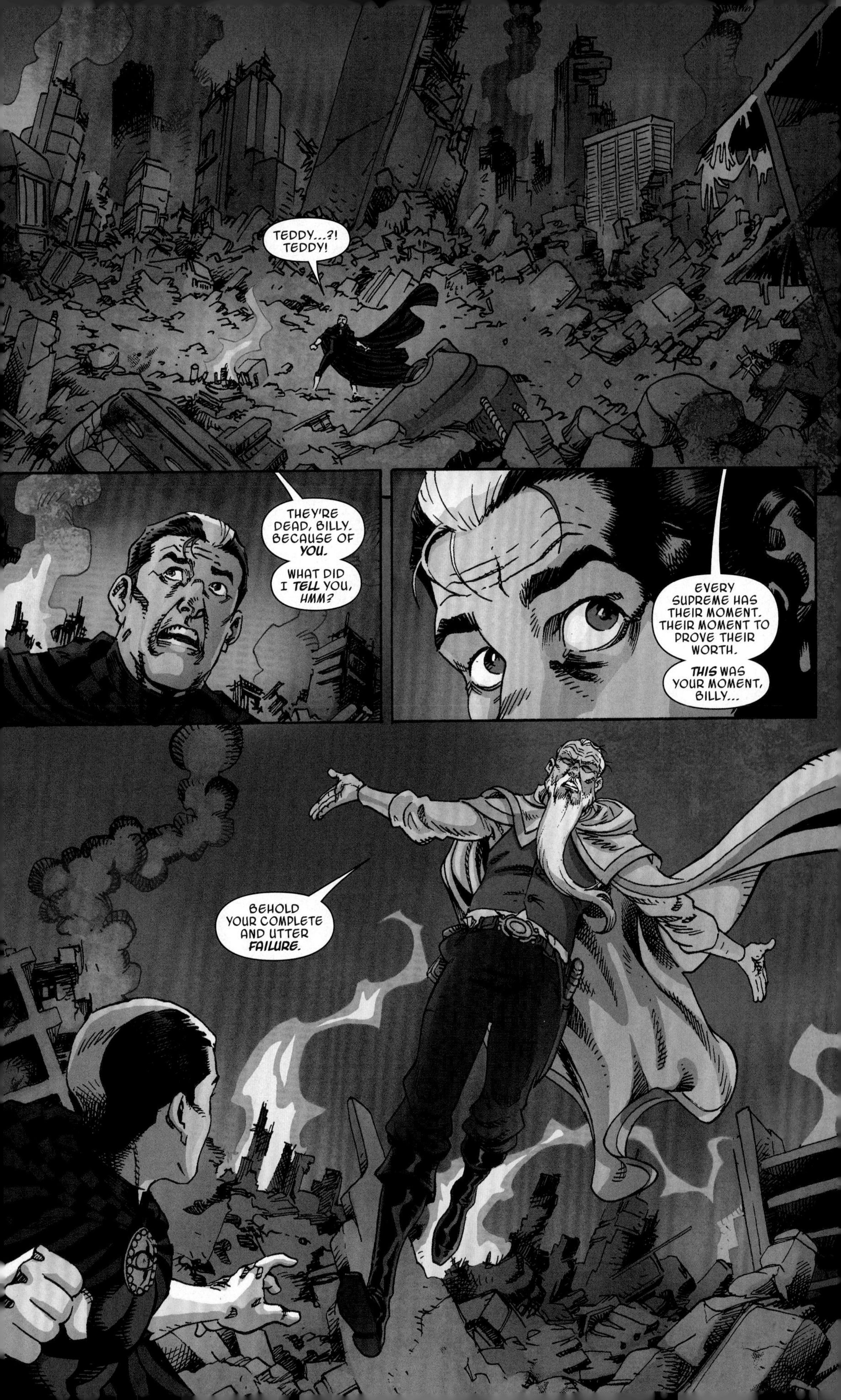
TEDDY...?! TEDDY!
THEY'RE DEAD, BILLY. BECAUSE OF *YOU.*
WHAT DID I *TELL* YOU, *HMM?*
EVERY SUPREME HAS THEIR MOMENT. THEIR MOMENT TO PROVE THEIR WORTH.
THIS WAS YOUR MOMENT, BILLY...
BEHOLD YOUR COMPLETE AND UTTER *FAILURE.*

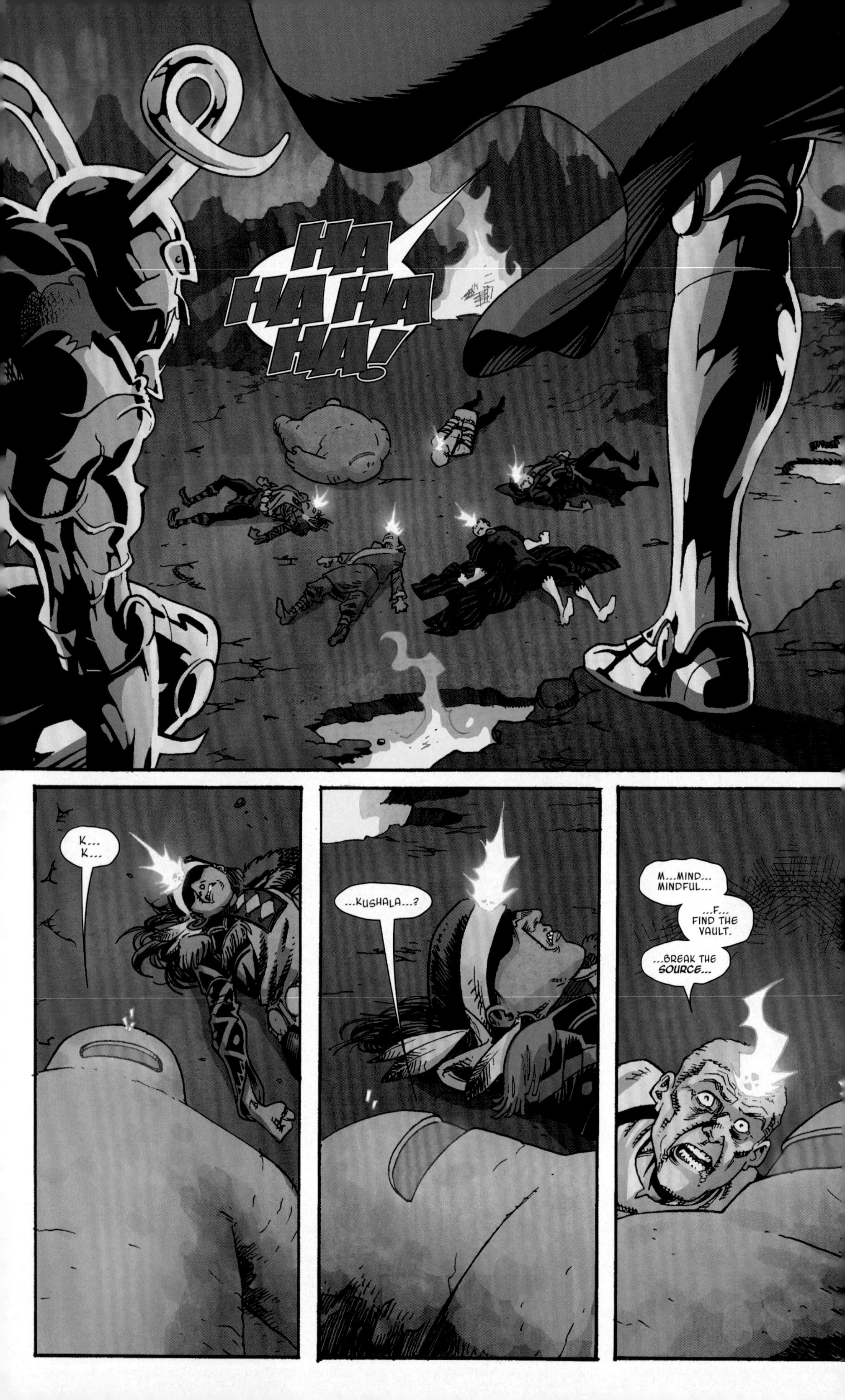
HA HA HA HA HA!
K...
K...
...KUSHALA...?
M...MIND...
MINDFUL...
...F...
FIND THE
VAULT.
...BREAK THE
SOURCE...

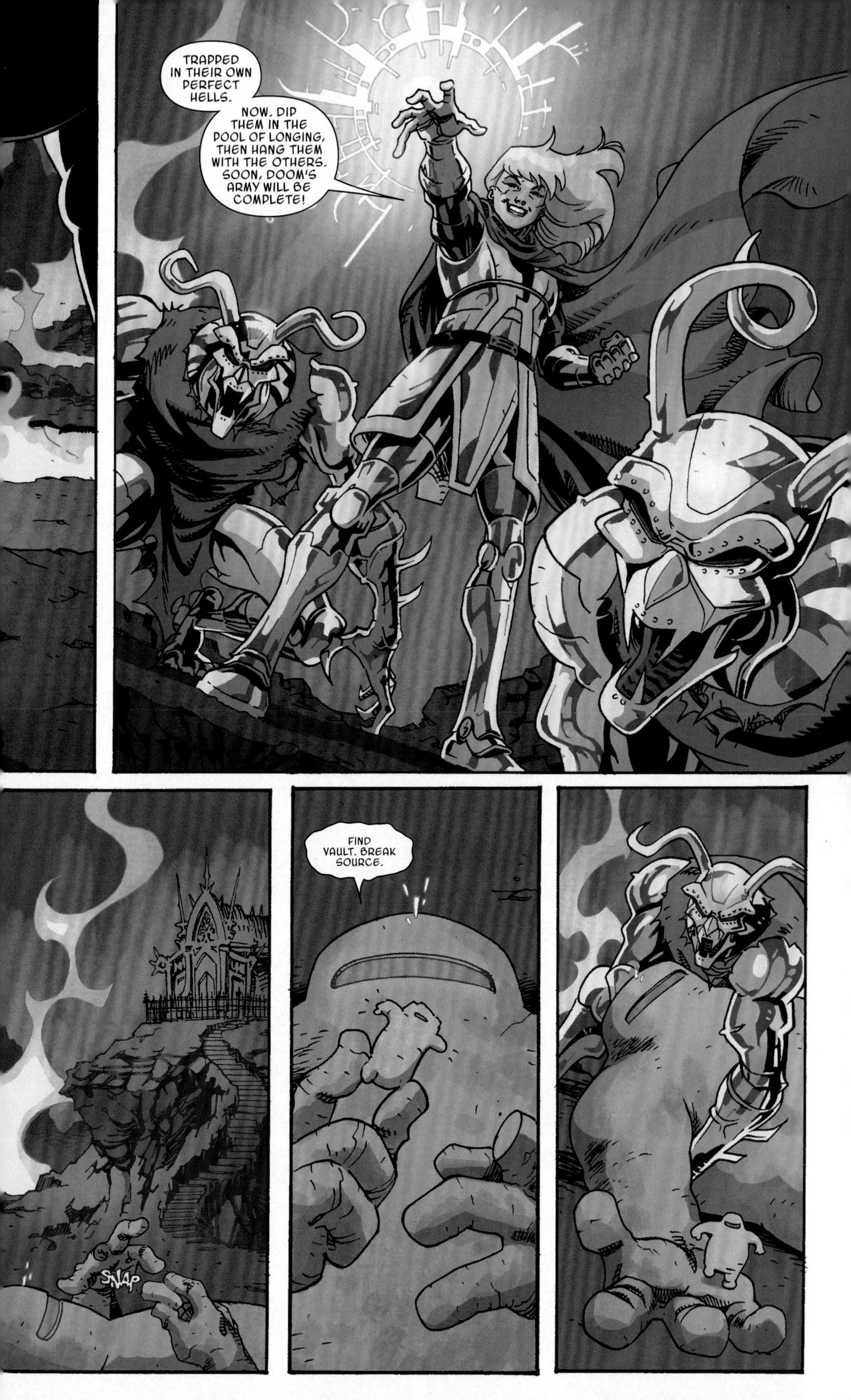
TRAPPED IN THEIR OWN PERFECT HELLS.
NOW. DIP THEM IN THE POOL OF LONGING, THEN HANG THEM WITH THE OTHERS. SOON, DOOM'S ARMY WILL BE COMPLETE!
SNAP
FIND VAULT. BREAK SOURCE.

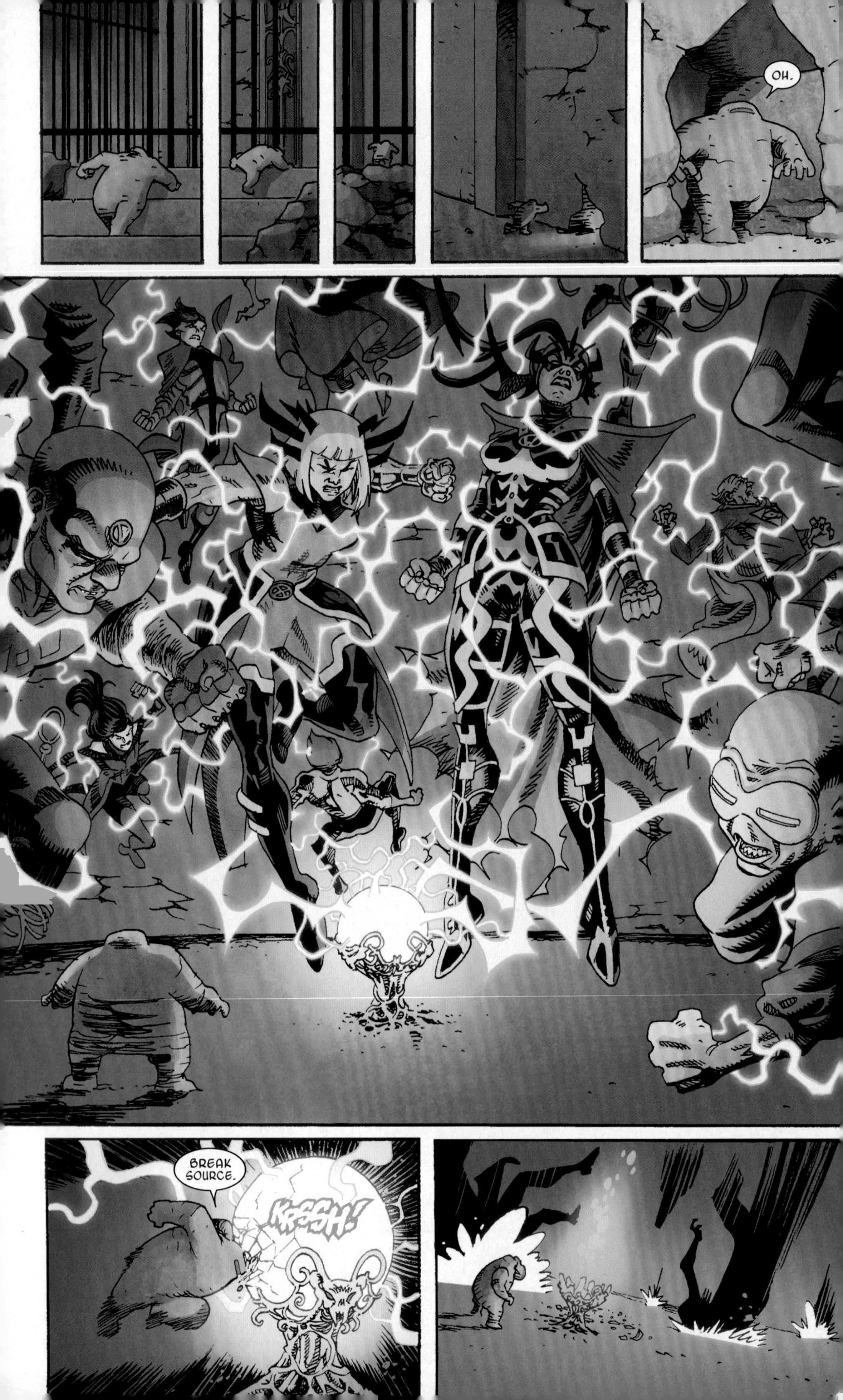
OH.
BREAK SOURCE.
KRSSH!

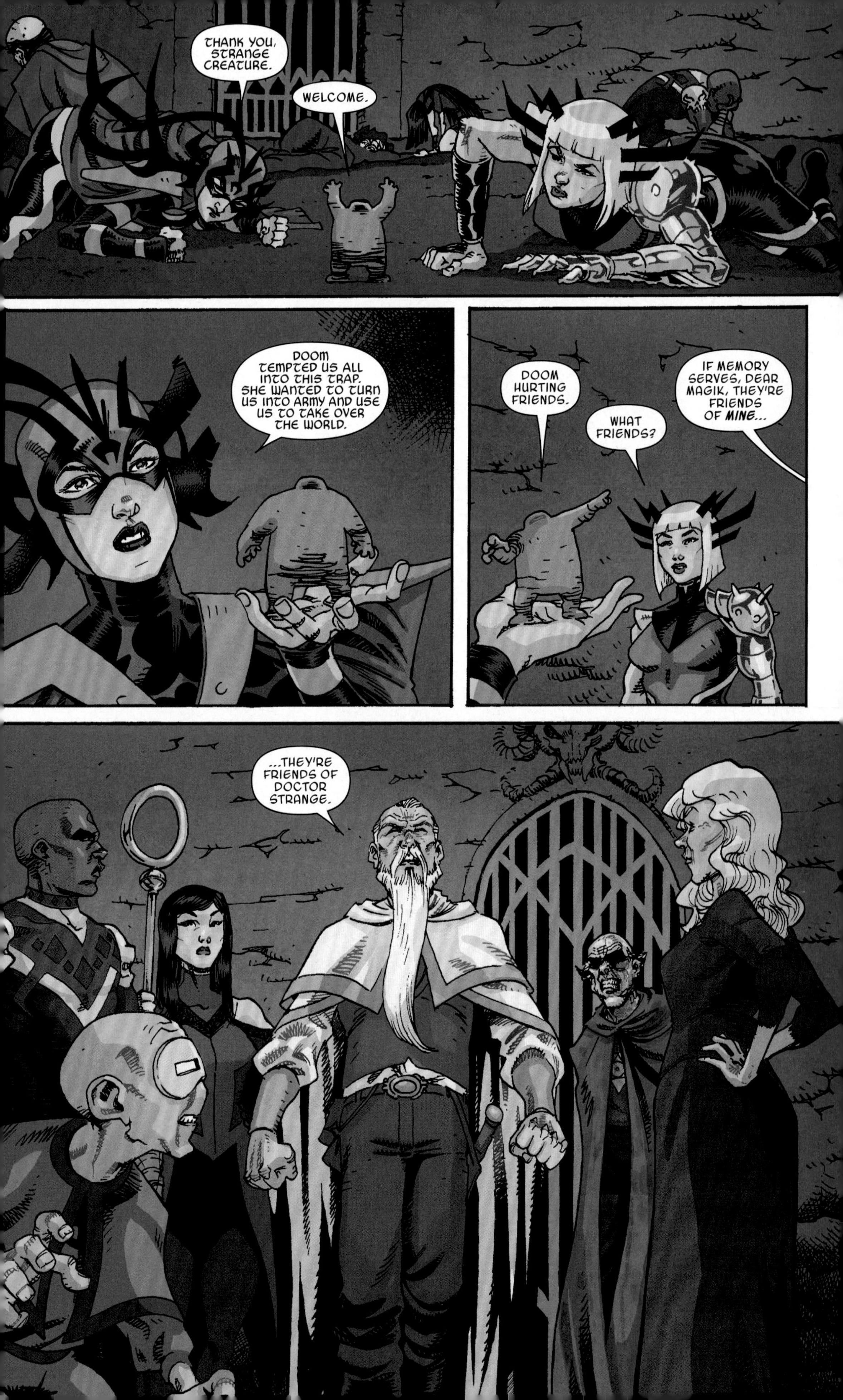
THANK YOU, STRANGE CREATURE.
WELCOME.
DOOM TEMPTED US ALL INTO THIS TRAP. SHE WANTED TO TURN US INTO ARMY AND USE US TO TAKE OVER THE WORLD.
DOOM HURTING FRIENDS.
WHAT FRIENDS?
IF MEMORY SERVES, DEAR MAGIK, THEY'RE FRIENDS OF MINE...
...THEY'RE FRIENDS OF DOCTOR STRANGE.

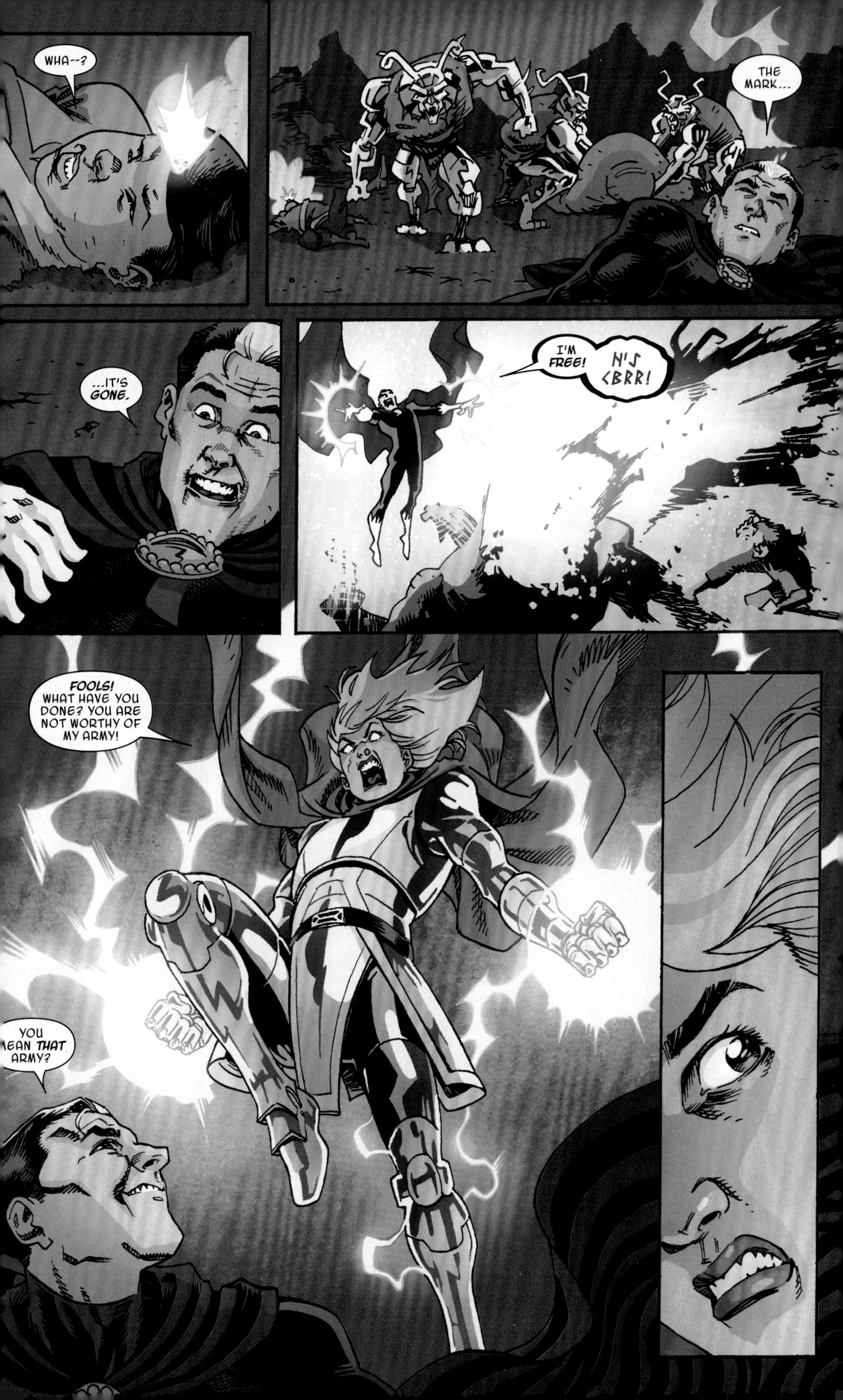
WHA--?
THE MARK...
...IT'S GONE.
I'M FREE!
FOOLS! WHAT HAVE YOU DONE? YOU ARE NOT WORTHY OF MY ARMY!
YOU EAN THAT ARMY?

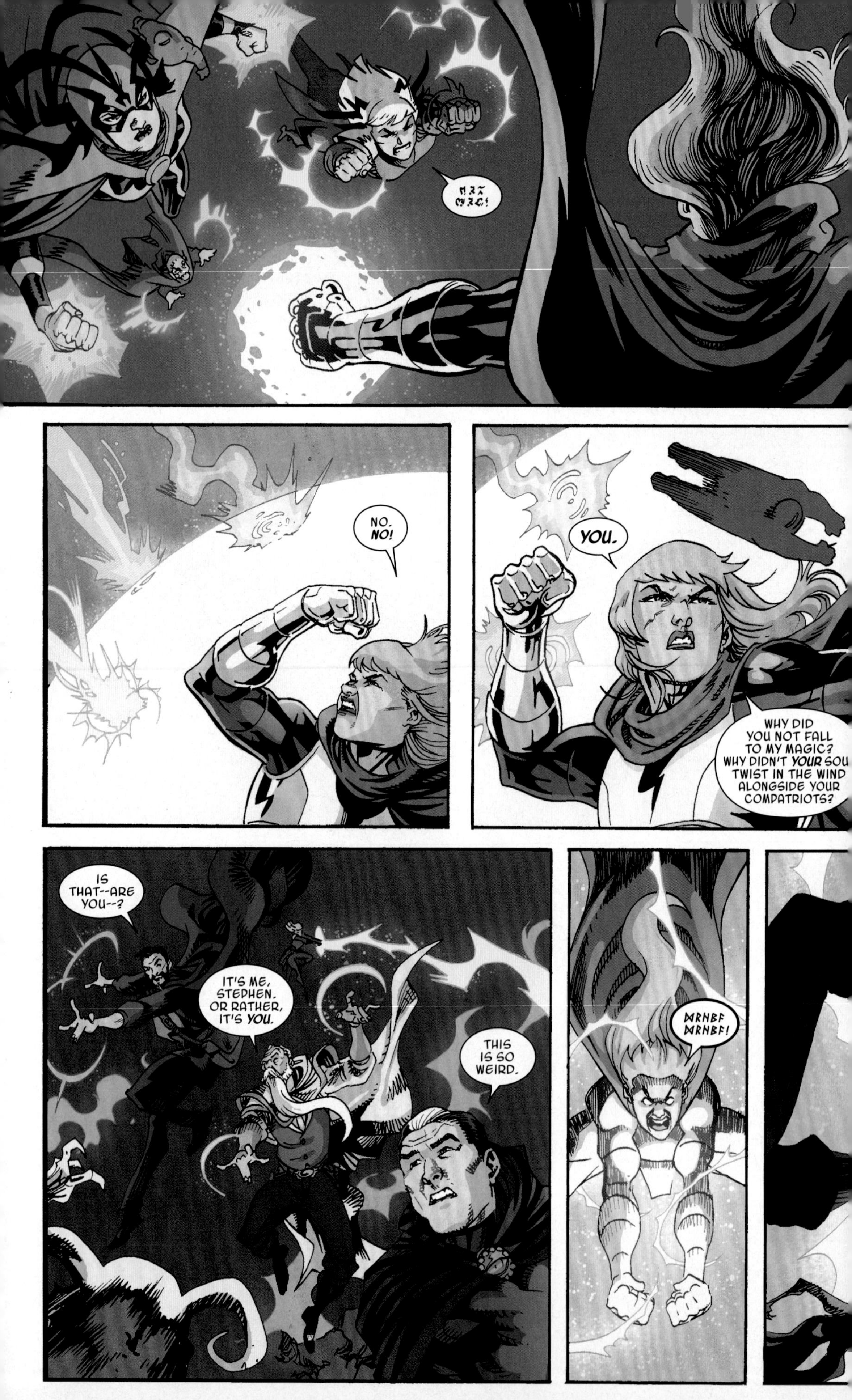
NO.
NO!
YOU.
WHY DID YOU NOT FALL TO MY MAGIC? WHY DIDN'T YOUR SOU TWIST IN THE WIND ALONGSIDE YOUR COMPATRIOTS?
IS THAT--ARE YOU--?
IT'S ME, STEPHEN. OR RATHER, IT'S YOU.
THIS IS SO WEIRD.

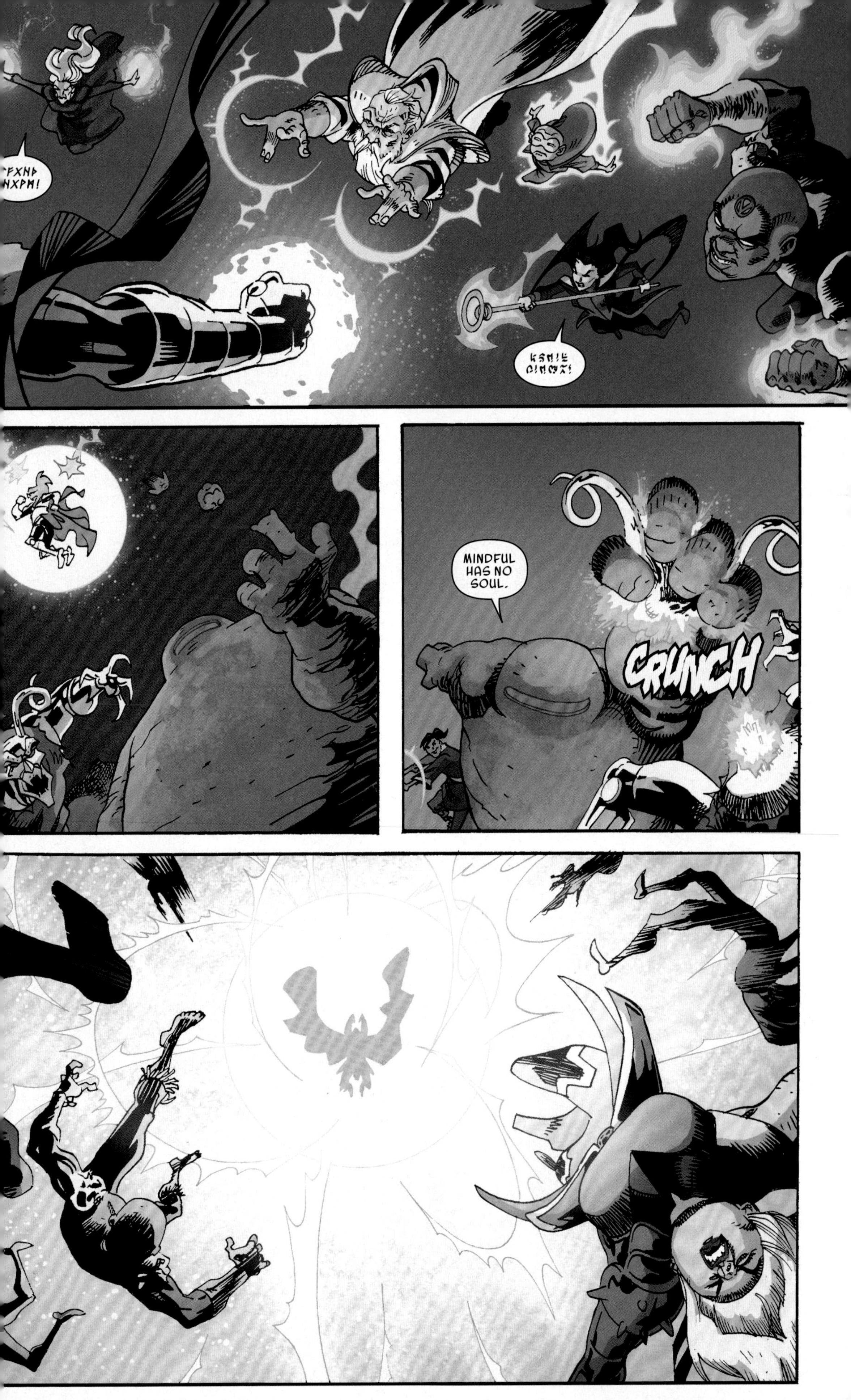
MINDFUL HAS NO SOUL.
CRUNCH

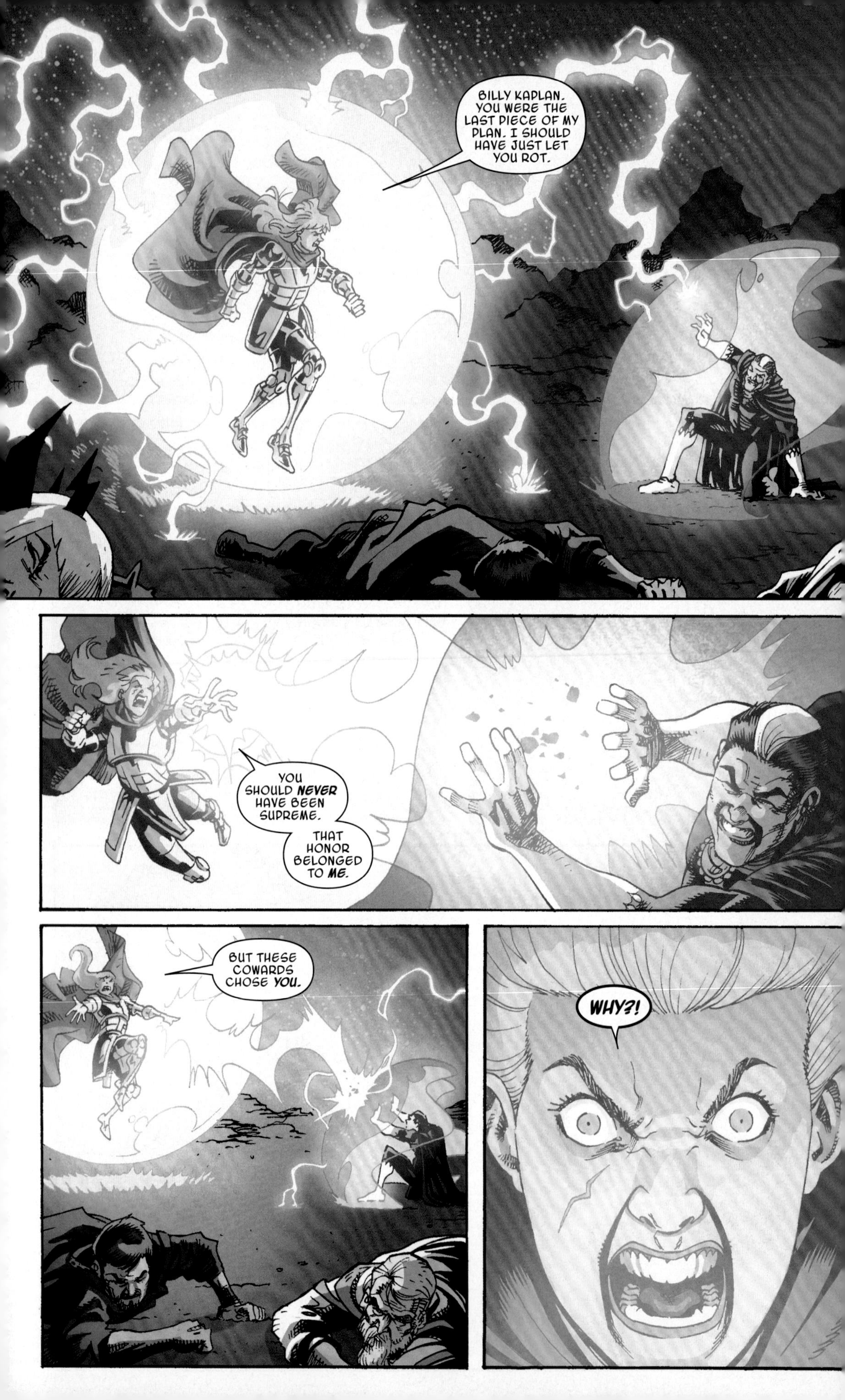

BILLY KAPLAN. YOU WERE THE LAST PIECE OF MY PLAN. I SHOULD HAVE JUST LET YOU ROT.
YOU SHOULD NEVER HAVE BEEN SUPREME.
THAT HONOR BELONGED TO ME.
BUT THESE COWARDS CHOSE YOU.
WHY?!

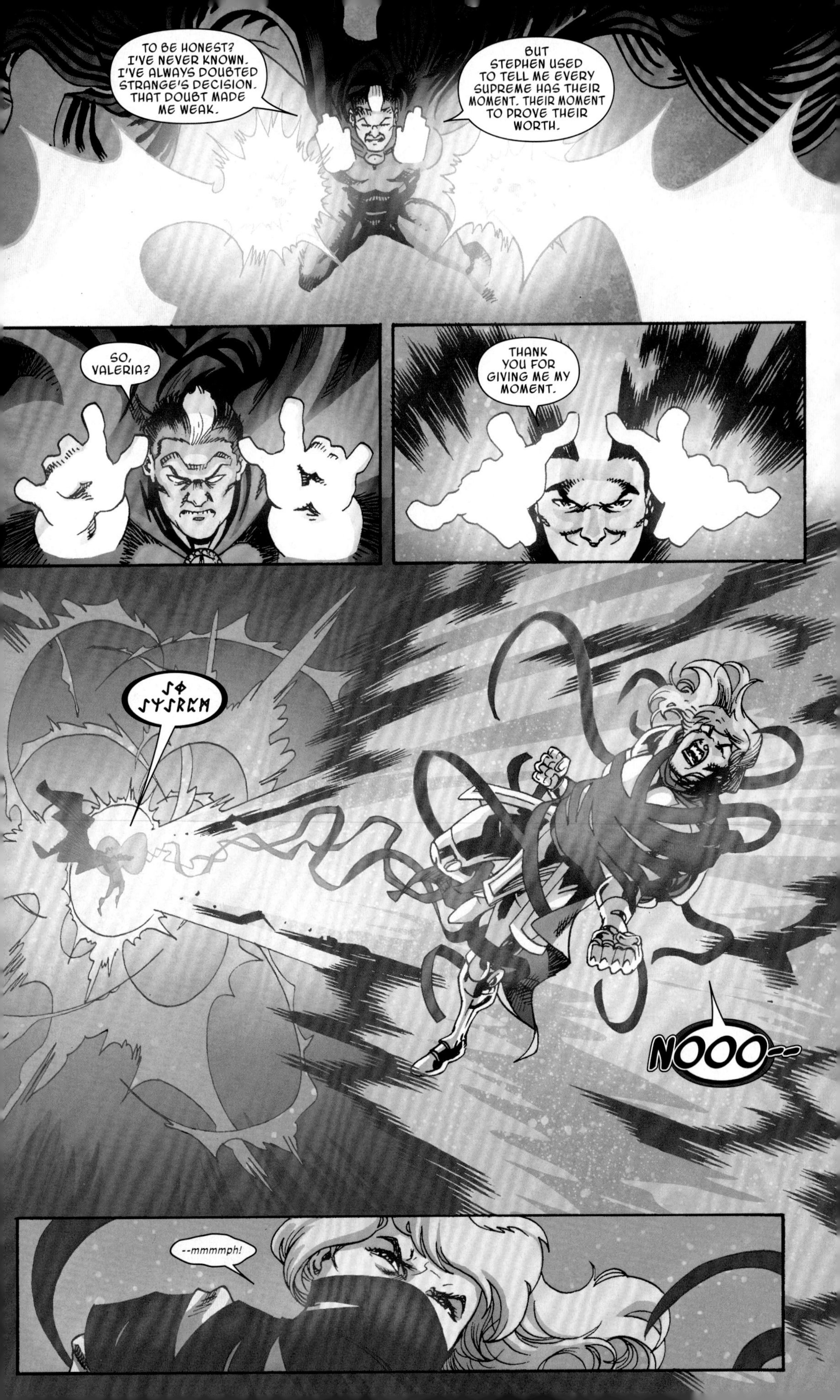
TO BE HONEST? I'VE NEVER KNOWN. I'VE ALWAYS DOUBTED STRANGE'S DECISION. THAT DOUBT MADE ME WEAK.
BUT STEPHEN USED TO TELL ME EVERY SUPREME HAS THEIR MOMENT. THEIR MOMENT TO PROVE THEIR WORTH.
SO, VALERIA?
THANK YOU FOR GIVING ME MY MOMENT.
NOOO--
--mmmmph!

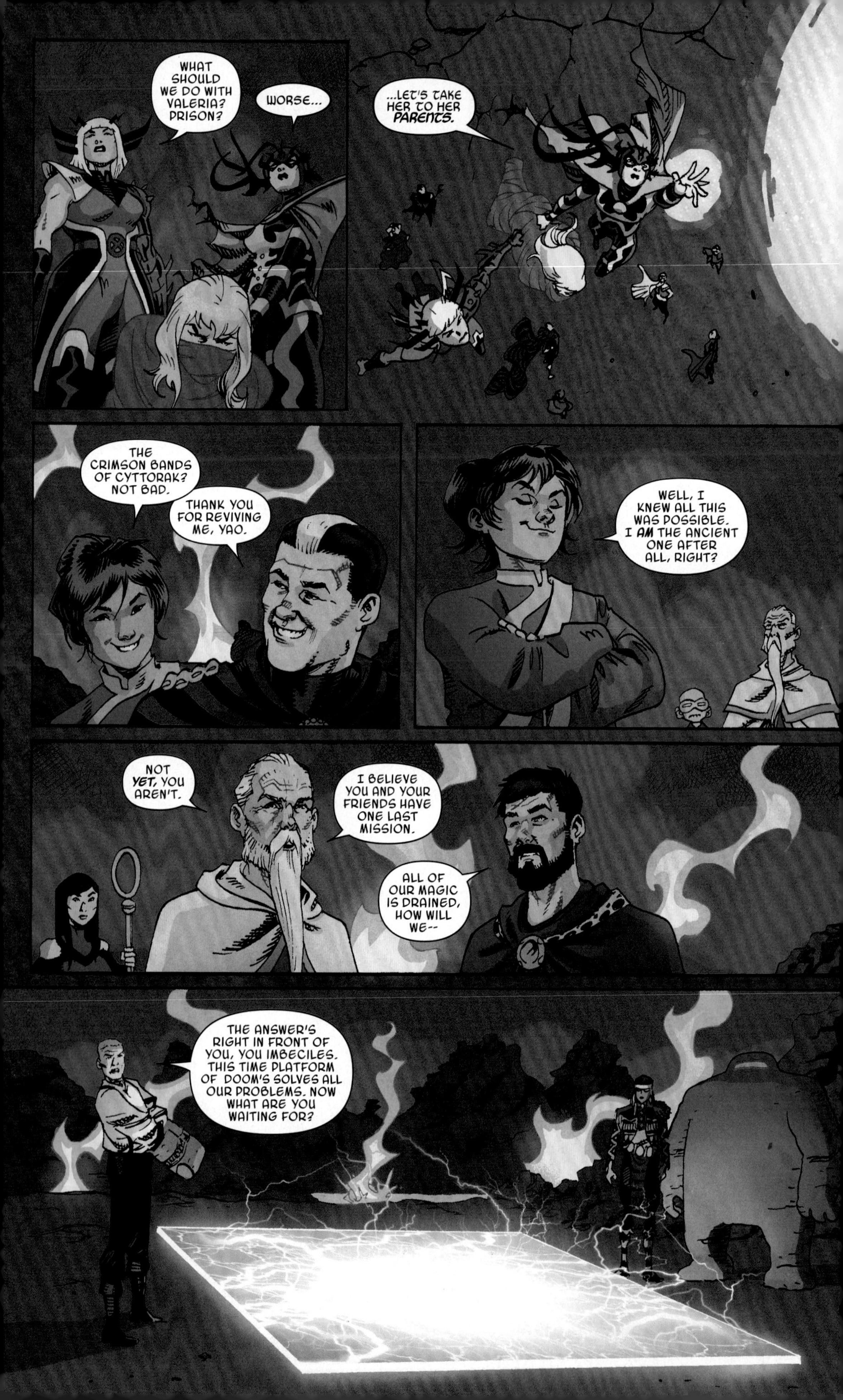

WHAT SHOULD WE DO WITH VALERIA? PRISON?
WORSE...
...LET'S TAKE HER TO HER PARENTS.
THE CRIMSON BANDS OF CYTTORAK? NOT BAD.
THANK YOU FOR REVIVING ME, YAO.
WELL, I KNEW ALL THIS WAS POSSIBLE. I AM THE ANCIENT ONE AFTER ALL, RIGHT?
NOT YET, YOU AREN'T.
I BELIEVE YOU AND YOUR FRIENDS HAVE ONE LAST MISSION.
ALL OF OUR MAGIC IS DRAINED, HOW WILL WE--
THE ANSWER'S RIGHT IN FRONT OF YOU, YOU IMBECILES. THIS TIME PLATFORM OF DOOM'S SOLVES ALL OUR PROBLEMS. NOW WHAT ARE YOU WAITING FOR?

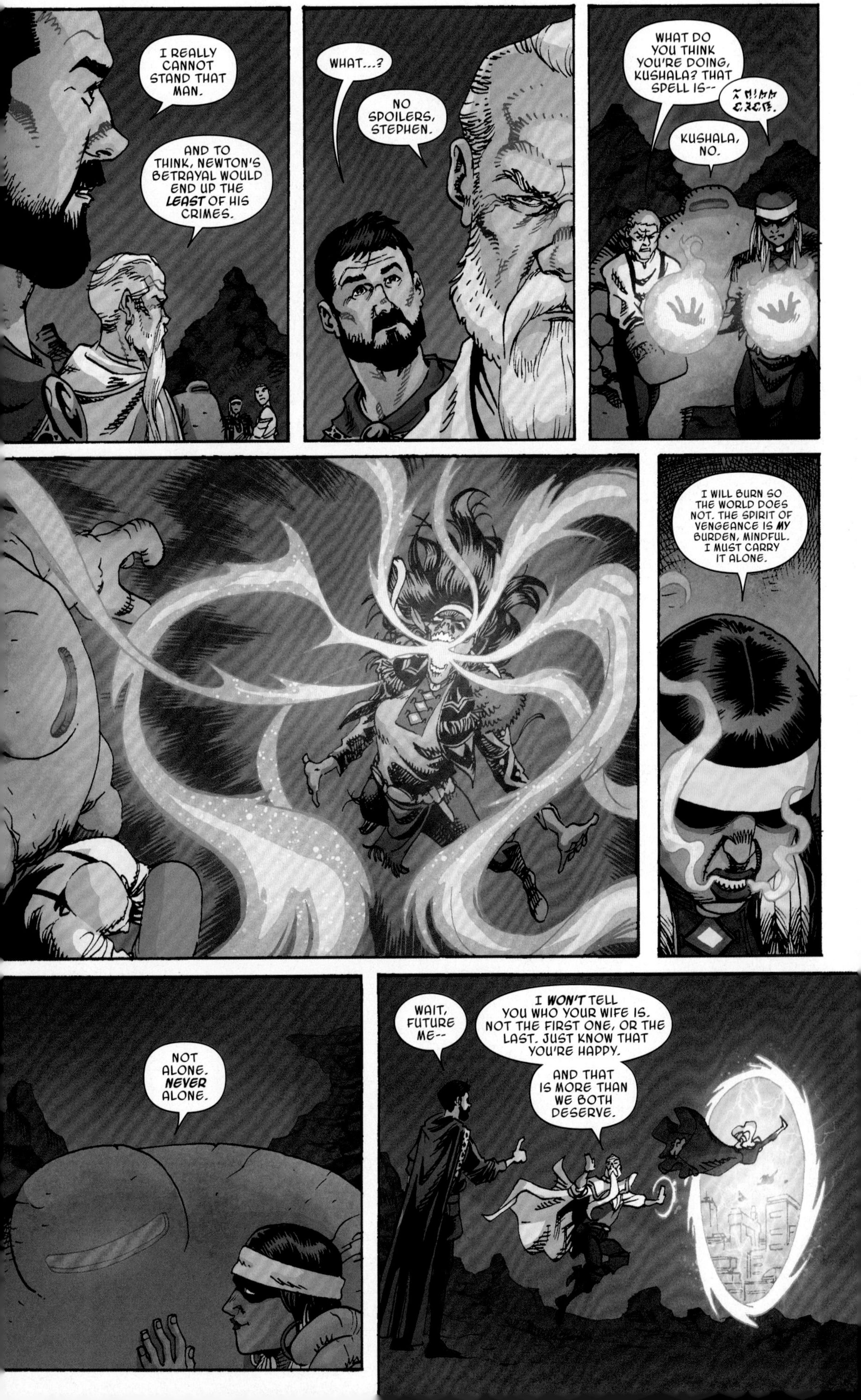
I REALLY CANNOT STAND THAT MAN.
AND TO THINK, NEWTON'S BETRAYAL WOULD END UP THE *LEAST* OF HIS CRIMES.
WHAT...?
NO SPOILERS, STEPHEN.
WHAT DO YOU THINK YOU'RE DOING, KUSHALA? THAT SPELL IS--
KUSHALA, NO.
I WILL BURN SO THE WORLD DOES NOT. THE SPIRIT OF VENGEANCE IS *MY* BURDEN, MINDFUL. I MUST CARRY IT ALONE.
NOT ALONE. *NEVER* ALONE.
WAIT, FUTURE ME--
I *WON'T* TELL YOU WHO YOUR WIFE IS. NOT THE FIRST ONE, OR THE LAST. JUST KNOW THAT YOU'RE HAPPY.
AND THAT IS MORE THAN WE BOTH DESERVE.

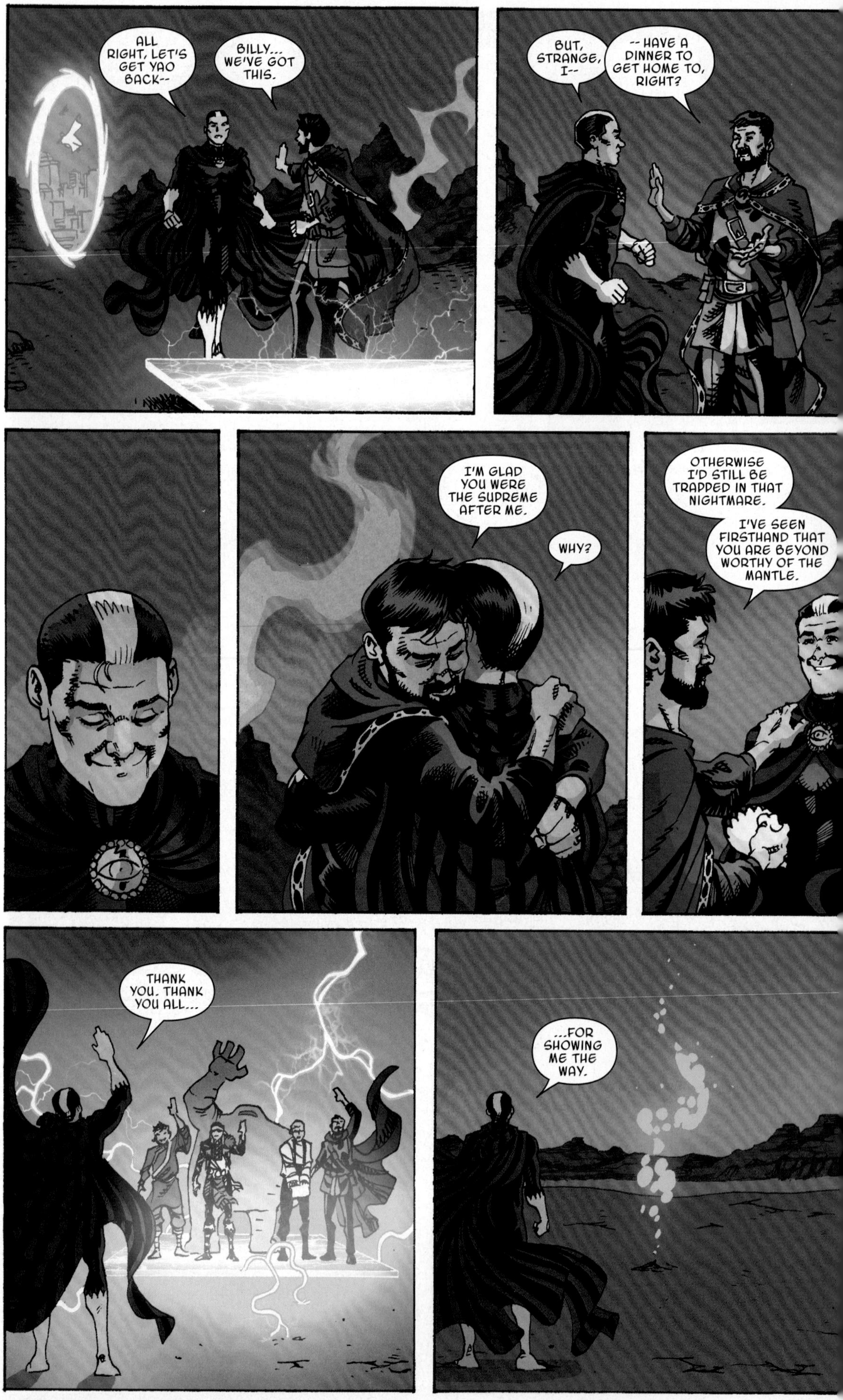
ALL RIGHT, LET'S GET YAO BACK--
BILLY... WE'VE GOT THIS.
BUT, STRANGE, I--
-- HAVE A DINNER TO GET HOME TO, RIGHT?
I'M GLAD YOU WERE THE SUPREME AFTER ME.
WHY?
OTHERWISE I'D STILL BE TRAPPED IN THAT NIGHTMARE.
I'VE SEEN FIRSTHAND THAT YOU ARE BEYOND WORTHY OF THE MANTLE.
THANK YOU. THANK YOU ALL...
...FOR SHOWING ME THE WAY.

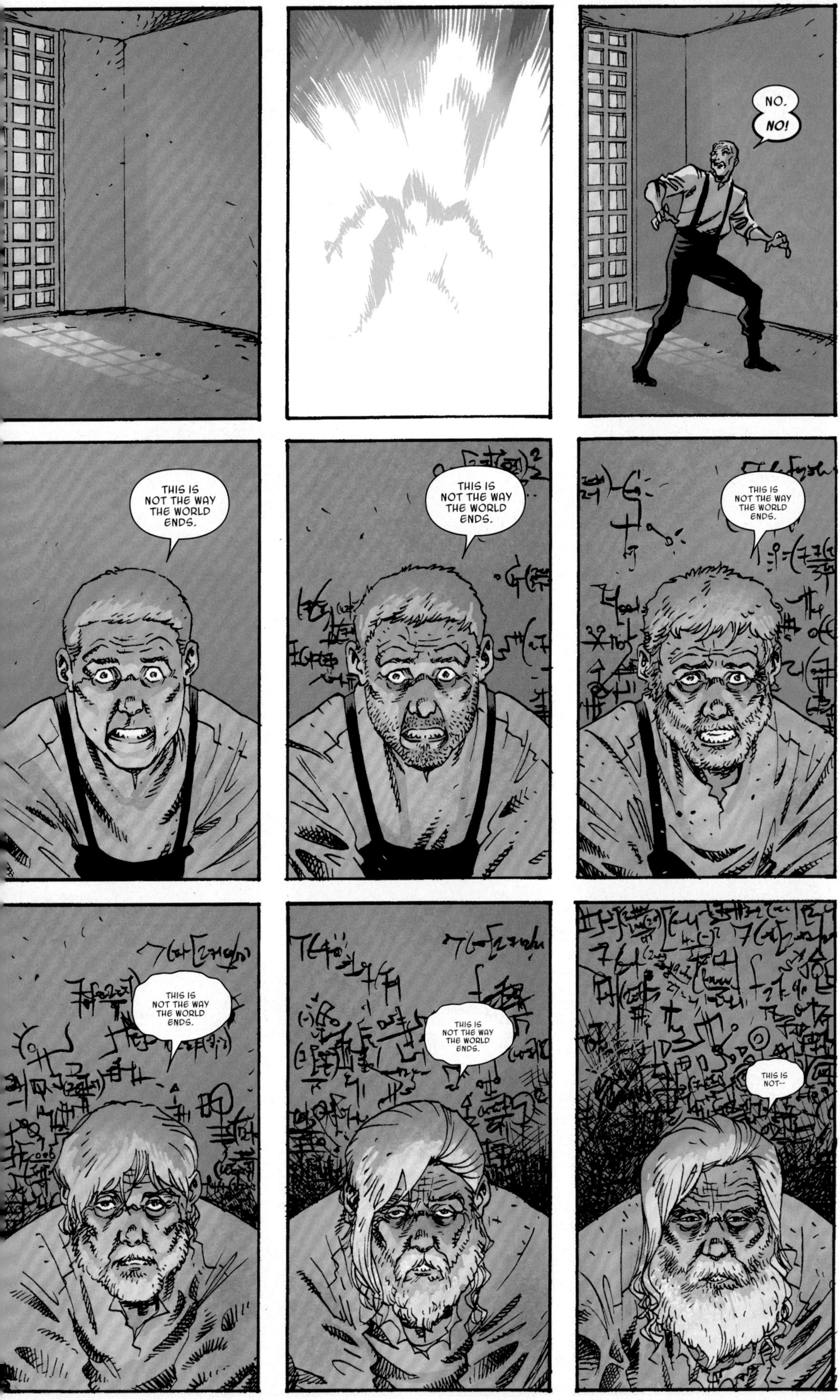

NO.
NO!
THIS IS NOT THE WAY THE WORLD ENDS.
THIS IS NOT THE WAY THE WORLD ENDS.
THIS IS NOT THE WAY THE WORLD ENDS.
THIS IS NOT THE WAY THE WORLD ENDS.
THIS IS NOT THE WAY THE WORLD ENDS.
THIS IS NOT--

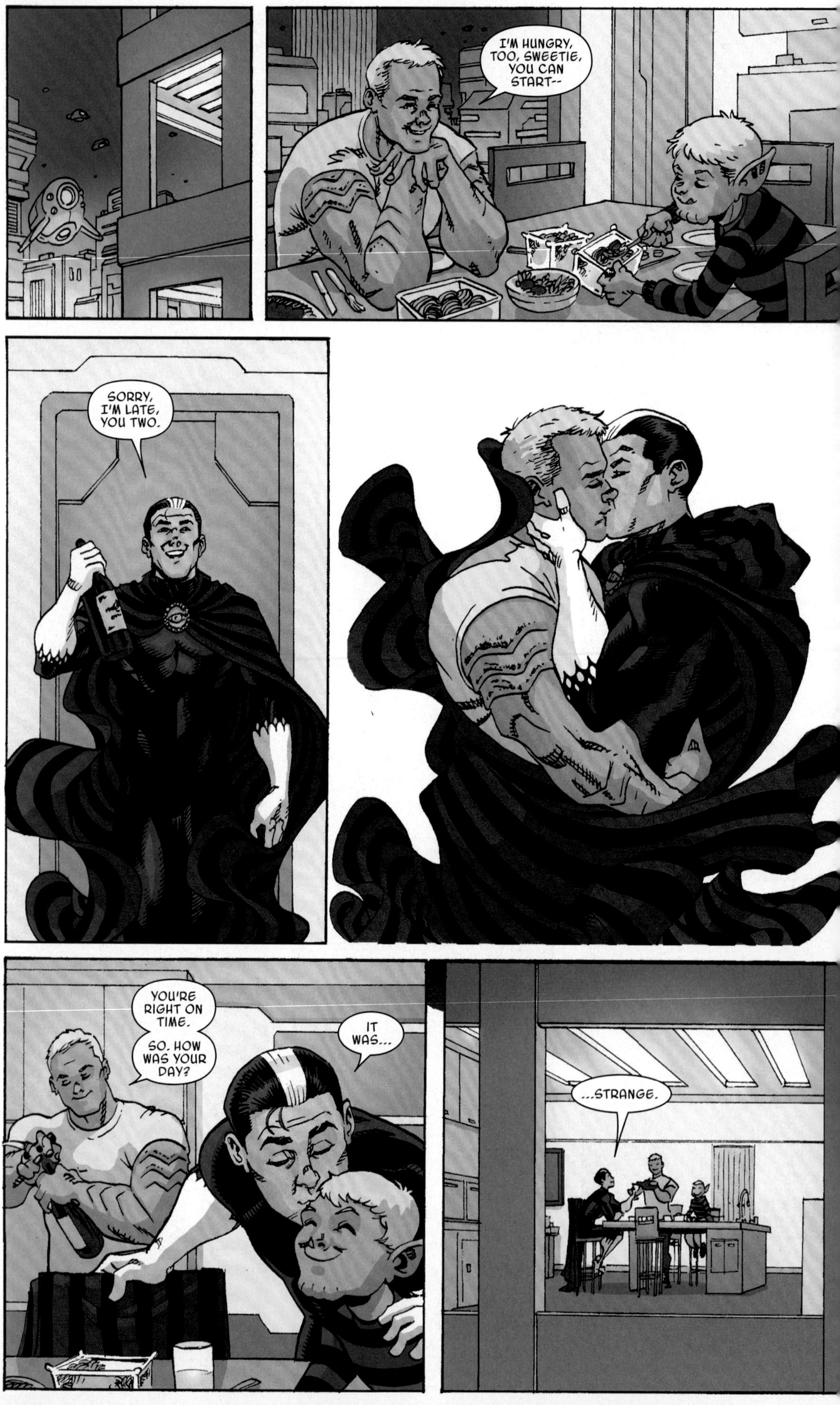
I'M HUNGRY, TOO, SWEETIE, YOU CAN START--
SORRY, I'M LATE, YOU TWO.
YOU'RE RIGHT ON TIME.
SO. HOW WAS YOUR DAY?
IT WAS...
...STRANGE.

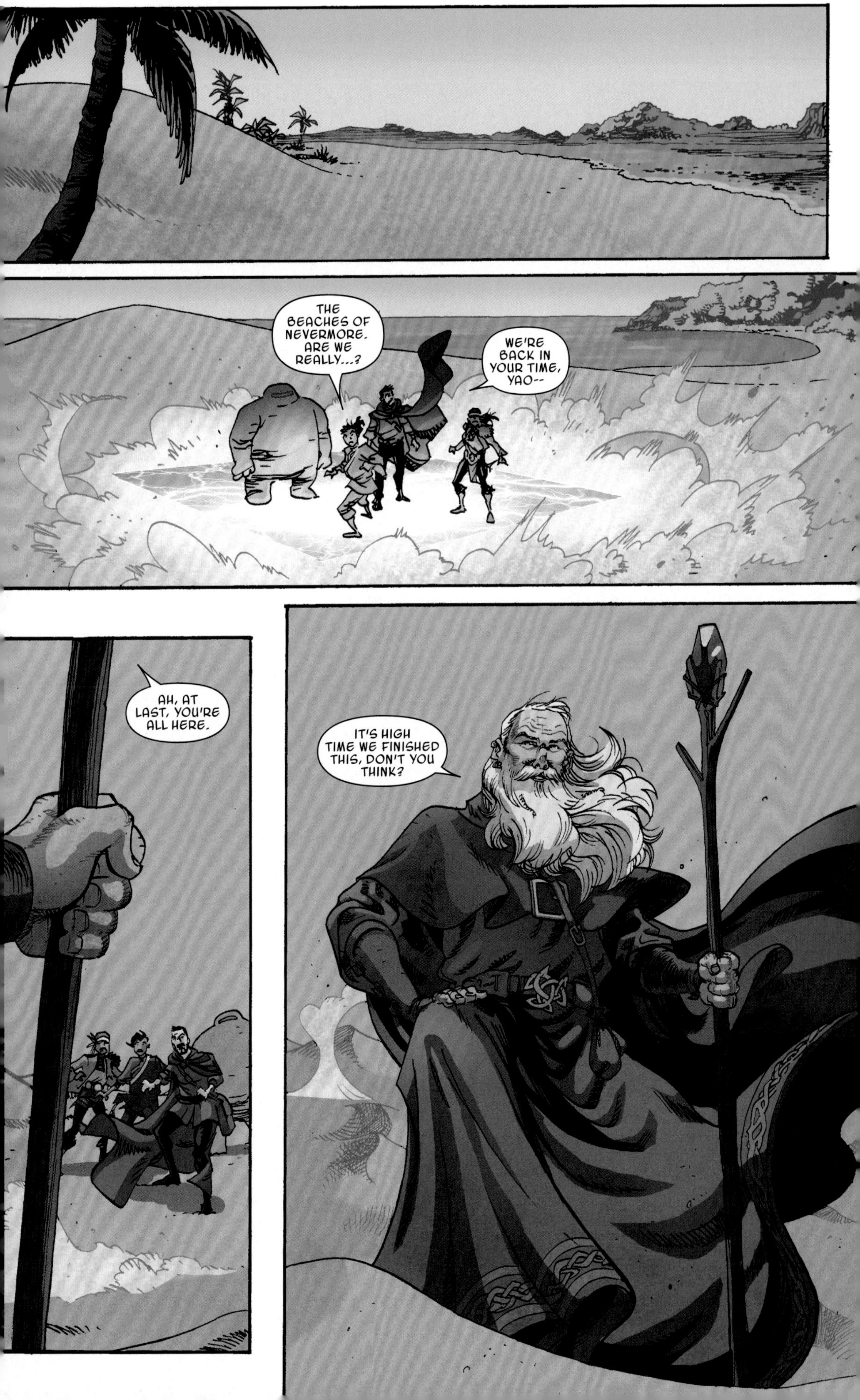
THE BEACHES OF NEVERMORE. ARE WE REALLY...?
WE'RE BACK IN YOUR TIME, YAO--
AH, AT LAST, YOU'RE ALL HERE.
IT'S HIGH TIME WE FINISHED THIS, DON'T YOU THINK?

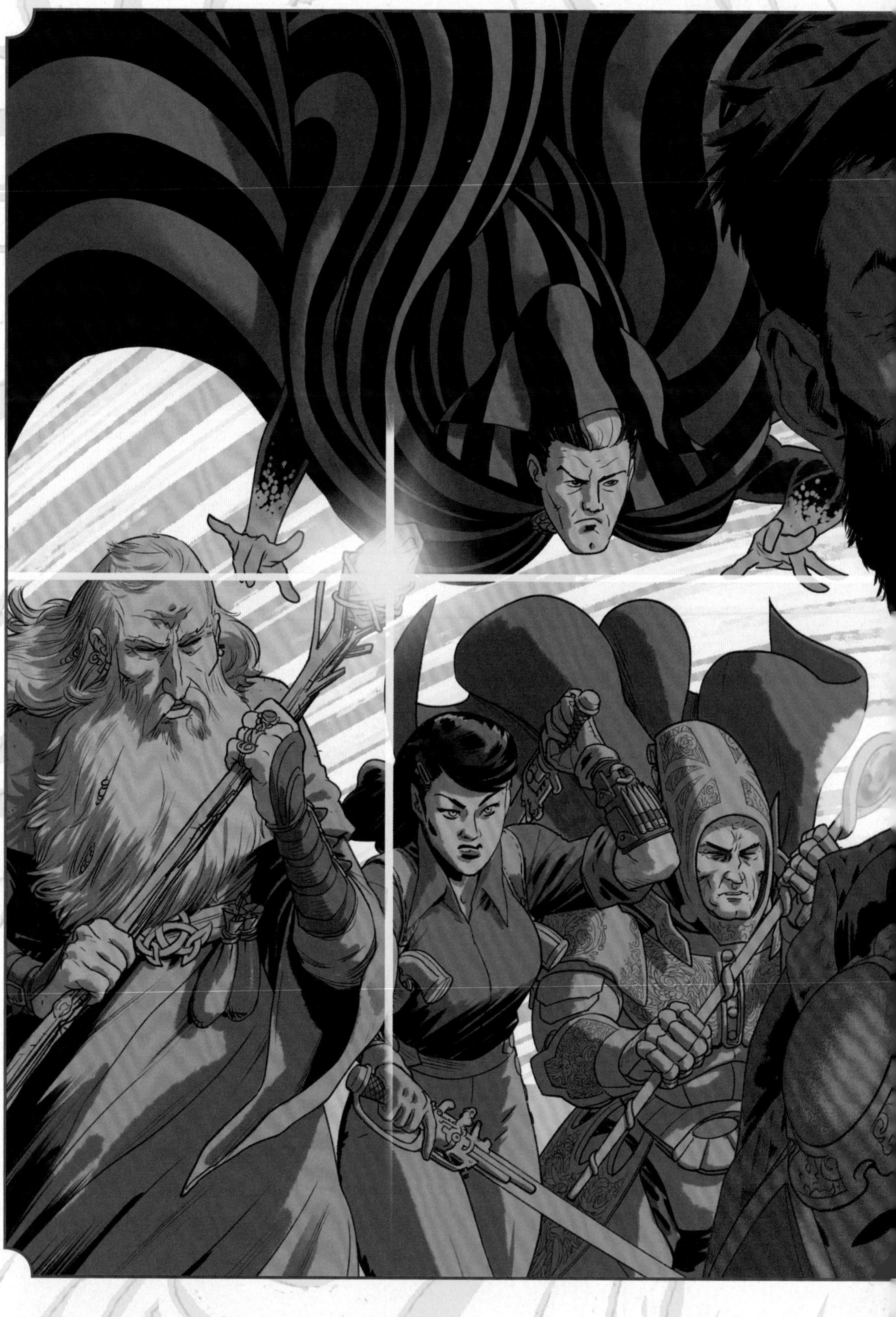

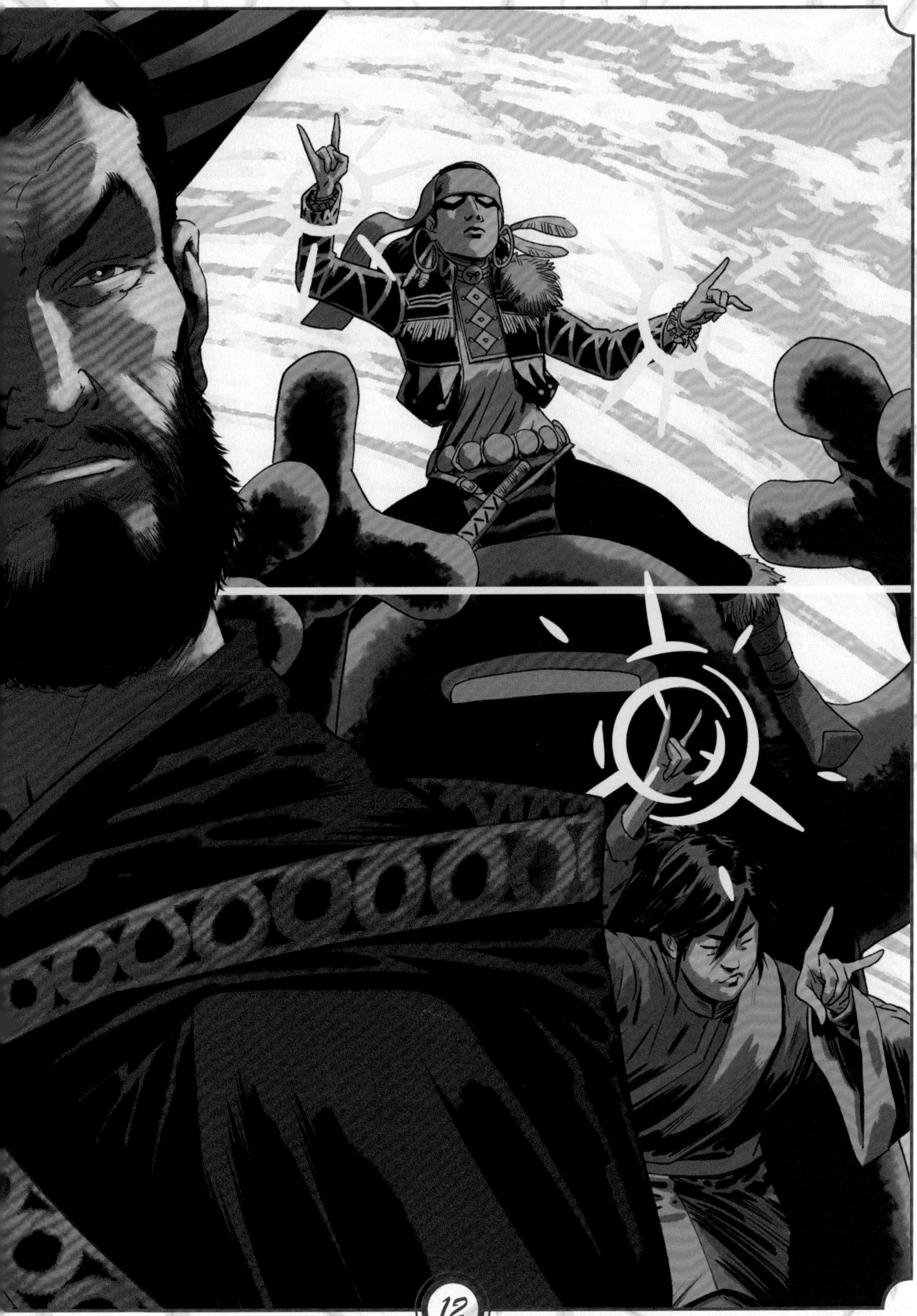

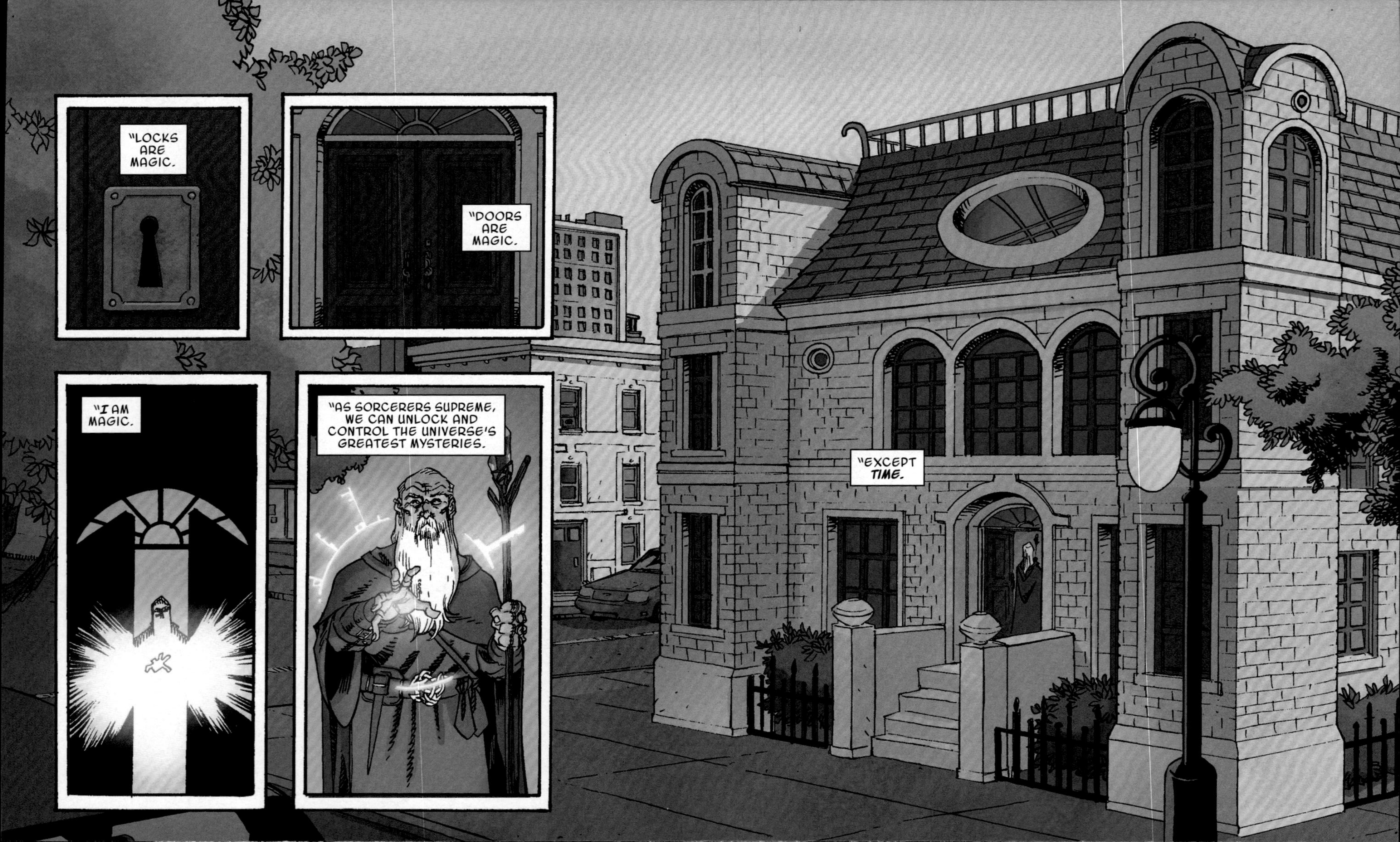
"LOCKS ARE MAGIC.
"DOORS ARE MAGIC.
"I AM MAGIC.
"AS SORCERERS SUPREME, WE CAN UNLOCK AND CONTROL THE UNIVERSE'S GREATEST MYSTERIES.
"EXCEPT *TIME*.

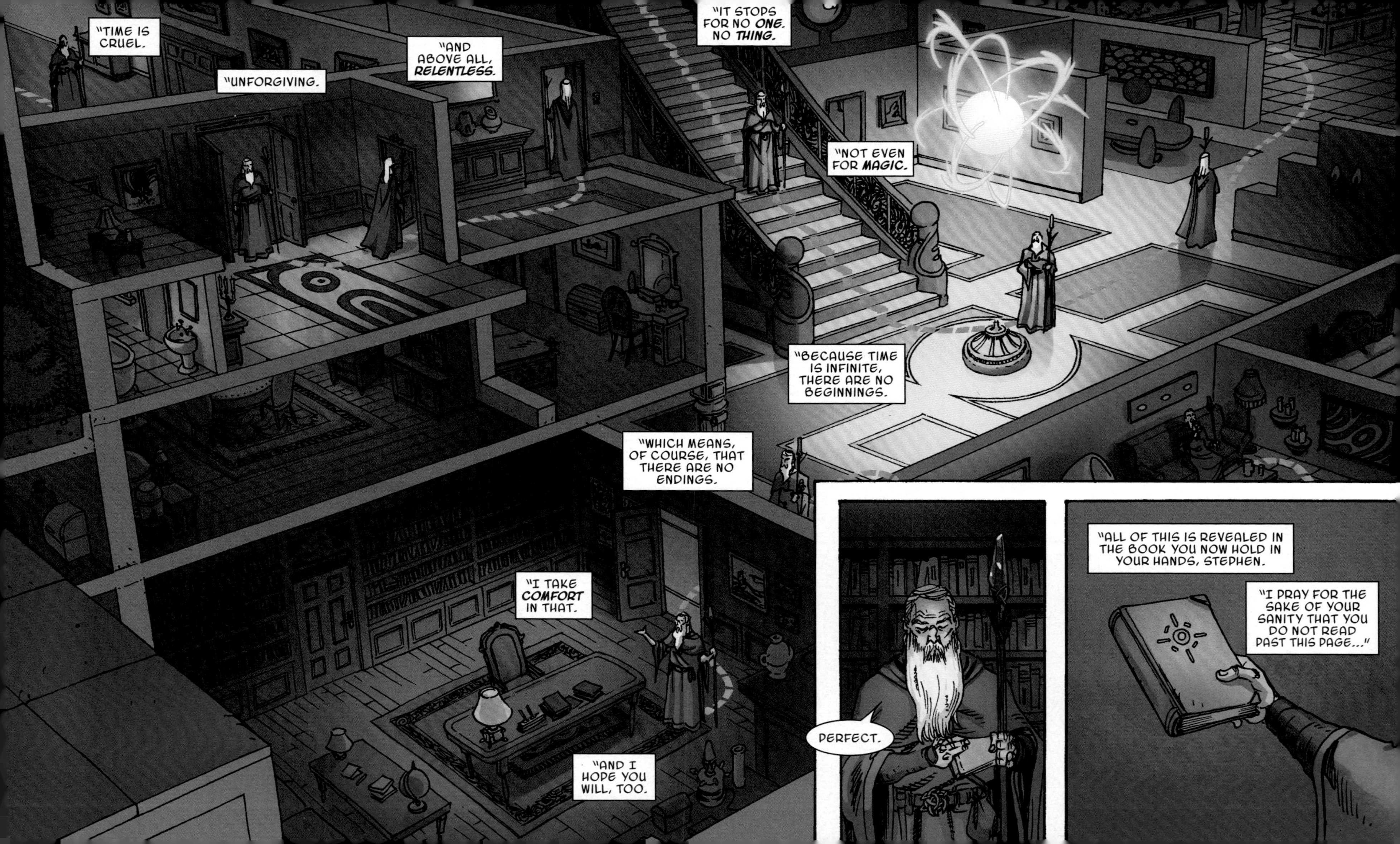
"TIME IS CRUEL.
"UNFORGIVING.
"AND ABOVE ALL, ***RELENTLESS.***
"IT STOPS FOR NO ***ONE.*** NO ***THING.***
"NOT EVEN FOR ***MAGIC.***
"BECAUSE TIME IS INFINITE, THERE ARE NO BEGINNINGS.
"WHICH MEANS, OF COURSE, THAT THERE ARE NO ENDINGS.
"I TAKE ***COMFORT*** IN THAT.
"AND I HOPE YOU WILL, TOO.
PERFECT.
"ALL OF THIS IS REVEALED IN THE BOOK YOU NOW HOLD IN YOUR HANDS, STEPHEN.
"I PRAY FOR THE SAKE OF YOUR SANITY THAT YOU DO NOT READ PAST THIS PAGE..."

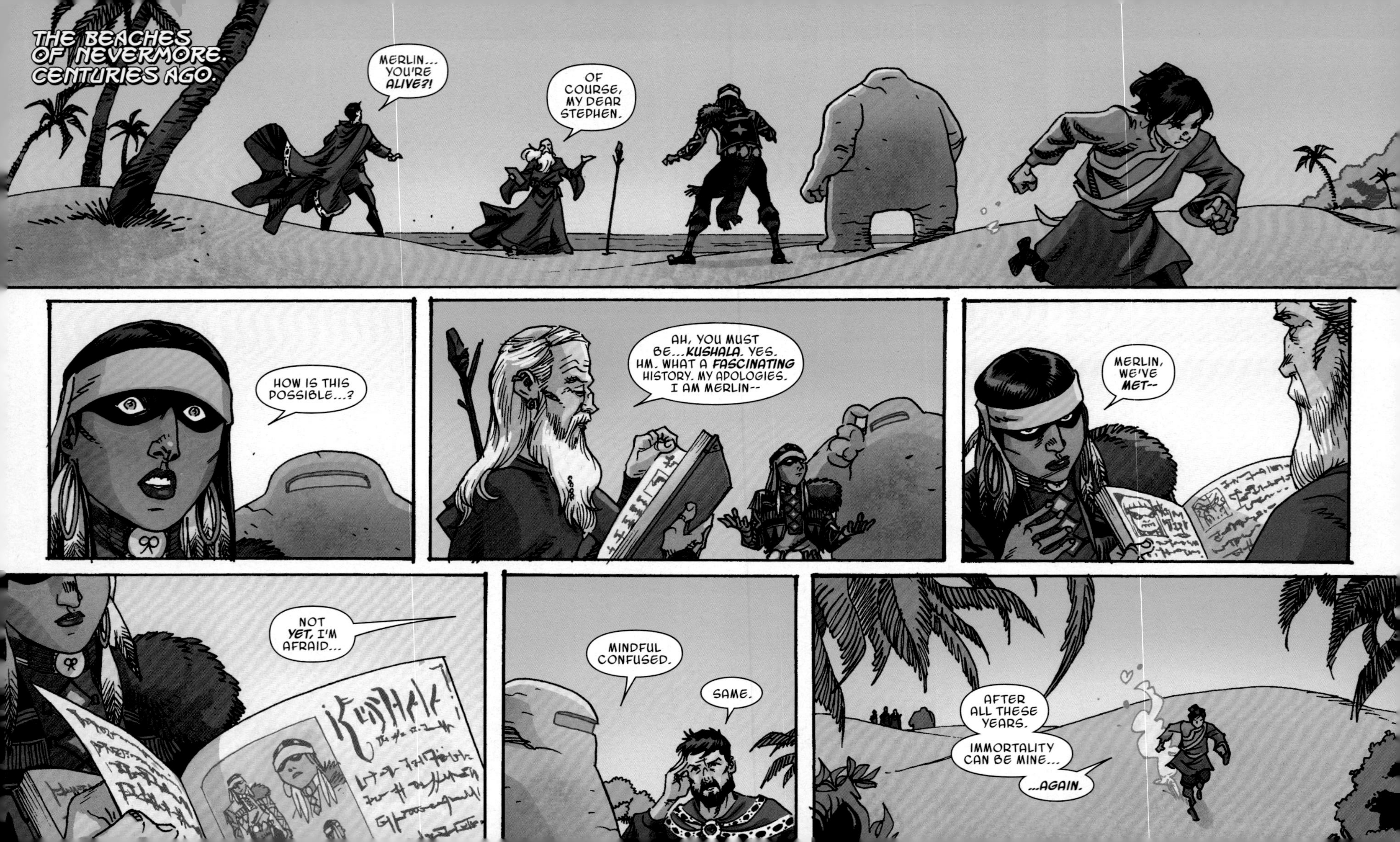

THE BEACHES OF NEVERMORE. CENTURIES AGO.
MERLIN... YOU'RE ALIVE?!
OF COURSE, MY DEAR STEPHEN.
HOW IS THIS POSSIBLE...?
AH, YOU MUST BE... KUSHALA. YES. HM. WHAT A FASCINATING HISTORY. MY APOLOGIES. I AM MERLIN--
MERLIN, WE'VE MET--
NOT YET, I'M AFRAID...
MINDFUL CONFUSED.
SAME.
AFTER ALL THESE YEARS.
IMMORTALITY CAN BE MINE...
...AGAIN.

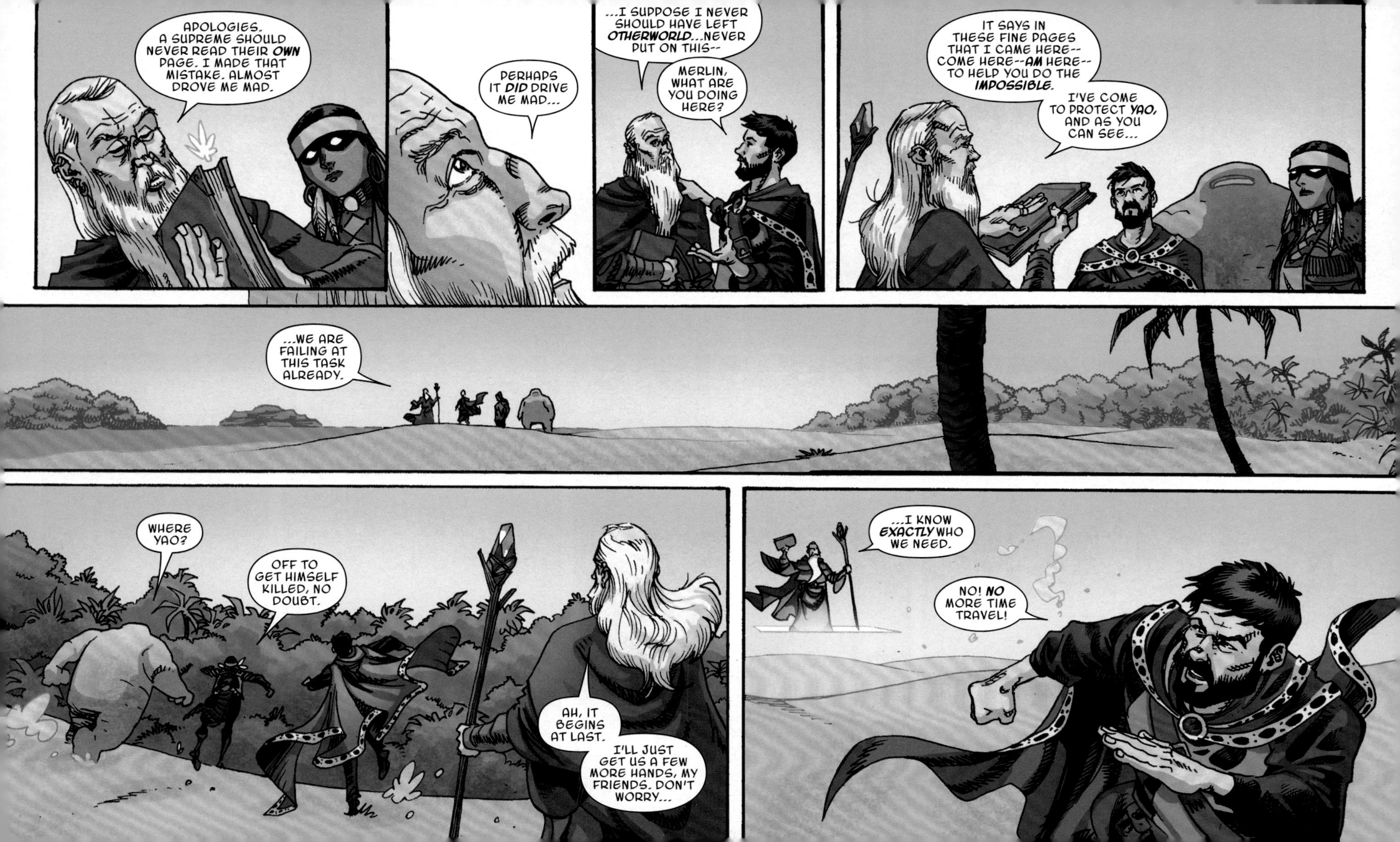
APOLOGIES. A SUPREME SHOULD NEVER READ THEIR OWN PAGE. I MADE THAT MISTAKE. ALMOST DROVE ME MAD.
PERHAPS IT DID DRIVE ME MAD...
...I SUPPOSE I NEVER SHOULD HAVE LEFT OTHERWORLD...NEVER PUT ON THIS--
MERLIN, WHAT ARE YOU DOING HERE?
IT SAYS IN THESE FINE PAGES THAT I CAME HERE--COME HERE--AM HERE--TO HELP YOU DO THE IMPOSSIBLE.
I'VE COME TO PROTECT YAO, AND AS YOU CAN SEE...
...WE ARE FAILING AT THIS TASK ALREADY.
WHERE YAO?
OFF TO GET HIMSELF KILLED, NO DOUBT.
AH, IT BEGINS AT LAST.
I'LL JUST GET US A FEW MORE HANDS, MY FRIENDS. DON'T WORRY...
...I KNOW EXACTLY WHO WE NEED.
NO! NO MORE TIME TRAVEL!

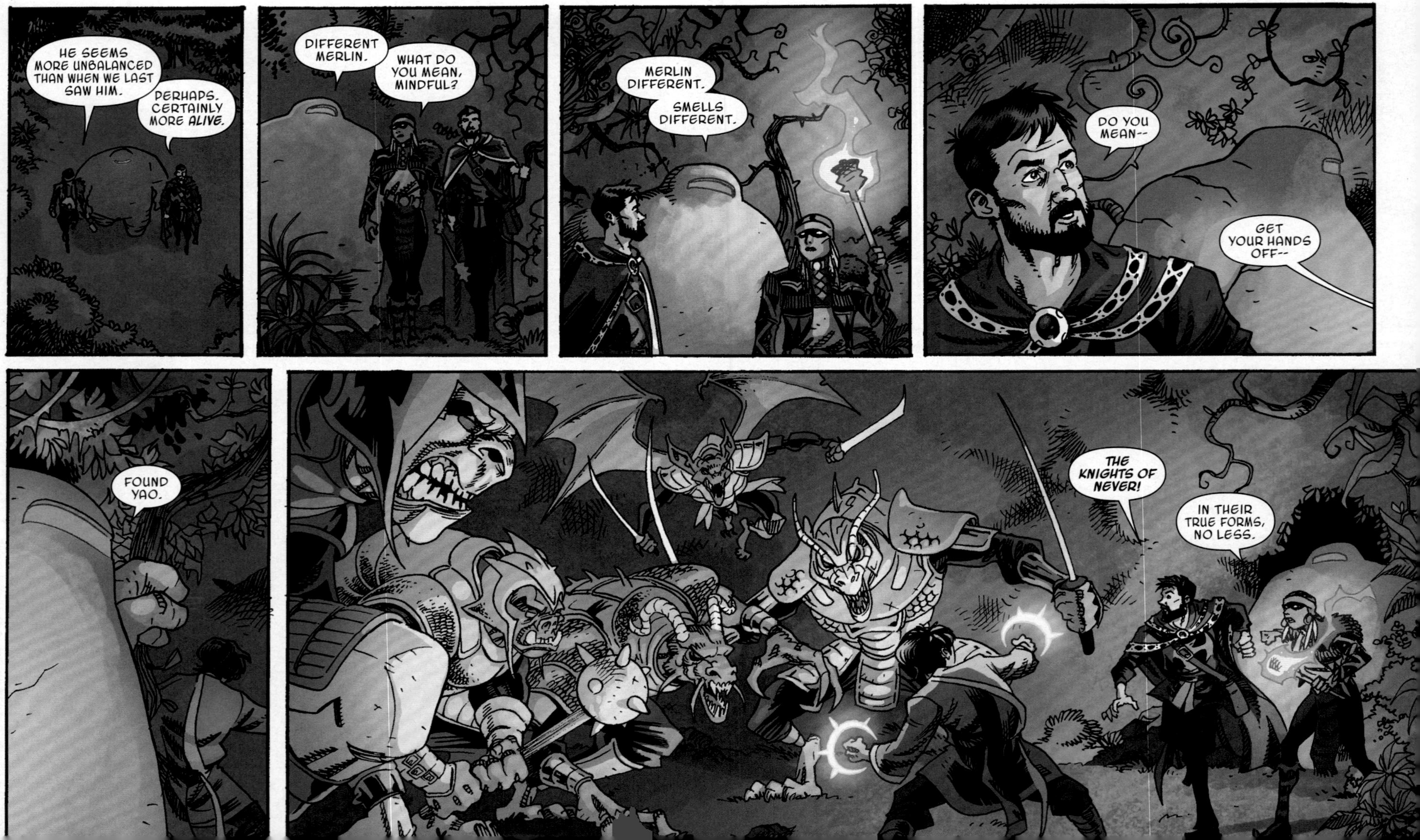
HE SEEMS MORE UNBALANCED THAN WHEN WE LAST SAW HIM.
PERHAPS. CERTAINLY MORE *ALIVE*.
DIFFERENT MERLIN.
WHAT DO YOU MEAN, MINDFUL?
MERLIN DIFFERENT.
SMELLS DIFFERENT.
DO YOU MEAN--
GET YOUR HANDS OFF--
FOUND YAO.
THE KNIGHTS OF NEVER!
IN THEIR TRUE FORMS, NO LESS.

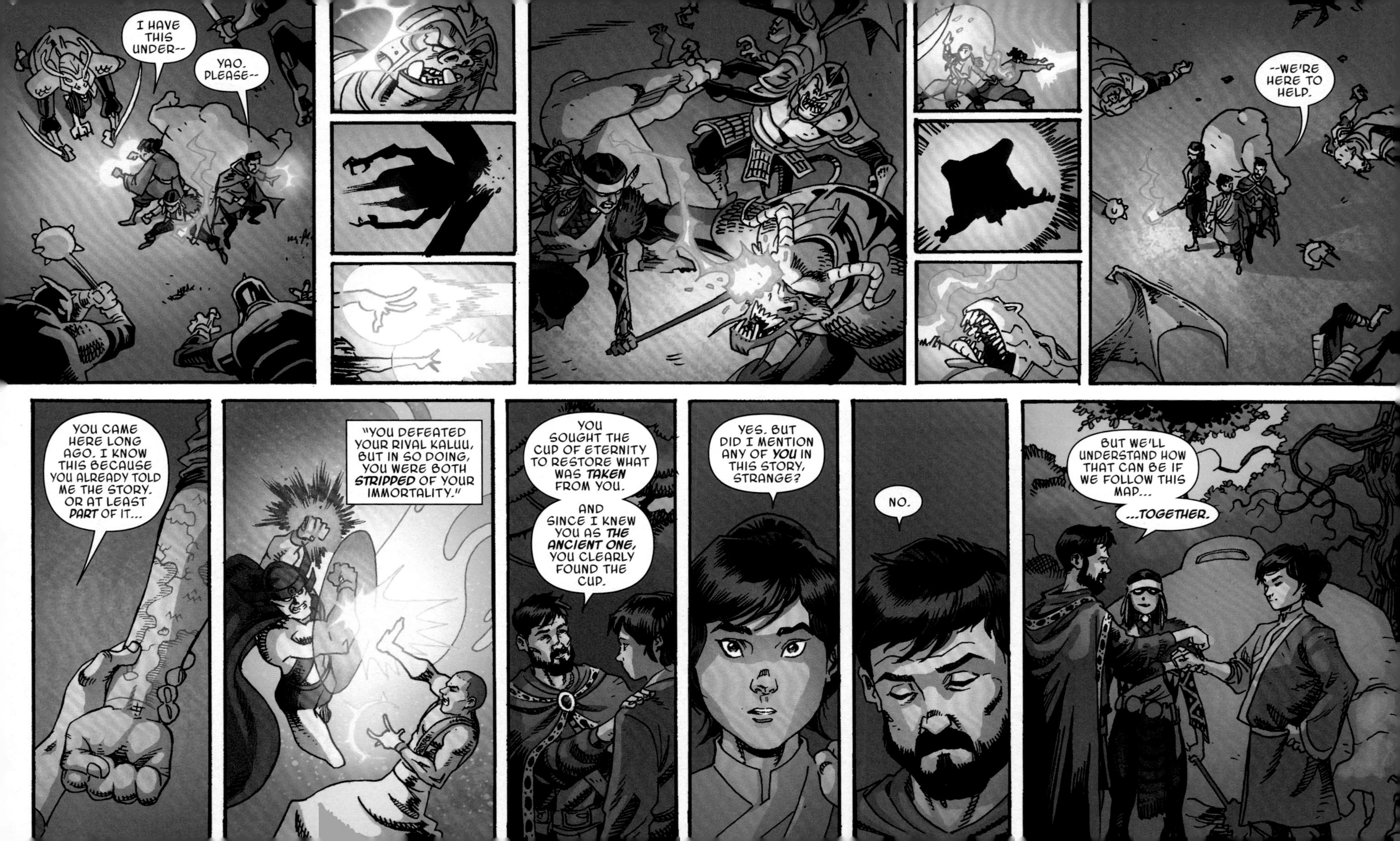
I HAVE THIS UNDER--
YAO. PLEASE--
--WE'RE HERE TO HELP.
YOU CAME HERE LONG AGO. I KNOW THIS BECAUSE YOU ALREADY TOLD ME THE STORY. OR AT LEAST *PART* OF IT...
"YOU DEFEATED YOUR RIVAL KALUU, BUT IN SO DOING, YOU WERE BOTH *STRIPPED* OF YOUR IMMORTALITY."
YOU SOUGHT THE CUP OF ETERNITY TO RESTORE WHAT WAS *TAKEN* FROM YOU.
AND SINCE I KNEW YOU AS *THE ANCIENT ONE,* YOU CLEARLY FOUND THE CUP.
YES. BUT DID I MENTION ANY OF *YOU* IN THIS STORY, STRANGE?
NO.
BUT WE'LL UNDERSTAND HOW THAT CAN BE IF WE FOLLOW THIS MAP...
...TOGETHER.

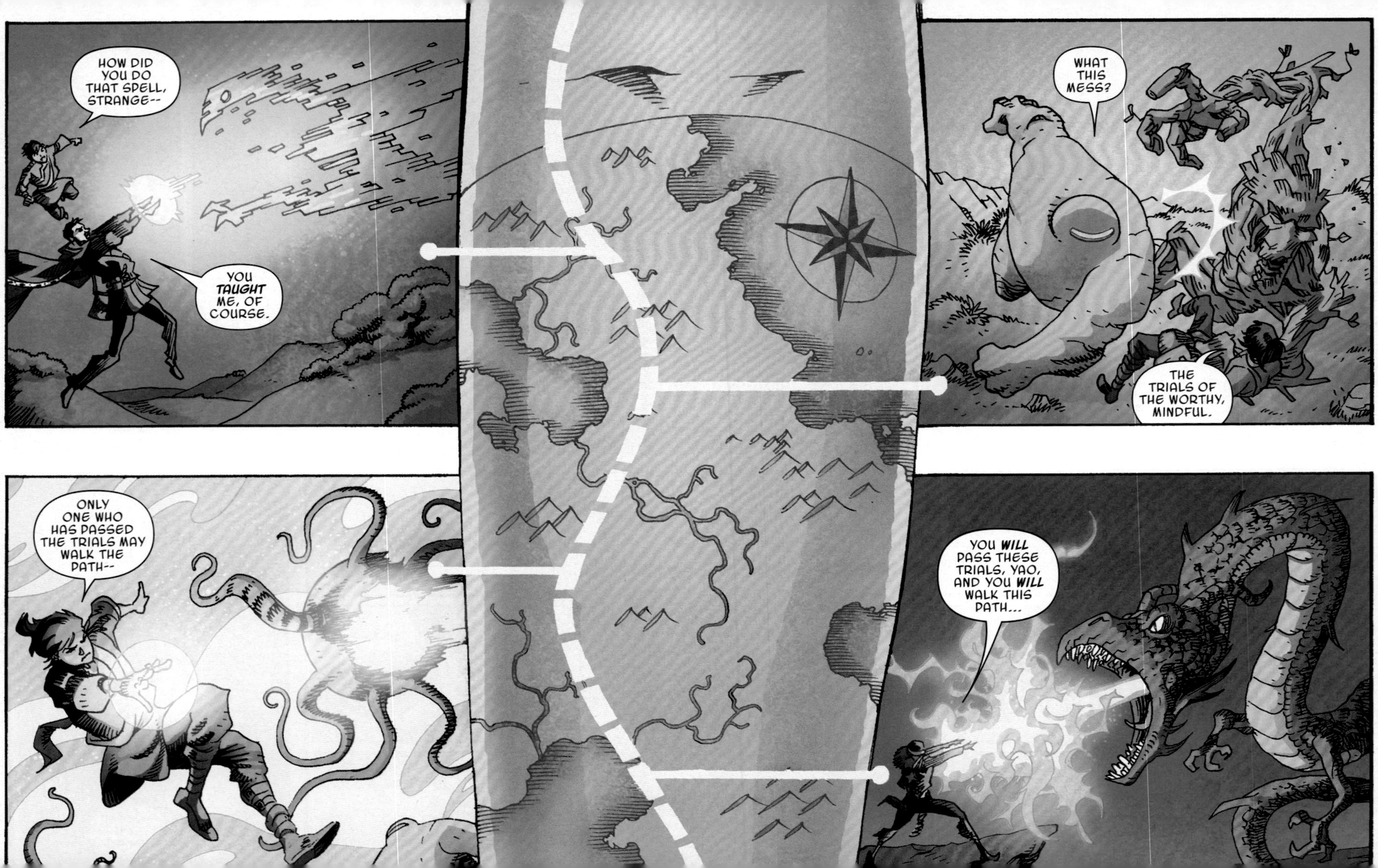
HOW DID YOU DO THAT SPELL, STRANGE--
YOU **TAUGHT** ME, OF COURSE.
WHAT THIS MESS?
THE TRIALS OF THE WORTHY, MINDFUL.
ONLY ONE WHO HAS PASSED THE TRIALS MAY WALK THE PATH--
YOU **WILL** PASS THESE TRIALS, YAO, AND YOU **WILL** WALK THIS PATH...

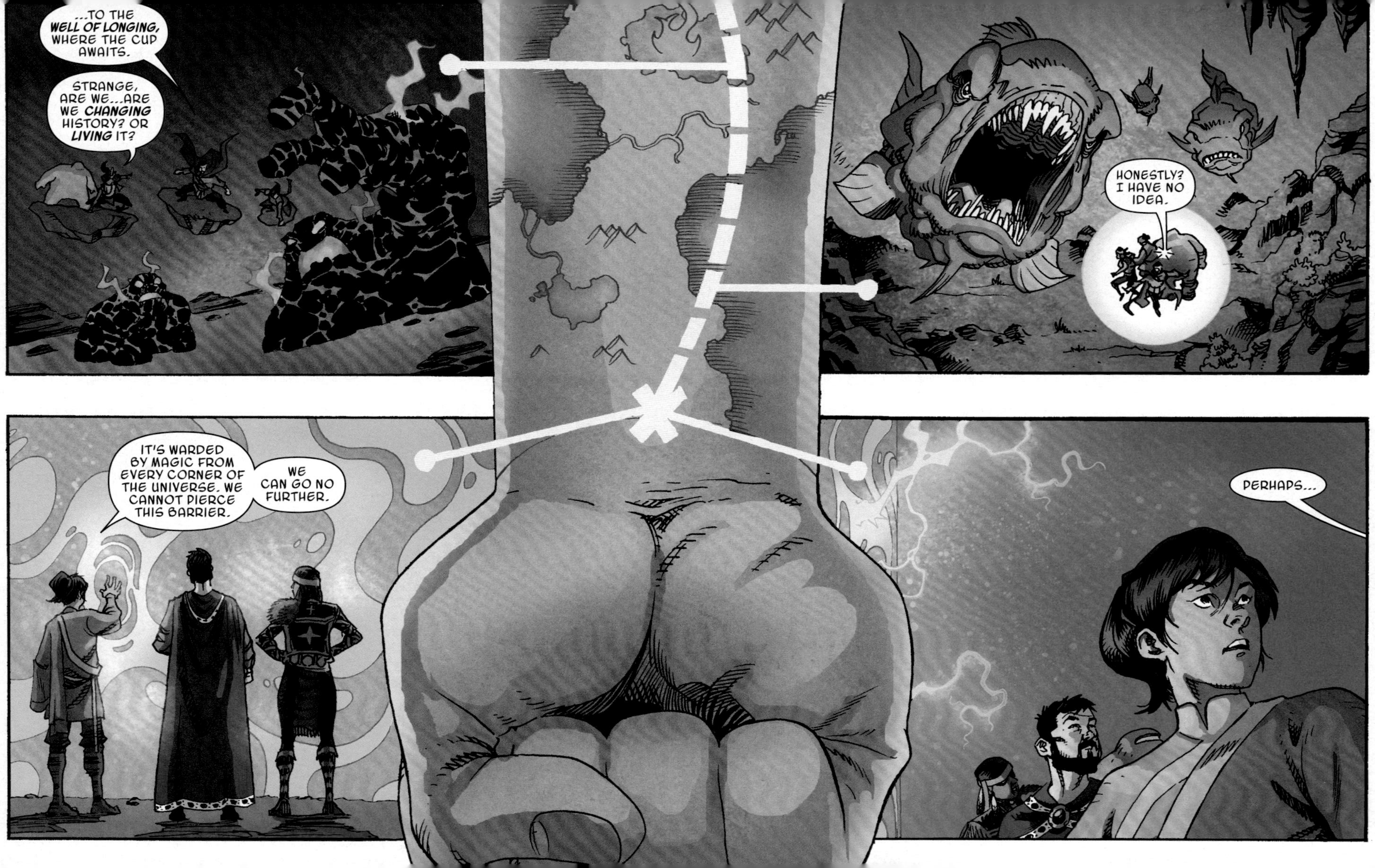

...TO THE WELL OF LONGING, WHERE THE CUP AWAITS.
STRANGE, ARE WE...ARE WE CHANGING HISTORY? OR LIVING IT?
HONESTLY? I HAVE NO IDEA.
IT'S WARDED BY MAGIC FROM EVERY CORNER OF THE UNIVERSE. WE CANNOT PIERCE THIS BARRIER.
WE CAN GO NO FURTHER.
PERHAPS...

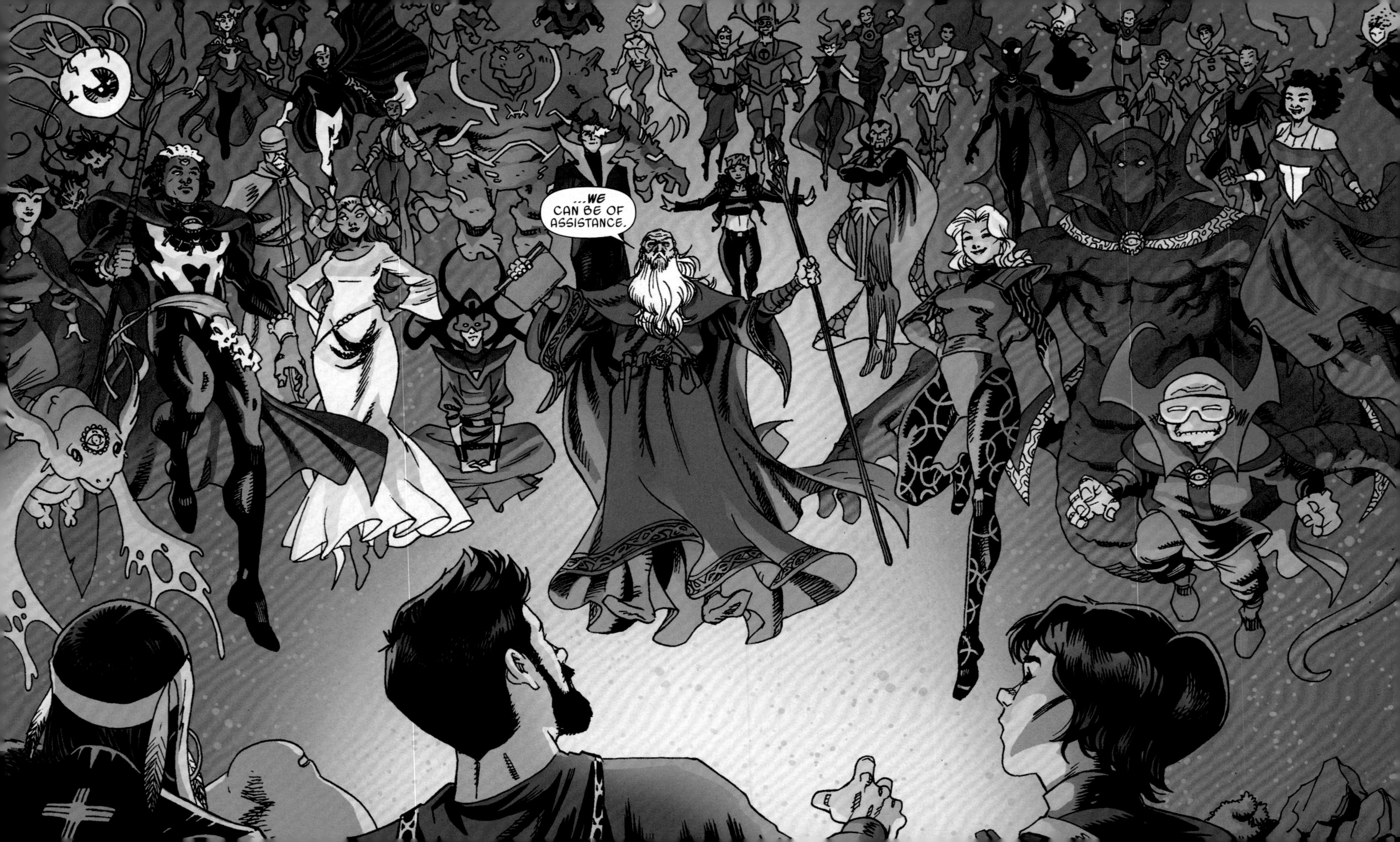
...WE CAN BE OF ASSISTANCE.

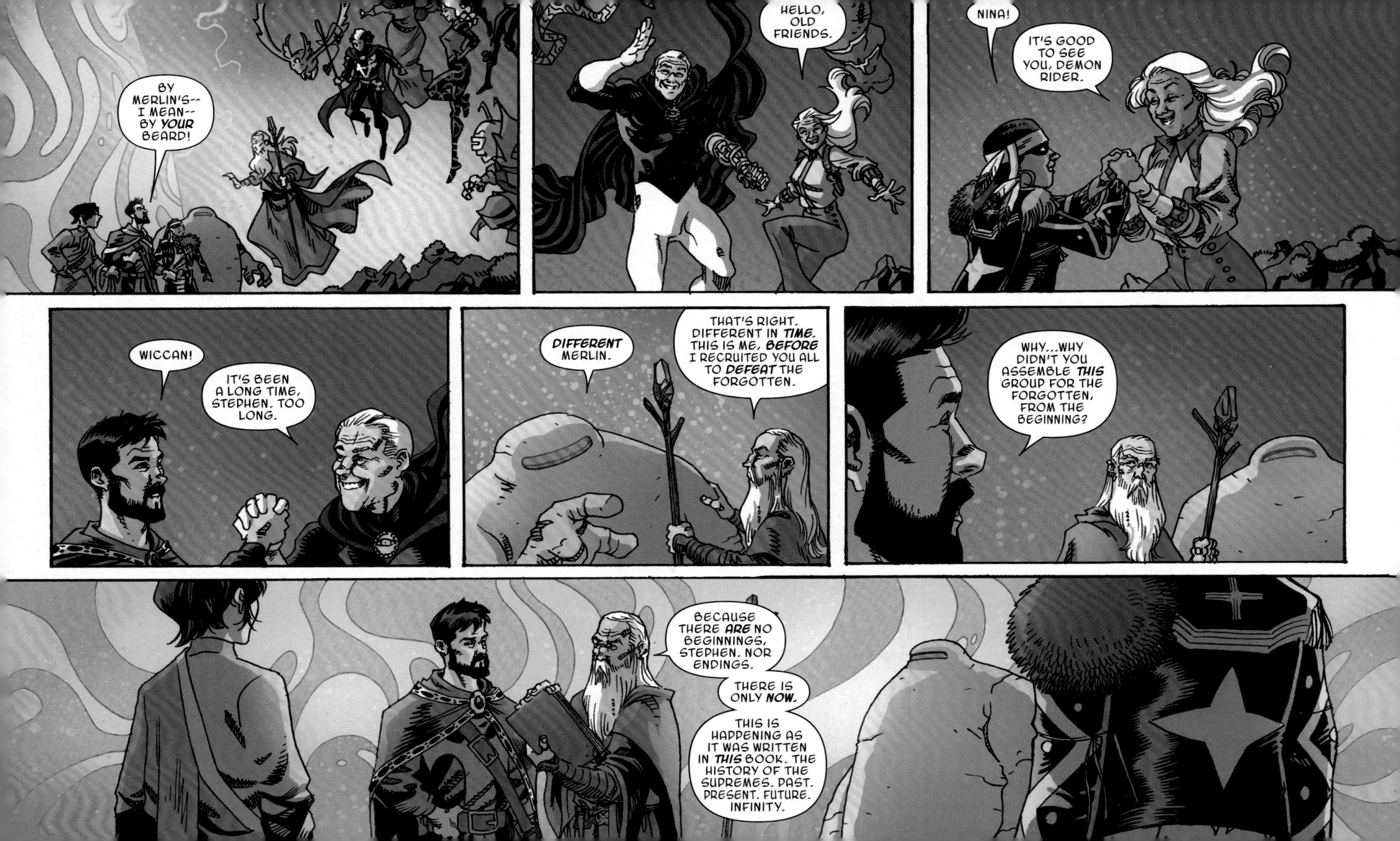
BY MERLIN'S-- I MEAN-- BY **YOUR** BEARD!
HELLO, OLD FRIENDS.
NINA!
IT'S GOOD TO SEE YOU, DEMON RIDER.
WICCAN!
IT'S BEEN A LONG TIME, STEPHEN. TOO LONG.
DIFFERENT MERLIN.
THAT'S RIGHT. DIFFERENT IN **TIME**. THIS IS ME, **BEFORE** I RECRUITED YOU ALL TO **DEFEAT** THE FORGOTTEN.
WHY...WHY DIDN'T YOU ASSEMBLE **THIS** GROUP FOR THE FORGOTTEN, FROM THE BEGINNING?
BECAUSE THERE **ARE** NO BEGINNINGS, STEPHEN. NOR ENDINGS.
THERE IS ONLY **NOW**.
THIS IS HAPPENING AS IT WAS WRITTEN IN **THIS** BOOK. THE HISTORY OF THE SUPREMES. PAST. PRESENT. FUTURE. INFINITY.

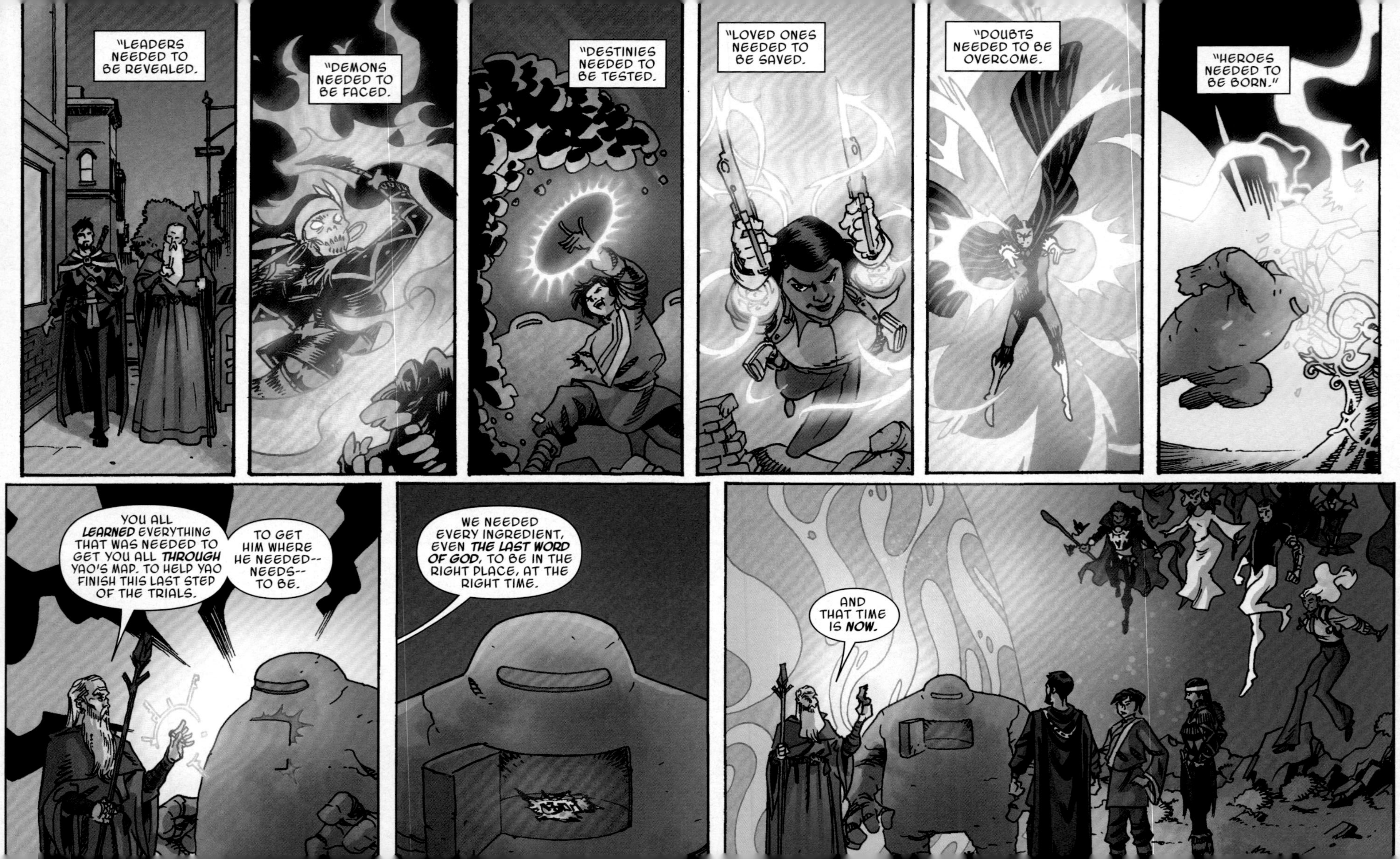
"LEADERS NEEDED TO BE REVEALED.
"DEMONS NEEDED TO BE FACED.
"DESTINIES NEEDED TO BE TESTED.
"LOVED ONES NEEDED TO BE SAVED.
"DOUBTS NEEDED TO BE OVERCOME.
"HEROES NEEDED TO BE BORN."
YOU ALL **LEARNED** EVERYTHING THAT WAS NEEDED TO GET YOU ALL **THROUGH** YAO'S MAP. TO HELP YAO FINISH THIS LAST STEP OF THE TRIALS.
TO GET HIM WHERE HE NEEDED-- NEEDS-- TO BE.
WE NEEDED EVERY INGREDIENT, EVEN **THE LAST WORD OF GOD**, TO BE IN THE RIGHT PLACE, AT THE RIGHT TIME.
AND THAT TIME IS **NOW**.

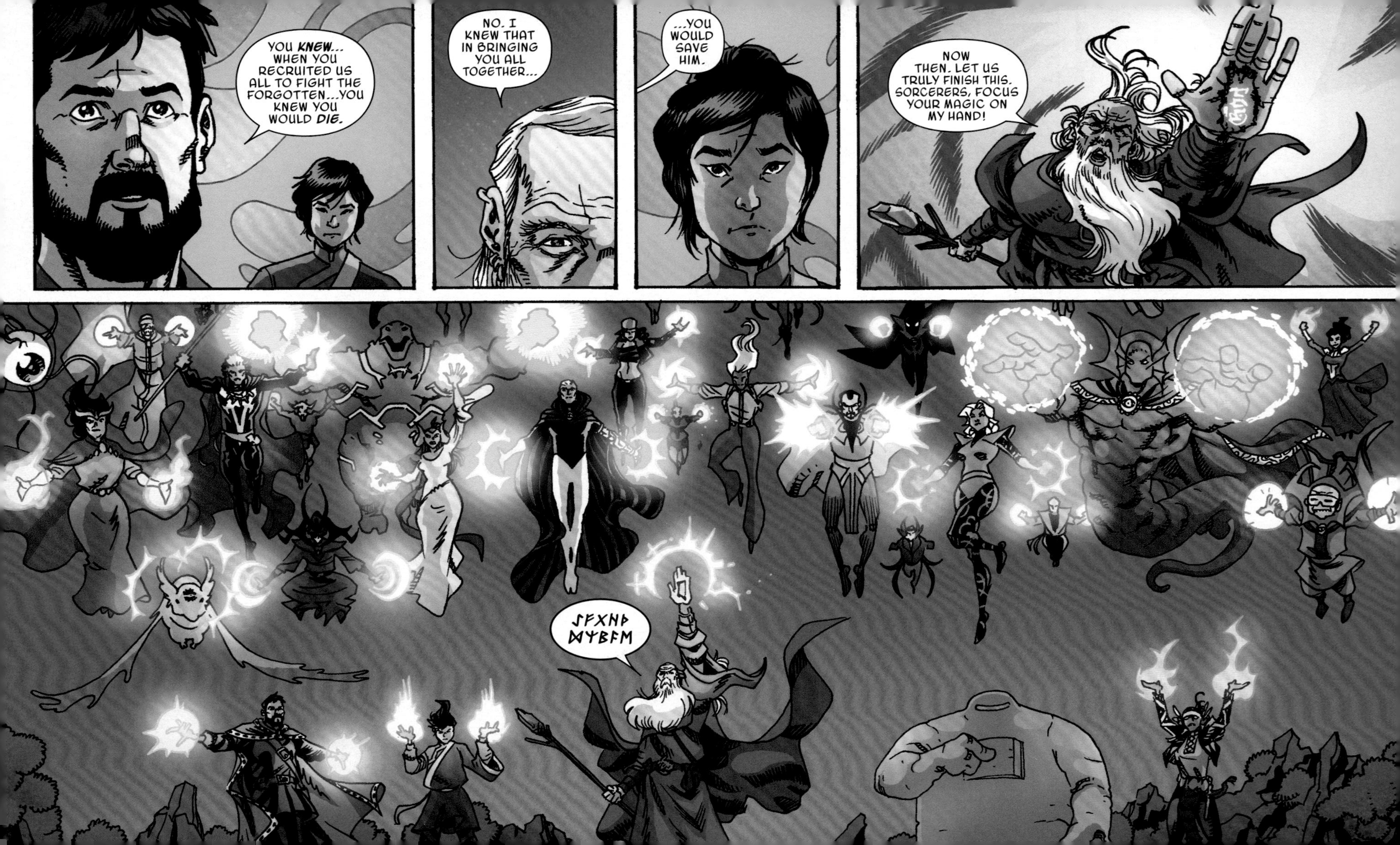
YOU KNEW... WHEN YOU RECRUITED US ALL TO FIGHT THE FORGOTTEN...YOU KNEW YOU WOULD DIE.
NO. I KNEW THAT IN BRINGING YOU ALL TOGETHER...
...YOU WOULD SAVE HIM.
NOW THEN. LET US TRULY FINISH THIS. SORCERERS, FOCUS YOUR MAGIC ON MY HAND!

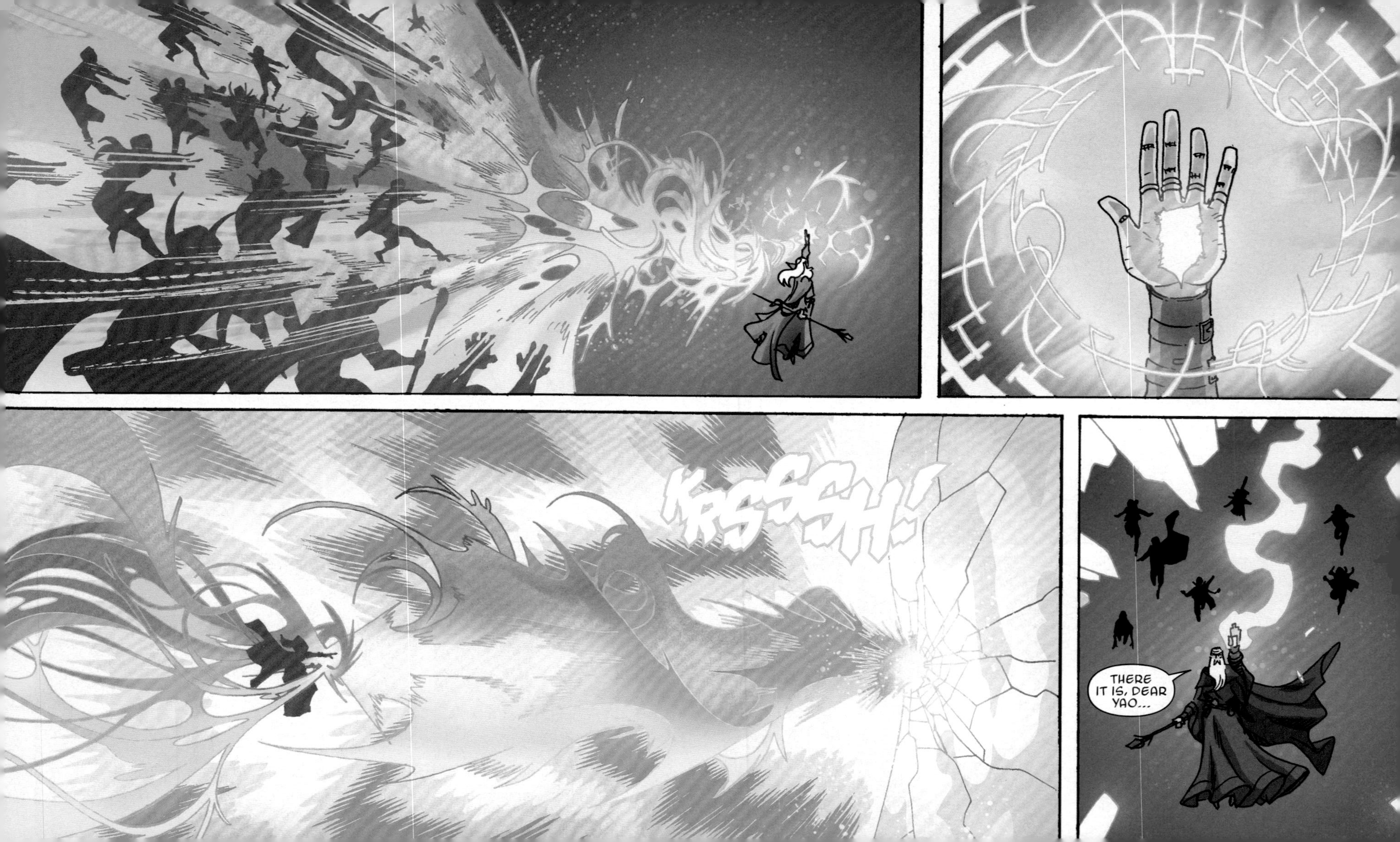
KRSSSH!
THERE IT IS, DEAR YAO...

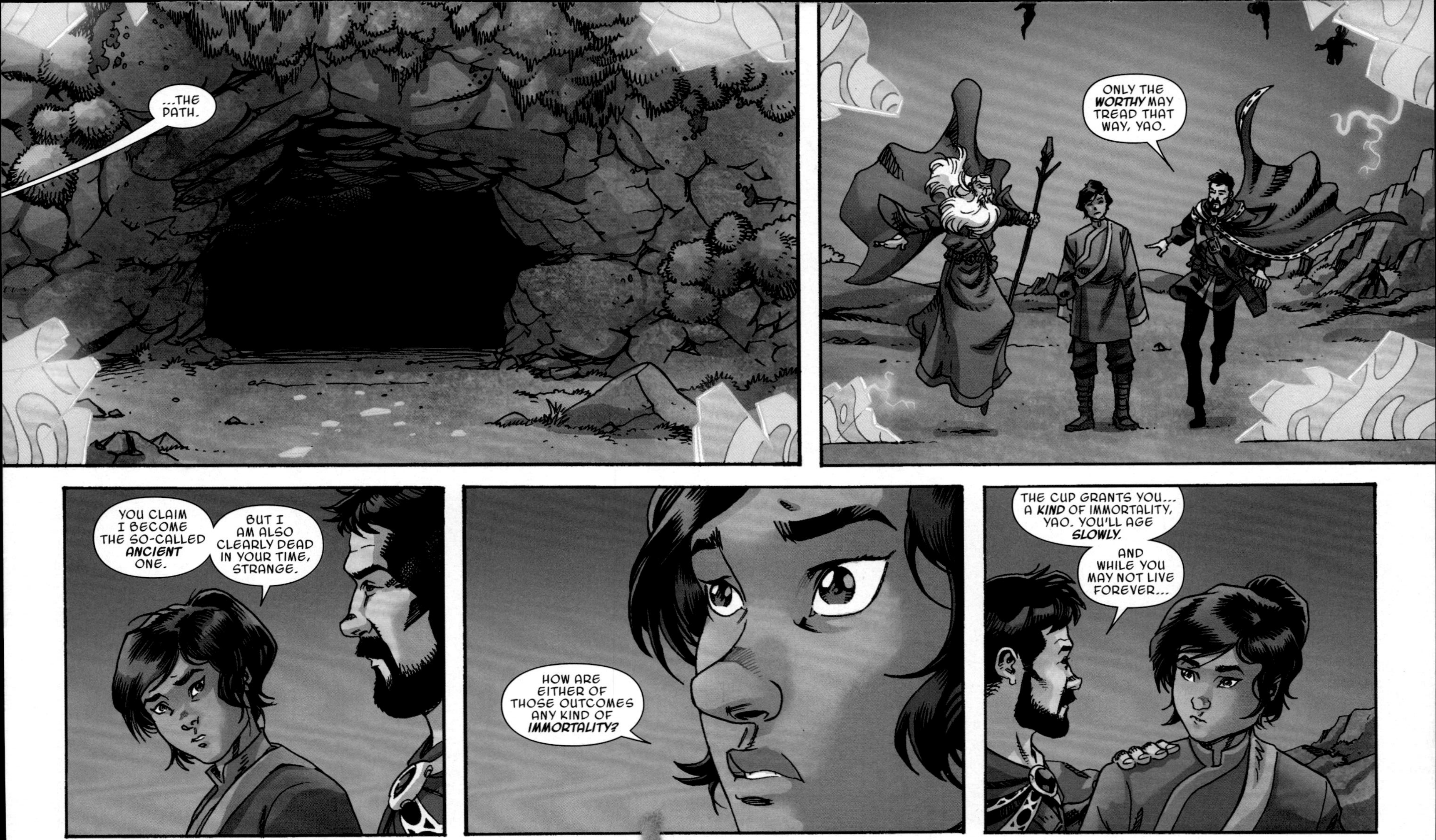
...THE PATH.
ONLY THE WORTHY MAY TREAD THAT WAY, YAO.
YOU CLAIM I BECOME THE SO-CALLED ANCIENT ONE.
BUT I AM ALSO CLEARLY DEAD IN YOUR TIME, STRANGE.
HOW ARE EITHER OF THOSE OUTCOMES ANY KIND OF IMMORTALITY?
THE CUP GRANTS YOU... A KIND OF IMMORTALITY, YAO. YOU'LL AGE SLOWLY.
AND WHILE YOU MAY NOT LIVE FOREVER...

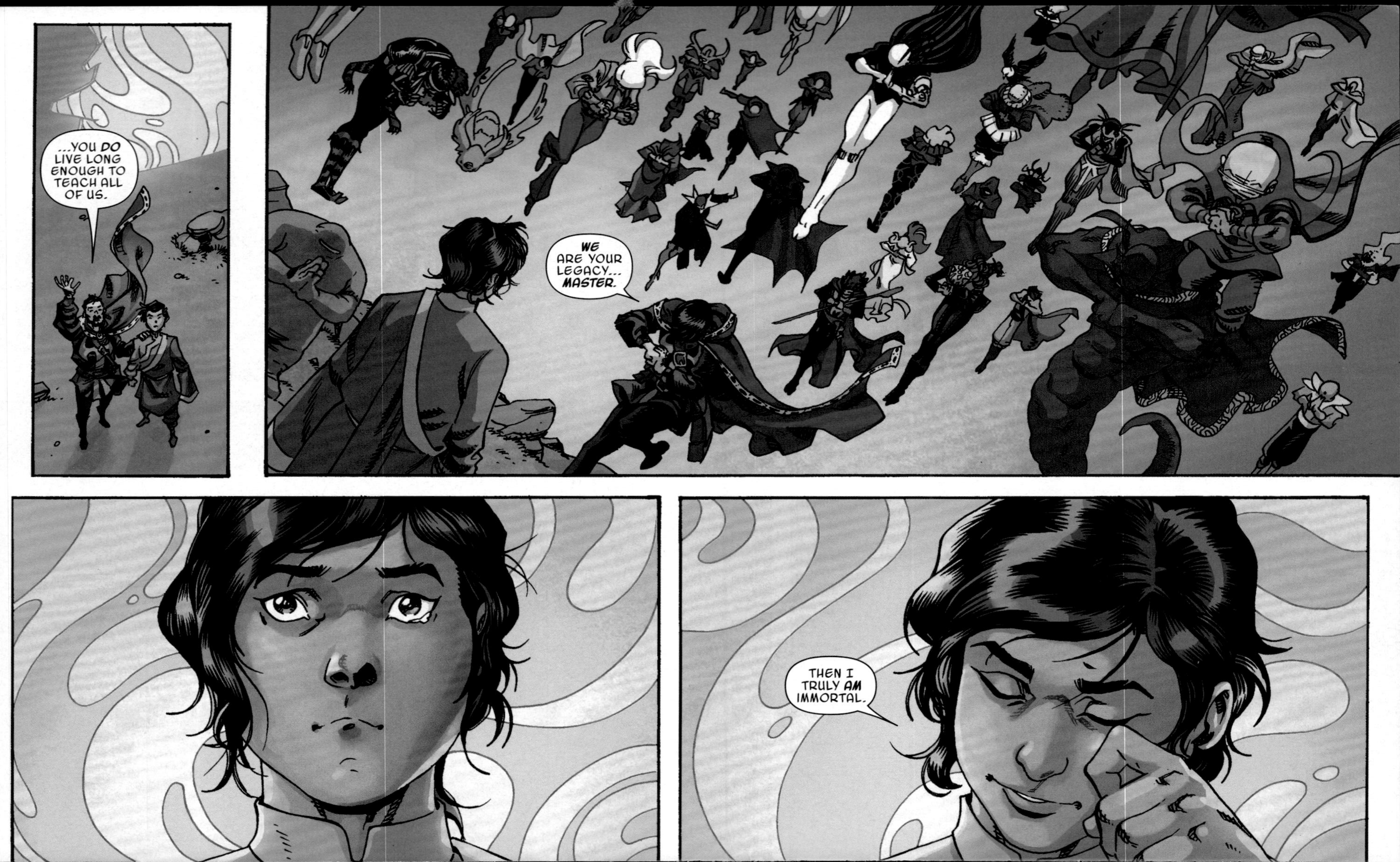
...YOU DO LIVE LONG ENOUGH TO TEACH ALL OF US.
WE ARE YOUR LEGACY... MASTER.
THEN I TRULY AM IMMORTAL.

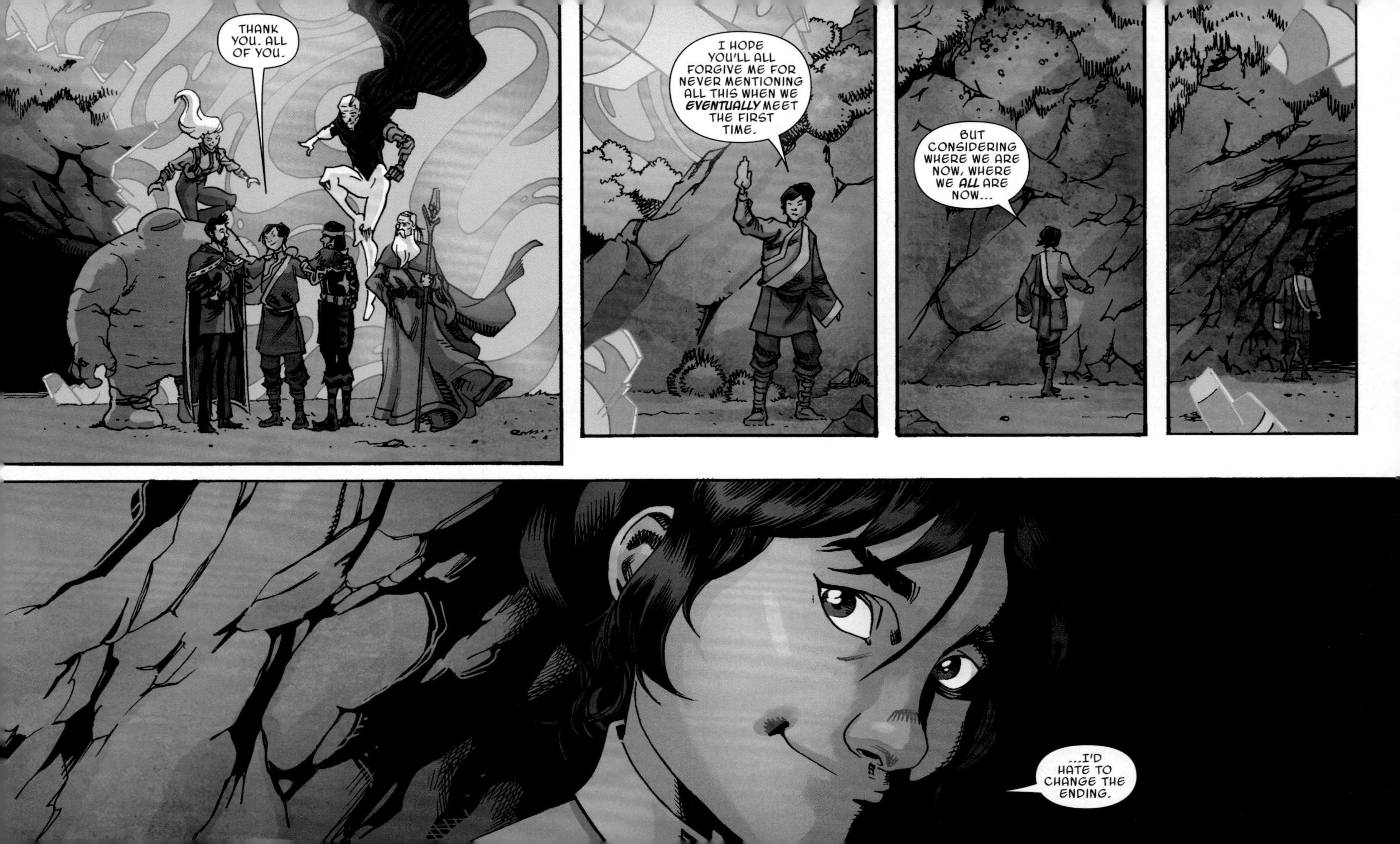
THANK YOU. ALL OF YOU.
I HOPE YOU'LL ALL FORGIVE ME FOR NEVER MENTIONING ALL THIS WHEN WE EVENTUALLY MEET THE FIRST TIME.
BUT CONSIDERING WHERE WE ARE NOW, WHERE WE ALL ARE NOW...
...I'D HATE TO CHANGE THE ENDING.

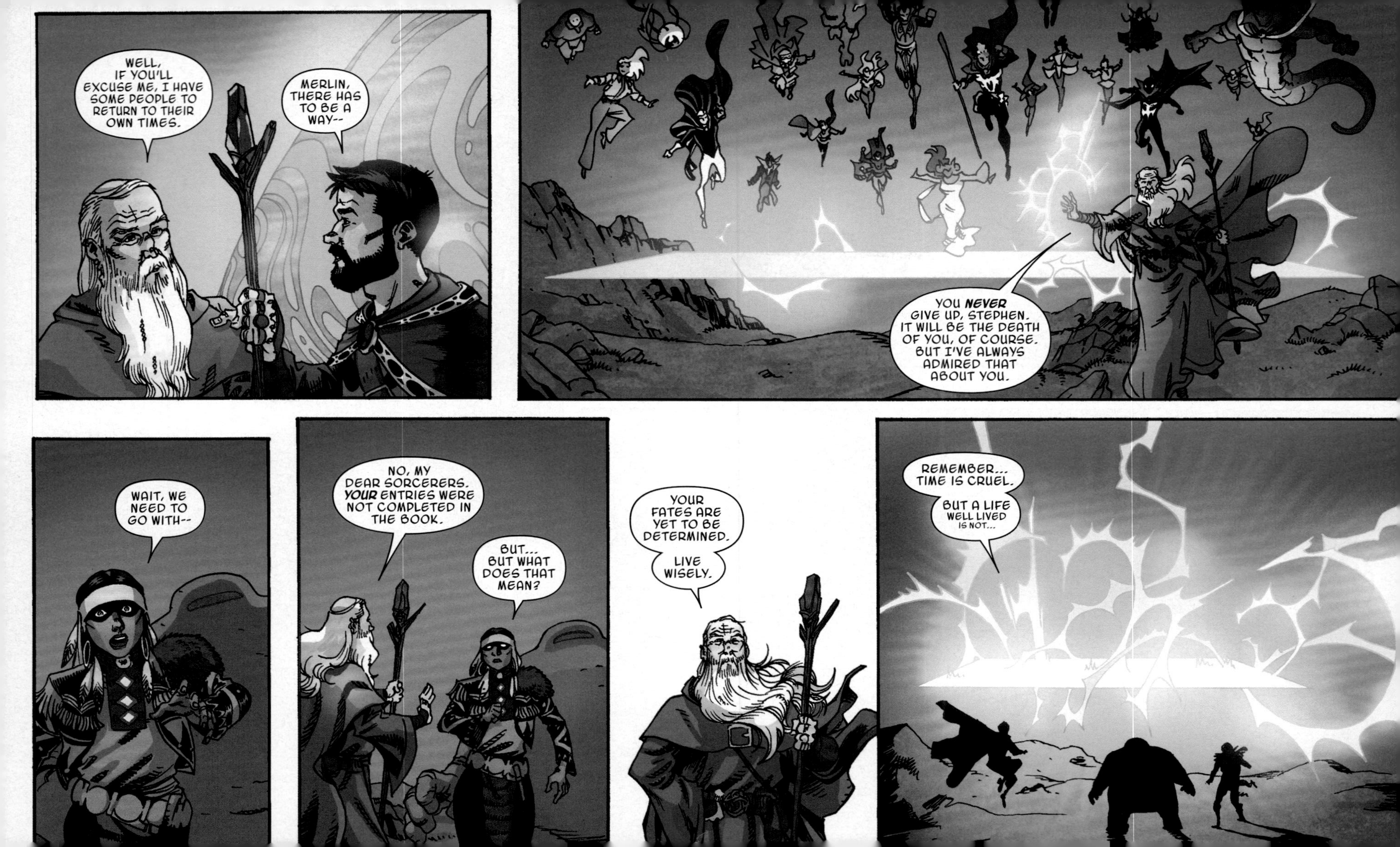
WELL, IF YOU'LL EXCUSE ME, I HAVE SOME PEOPLE TO RETURN TO THEIR OWN TIMES.
MERLIN, THERE HAS TO BE A WAY--
YOU **NEVER** GIVE UP, STEPHEN. IT WILL BE THE DEATH OF YOU, OF COURSE. BUT I'VE ALWAYS ADMIRED THAT ABOUT YOU.
WAIT, WE NEED TO GO WITH--
NO, MY DEAR SORCERERS. **YOUR** ENTRIES WERE NOT COMPLETED IN THE BOOK.
BUT... BUT WHAT DOES THAT MEAN?
YOUR FATES ARE YET TO BE DETERMINED.
LIVE WISELY.
REMEMBER... TIME IS CRUEL.
BUT A LIFE WELL LIVED IS NOT...

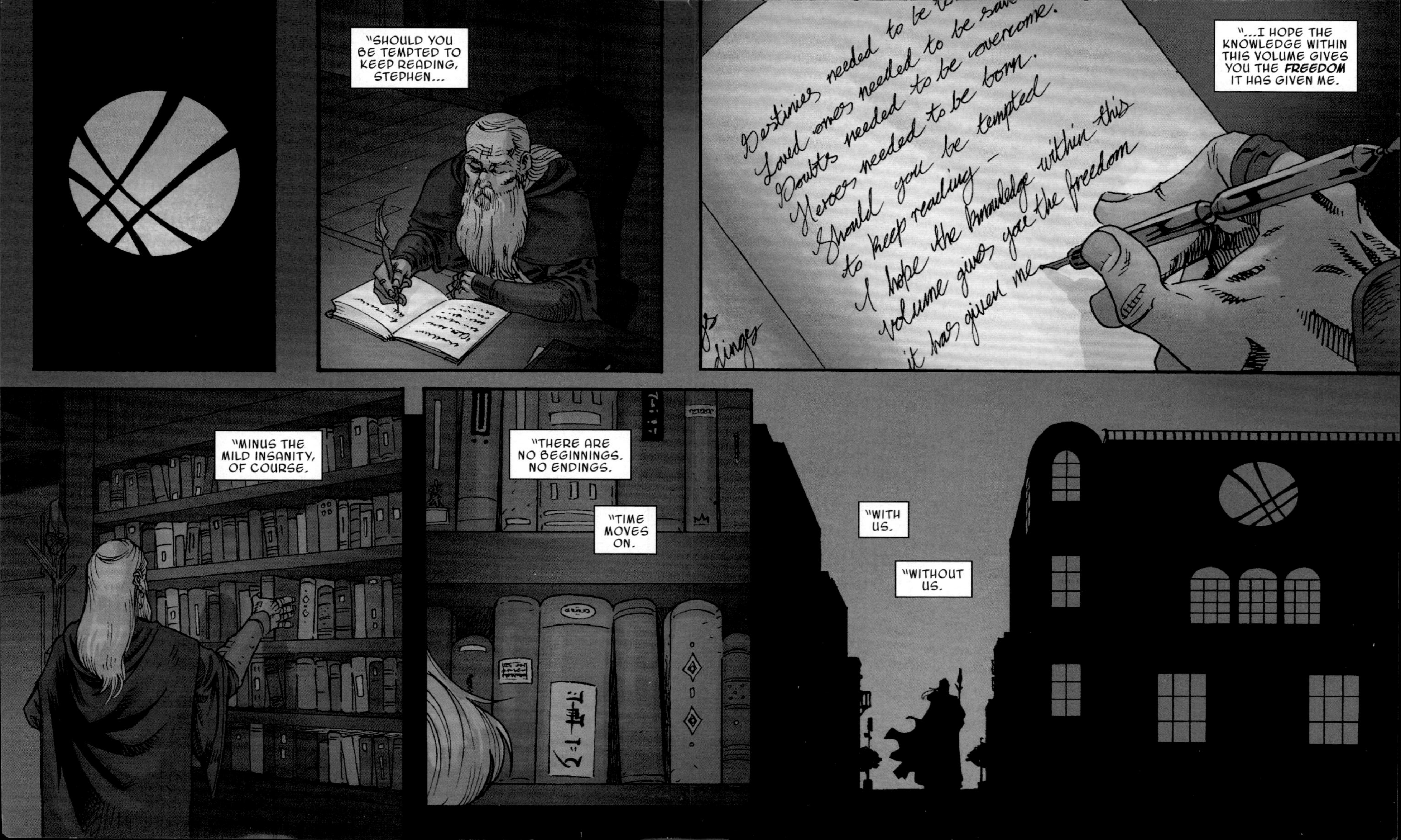
"SHOULD YOU BE TEMPTED TO KEEP READING, STEPHEN...
Destinies needed to be
Loved ones needed to be
Doubts needed to be overcome.
Heroes needed to be born.
Should you be tempted
to keep reading —
I hope the knowledge within this
volume gives you the freedom
it has given me.
"...I HOPE THE KNOWLEDGE WITHIN THIS VOLUME GIVES YOU THE ***FREEDOM*** IT HAS GIVEN ME.
"MINUS THE MILD INSANITY, OF COURSE.
"THERE ARE NO BEGINNINGS. NO ENDINGS.
"TIME MOVES ON.
"WITH US.
"WITHOUT US.

WHERE HAVE YOU BEEN?

"...ARE THE PEOPLE WE MEET IN BETWEEN..."

PERFECT.

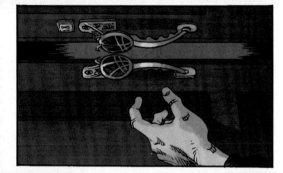

NO TIME FOR INTRODUCTIONS! THERE'S AN INTER-DIMENSIONAL PSYCHO-POMP FEEDING ON SOULS IN WASHINGTON HEIGHTS!

"ALL THAT MATTERS, IN THE END..."

THANK YOU, STRANGE.

THAT IT IS, MINDFUL.

HOME NICE.

KUSHALA, MINDFUL, THIS IS THE ALWAYS-WELCOMING ZELMA STANTON.

GOOD TO SEE YOU, TOO.

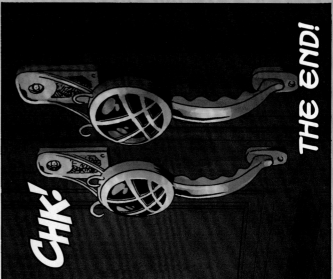

THE END!

CHK!

ESPECIALLY YOU, MINDFUL...

EVEN ME?

"...AND THE MOMENTS WE ARE LUCKY ENOUGH TO SHARE WITH THEM."

WHEN WE RETURN. NOW, YOU ARE BOTH WELCOME TO STAY AS LONG YOU'D LIKE. NO KEYS REQUIRED. THIS DOOR IS ALWAYS OPEN TO ANY WHO HAVE MAGIC WITHIN THEM.

Magic.

That's what all of you who are reading this are: magic.

This book shouldn't exist. But twelve issues exist because of your magic. From the bottom of my cold, robotic heart, thank you for supporting this book, and for sharing its story with us.

I knew I wanted to pitch for this book the second Editor Nick Lowe said the words "Doctor Strange," but when he laid out the crazy premise and ended it with, "And then, at the end of issue #1, Merlin gets killed!" I was desperate to work on this comic. Who among us *hasn't* wanted to kill Merlin? Nick built an amazing team of artists to bring this book to life. He also brought on Quinn Bradley as a Native American consultant to help us create Kushala. Thank you, Nick, for your amazing ideas, your relentless positivity, and as always, for your sweet, sweet singing voice.

I've had the good fortune to work with Editor Darren Shan on a couple books now, and from the opening recap to the teaser for the next issue, he's always looking for ways to make the book the best it can be. He has an incredible attention to detail, a wealth of ideas and a fantastic grasp on story. Thank you, Darren, for all of your hard work and for consistently making each issue shine.

Thank you, Assistant Editor Allison Stock. Allison is as passionate as she is diligent, and she helped make this book run seamlessly. She always kept each deadline fresh in my mind without making me terrified, and made sure every piece of material sailed through the process with ease.

Thank you, Joe Caramagna, one of the best letterers in the business. Despite his passion for the New Jersey Devils over the Detroit Red Wings, we've worked together on two books now, and I'm grateful for everything Joe brings to a story. Joe brought each character's voice to life and added magical words, effects and other sorcery to every page.

I worked with superstar Jordie Bellaire on SPIDER-WOMEN ALPHA and admired her colors from afar, but getting to see her work on a monthly book blew me away. She tells a story with each color, moving your eye where it needs to go and bringing characters and moments to life in every panel. She turned each stunning page we received into true masterpieces. Notes were variations on "Wow!" "Gorgeous!" "OMG!" "Amazing!" Thank you, Jordie, for your light, and for being such a great storytelling partner.

Thank you to Tamra Bonvillain for your stunning colors on two issues of this book. You stepped in and helped us not miss a beat, keeping the colors gorgeous and making the book your own.

Thank you, Jim Campbell, for bringing your fantastic coloring to the final run of this book. I was lucky enough to collaborate with Jim on SPIDEY, and he brings out the best in each issue, and works perfectly with...

...Nate Stockman, my once and future partner in crime. I've worked with Nate on two books and he's tenacious, passionate and brilliant. He's also fearless, always willing to try something completely new or different, from character designs to plotting. Please never tell him I said this, but he's a rising star in comics, and I hope I'm lucky enough to work with him again on another book soon.

Thank you, Álvaro López, for your shadows, incredible detail and unbelievable work on this comic. Álvaro's inks are some of the best I've ever seen, and he brought his signature style to every page. We would get amazing pencils each week, and then get to watch Álvaro work his magic. He and Javier are the perfect dance partners, and witnessing their work from front-row seats was truly magical.

And last and most certainly not least, I want to thank the Sorcerer Supreme himself: Javier Rodríguez. Javier is a true genius and master of sequential art. Right from the jump, it was clear he was the reason the book had a shot at working — from his first cover to his initial character designs, which brought every character to life in a single page before anything had been written. SPIDER-WOMAN was one of my favorite Marvel books, so I reached out to Dennis Hopeless to ask about Javier. Dennis had the best advice — get out of Javier's way. I also got great help from Nick, who sent me Jason Aaron's awesome scripts for DOCTOR STRANGE, which showed how he was working with artist Chris Bachalo. It was a looser style, less about panel breakdowns and more about telling the story together. Using Dennis' advice and Jason's scripts as a template, Javier and I exchanged a bunch of emails and started figuring the story out together. Then, my wife and I had the pleasure of spending the day with Javier's beautiful family last year. We talked about everything from music, to movies, to politics, and of course comics. Javier and his family are as fantastic and wonderful as his art. I'd send him the scripts early and he always had the best ideas and suggestions to push the book to be more and more visual, to make it more purely a comic, to make the characters and plot more magical. He took what was on the page and used it as a springboard to create stunning artwork. From his first issue to his last, he always found a way to make a jaw-dropping two-page spread, to push the boundaries of layouts and character design. Javier had an impact on the comic even after leaving it! When he handed in his cover for issue #12, showing all the Supremes together again, I was so struck by the image that I threw out the script I had written and rewrote it completely to feature the gang together once more. Once again, his imagery told the story the best way. So, thank you, Javier, for your outstanding work on this book. I am grateful for everything you taught me about comics, and I cannot wait to learn more from you in the future.

And now, for our final trick, we disappear! Thank you all so much, and I hope you enjoyed the show!

-Robbie Thompson

DOCTOR STRANGE AND THE SORCERERS SUPREME was a challenge. It was a festival of characters, with eight individual Sorcerers Supreme: Strange, Newton, Mindful One, Nina, Kushala, Yao, Merlin and Wiccan. All of them needed either updated looks or to be created altogether. There were constantly new guest stars appearing, bizarre backgrounds, thousands of magicians, weird creatures, scary monsters... Each issue was conceived to blow up the reader's mind. We were exploring and testing the comic language anytime that we had an opportunity. We were looking for fun all the time, everywhere.

It was a lot of work. Thousands of hours expended. This project is the result of the titanic efforts of Robbie, Álvaro, Jordie, Joe, Nathan, Tamra, Nick, Darren and Allison. I'm so grateful to all of them. I would like to show my gratitude to this group of fantastic people for letting me be part of this magical trip, and to you as well, fellow reader. Thanks for being there till the end.

All the very best,
Javier Rodríguez

Sometimes chance comes across, puts his hand on your shoulder and the next thing you know you're down the rabbit hole, fighting a monster you thought dead, buried and forgotten. Sometimes you happen to an old friend's new face, or find yourself surrounded by new companions. Sometimes you feel powerless, only to discover what you're capable of. Sometimes the biggest adventure of your life is right there, smiling at you.

I've enjoyed working on this book as much as Stephen has struggled through it. Like him, I was surrounded by an unbeatable team. They all had my back when I managed to pull off my biggest trick.

Read, dream and remember: Magic is just around the corner!

-Álvaro López

Thanks to Robbie, Javier, Álvaro, Joe Caramagna, Nick, Allison and Darren — this book was a satisfying, crazy journey and I'm so happy we all did it together along with our awesome kickass backups by the talented team of Nate Stockman and Tamra Bonvillain. I like them.

I would also like to say that I personally dedicate this work to Tim O'Shea. I have a feeling this wild, magical comic would have been something he'd like. Miss you, Tim. Thanks for everything.

-Jordie Bellaire

When I first got the fax with the offer to join in on SORCERERS SUPREME, I thought, "That's weird. I don't even have a fax machine." I took that as a sign and that's when I knew I couldn't refuse. (And also because my soul is being held hostage in an urn in the Marvel offices. Always read your contracts, folks!)

The past few months have been some of the most rewarding creatively of my career. And I'm not just saying that to try and get my soul back. Nick, Javier, Álvaro and Jordie all gave me a warm welcome and kind words when I took over. What a team to try and follow! But thankfully Robbie, Darren, Allison, Tamra and Jim are some of the best people you could ever hope to work with and I loved working with them on every panel of every page of this book. I'm very fortunate to be surrounded by people who pick me up and bring out the best work from me. Alas, our magical journey together has come to an end. But as we learned in this issue, endings are just beginnings that we... start over again? Something like that, right? To be honest, I just glanced over the script.

-Nathan Stockman

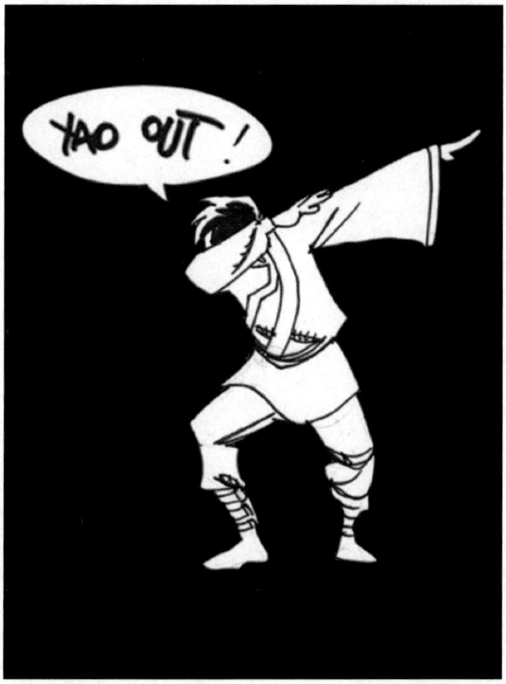
YAO OUT!